Contemporary Co-housing in Europe

This book investigates co-housing as an alternative housing form in relation to sustainable urban development.

Co-housing is often lauded as a more sustainable way of living. The primary aim of this book is to critically explore co-housing in the context of wider social, economic, political and environmental developments. This volume fills a gap in the literature by contextualising co-housing and related housing forms. With focus on Denmark, Sweden, Hamburg and Barcelona, the book presents general analyses of co-housing in these contexts and provides specific discussions of co-housing in relation to local government, urban activism, family life, spatial logics and socio-ecology.

This book will be of interest to students and researchers in a broad range of social-scientific fields concerned with housing, urban development and sustainability, as well as to planners, decision-makers and activists.

Pernilla Hagbert holds a PhD in Architecture and is currently a researcher at KTH Royal Institute of Technology, Sweden. Her research explores home-related practices and everyday life, interpretations of sustainability in housing and urban development, and norm-critical, alternative ways of living, as part of sustainability transitions.

Henrik Gutzon Larsen teaches Human Geography at Lund University, Sweden. His research addresses urban geography and housing, political geography and history of geographical thought.

Håkan Thörn is Full Professor of Sociology at University of Gothenburg, Sweden. His research is concerned with social movements, urban governance and globalization, and he has published a number of articles and books on these topics, including *Urban Uprisings: Challenging Neoliberal Urbanism in Europe* (co-edited, 2017) and *Christiania 1971–2011: Space for Urban Alternatives* (co-edited, 2011).

Cathrin Wasshede is positioned at the Department of Sociology and Work Science at the University of Gothenburg, Sweden. Her research addresses gender and sexuality, resistance and (urban) social movements.

Contemporary Co-housing in Europe

Towards Sustainable Cities?

Edited by
Pernilla Hagbert, Henrik Gutzon Larsen, Håkan Thörn and Cathrin Wasshede

Routledge
Taylor & Francis Group
LONDON AND NEW YORK

First published 2020
by Routledge
2 Park Square, Milton Park, Abingdon, Oxon OX14 4RN

and by Routledge
52 Vanderbilt Avenue, New York, NY 10017

Routledge is an imprint of the Taylor & Francis Group, an informa business

First issued in paperback 2021

British Library Cataloguing-in-Publication Data
A catalogue record for this book is available from the British Library

Library of Congress Cataloging-in-Publication Data
Names: Hagbert, Pernilla, editor.
Title: Contemporary co-housing in Europe : towards sustainable cities? / edited by Pernilla Hagbert, Henrik Gutzon Larsen, Håkan Thörn, and Cathrin Wasshede.
Description: Milton Park, Abingdon, Oxon ; New York, NY : Routledge, 2020. | Includes bibliographical references and index.
Identifiers: LCCN 2019050110 (print) | LCCN 2019050111 (ebook) |
Subjects: LCSH: Housing, Cooperative--Europe, Western. | City planning--Europe, Western. | Cities and towns--Europe, Western--Growth.
Classification: LCC HD7287.72.E85 C66 2020 (print) | LCC HD7287.72.E85 (ebook) | DDC 344/.1094--dc23
LC record available at https://lccn.loc.gov/2019050110
LC ebook record available at https://lccn.loc.gov/2019050111

ISBN: 978-1-138-32591-3 (hbk)
ISBN: 978-1-03-208523-4 (pbk)
ISBN: 978-0-429-45017-4 (ebk)

Typeset in Times New Roman
by Taylor & Francis Books

Contents

Illustrations

Figure

Tables

Acknowledgements

This book is based on the research project 'Co-housing and sustainable urban development: cases from Denmark, Germany, Spain and Sweden', funded by Riksbankens Jubileumsfond (The Swedish Foundation for Humanities and Social Sciences). We are greatly indebted to all our informants who generously dedicated time to answer our questions, and in some cases invited us to their homes and shared meals with us. In addition to the project member and contributor to this book, Claes Caldenby, the editors would also like to thank David Scheller, Lorenzo Vidal and Peter Jakobsen, who all played important roles in our team by assisting with field work, participating in meetings and giving us valuable feedback on the research process. Sofia Björk provided constructive and helpful comments on Chapter 7.

Co-housing, sustainable urban development and governance

An introduction

Håkan Thörn, Henrik Gutzon Larsen, Pernilla Hagbert and Cathrin Wasshede

This book is a critical contribution to the growing research field that has emerged in connection with a new wave of co-housing that has been identified in both the United States and Europe in the 2000s (Williams 2005; Sargisson 2012; Tummers 2016; Lang et al. 2018). It provides an analysis of different forms of co-housing in relation to contemporary discourses on urban development, housing provision and sustainability, and how co-housing is realized in the context of local urban governance. With rising real estate values in cities, de-regulations of housing markets and what increasingly appears to be a permanent and global housing crisis (Aalbers 2015; Madden and Marcuse 2016), it has become even more difficult for low-income groups to access affordable housing. In addition, rising concerns over climate change and other ecological and social impacts of modern ways of living have contributed to a growing interest in developing more socially, ecologically and economically sustainable modes of living. Co-housing is often lauded as an alternative housing form with the potential to meet these challenges. This book takes its departure from the need for a critical exploration of co-housing in the context of sustainable urban development.

All the contributors to the book were part of a research team involved in a four-year research project centred on in-depth studies of co-housing in and around major cities in Sweden, Denmark, Germany and Spain. While we do not compare co-housing in these countries according to a conventional national-comparative approach, these four countries were chosen to explore how co-housing developments can be understood and contextualized in urban sustainability discourses and policies in Europe today. In particular, aspects such as diverse housing policies, varying cultural traditions of co-housing, tenure and ownership forms, and processes of individualization, were seen as relevant starting points. However, we also argue that an analysis of co-housing needs to consider not just the national, but also the specific municipal, and the more general global context at the same time.

Our field work was carried out in a European context. In this respect, the research has a clear Western European focus, at least empirically. Nevertheless, we also treat co-housing practices and their interaction with local government and national contexts as responses to, and articulations of, wider developments, particularly those that have been conceptualized as neoliberal urbanism (Mayer 2016). We argue that our research is relevant for an understanding of contemporary housing politics, not only in Europe, but more generally in advanced capitalist countries where neoliberal urbanism has created housing crises of different shapes, and where sustainable urban development has been adopted as an agenda for urban governance. Questions explored in this book centre on aspects such as the socio-political contextualization of co-housing; concepts of sustainability; strategies of, and relations between, different actors in promoting co-housing; gentrification, inclusion and exclusion.

Based on Danish experiences with *bofællesskaber*, the concept of 'co-housing' (sometimes spelled 'cohousing') was introduced internationally in the late 1980s by McCamant and Durrett (1988). In this book, however, we highlight a few significant historical predecessors to co-housing in the early twentieth century (see Chapters 2, 3 and 8), demonstrating that the empirical phenomena it refers to tend to reappear in periods when capitalist society is in various forms of crisis (economic, social, cultural or ecological). Importantly, these phenomena have been considered by the involved practitioners, and by many researchers and policy makers, as *alternatives* to dominant forms of housing available on the housing market or provided by governments. Key recurring values in definitions and practices of co-housing are (intentional) *community, autonomy* (as in self-governance), *affordability* and, since the 1970s, *ecology* (as in resource-saving, ecological housing and lifestyle). Since the 2010s, these values have tended to be subsumed under the umbrella of 'sustainability' and its different dimensions – social, ecological and economic.

As will be evident in this book, definitions of co-housing and sustainability vary, and there is great variation in the values that define and are realized by different co-housing projects. One of our aims is therefore to chart and examine the meanings ascribed to both 'co-housing' and 'sustainability' in the context of co-housing projects and (local) government support for co-housing. Rather than suggesting a 'correct' definition in our concluding chapter, we will provide a contextualization and an analysis of the different meanings of co-housing. We will demonstrate that differences in meanings and practices depend on different historical, political, economic and cultural contexts.

This being said, our empirical research required a basic, if open, definition in order to know what to look for. We have limited this definition to three elements. First, we understand co-housing as 'a stress on collectivity in everyday life' (Droste, 2015: 79). Second, our understanding of co-housing involves a significant element of self-organization, which also implies that the co-housing community is intentional and has established procedures for self-governance. Third, co-housing is understood to entail a spatially relational aspect, with individual housing units organized in a (at least somewhat) collective spatial setting. Beyond these criteria, co-housing could involve a number of different ownership and tenure forms, ways of organizing everyday life, forms of collective identity and self-governance, architectural forms, etc. While broad, these criteria make our focus more specific than the wide-ranging term 'collaborative housing'. At the same time, the criteria also allow us to distinguish co-housing from the multitude of often small living arrangements that could be termed 'communes' (cf. Vestbro 2010a). Beyond these specifications, the open definition serves our purposes of empirically examining meanings ascribed to co-housing in different contexts. Importantly, however, our explanations and interpretations are based on structural and contextual analyses.

Researching co-housing: beyond a normative approach

It is no coincidence that the first ever international conference on co-housing was held in Sweden in 2010. The conference reflected a renewed interest in co-housing around the world, but it was also a result of the research conducted in Sweden on co-housing over a long period. As early as 1982, Dick-Urban Vestbro, the editor of the conference proceedings (Vestbro 2010b), published a comprehensive book on the history of collective housing ideas, including co-housing (Vestbro 1982). Vestbro's agenda was clearly activist in nature, in support of co-housing.

Co-housing research is still, to some extent, often characterized by such a normative approach. The current resurgence of interest in co-housing, also among politicians and urban planning and housing practitioners, can be seen in light of co-housing activists and activist-researchers successfully utilizing the political opportunities opened by the discourse on sustainable urban development to promote co-housing. Tellingly, 'planning for sustainable lifestyles' was a central theme of the 2010 co-housing conference in Stockholm (Vestbro 2010b). This renewed interest in co-housing reflects sustainability agendas that have different emphases, as co-housing is examined and analysed in terms of environmental, social as well as economic sustainability benefits. Recent co-housing literature has dealt with these different dimensions in various ways, for example: exploring co-housing as conceived in Low Impact Living Affordable Community developments (Chatterton 2013); the potential for reducing energy use as a result of sharing common areas (Kido and Nakajima 2012); as self-managed housing (Tummers 2016); in building social capital (Ruiu 2016); as a desirable alternative for older people (Scanlon and Arrigoitia 2015); an opportunity for municipalities to foster socially inclusive urban development (Droste 2015); recreating a (lost) sense of community (Jarvis and Bonnett, 2013); in relation to designing for gender equality (Vestbro and Horelli, 2012); living together privately (Chiodellia and Baglione 2013); as well as offering improvements in individuals' health, care needs and well-being, and strengthening neighbourhood support and associational involvement (Kehl and Then 2013). A special issue of *Built Environment* devoted to co-housing discusses co-housing both as contributing to urban renewal and as a way of achieving sustainability in a broader sense (Krokfors 2012). The renewed research interest in co-housing (and collaborative housing) has also generated a special issue of *Urban Research & Practice* (Tummers 2015) and a forthcoming special issue of *Housing, Theory and Society.*

Richard Lang, Claire Carriou and Darinka Czischke (2018) present a comprehensive overview of research on collaborative housing in Europe during the period 1990–2017. While their scope is broader than ours, since they consider co-housing as only one, though significant, form of collaborative housing, we believe that their conclusions are highly relevant for co-housing research. The authors not only ask for more research on collaborative housing in general. They also argue that there is a lack of studies with perspectives that are non-normative and that pay attention to historical and societal contexts. Further, they point to a number of under-researched empirical themes, including what needs and ideological motivations drive housing projects, the socio-economic attributes of inhabitants, and to what extent housing projects involve 'radical living'.

We share this analysis of the field, and our book addresses some of the gaps identified by Lang, Carriou and Czischke. In particular, we emphasize contextual aspects, which we believe are not only under-researched but also under-theorized in contemporary co-housing research. Further, our approach differs from co-housing research that normatively starts with the assumption that, if successful, co-housing is a positive thing in itself because it is practiced with intentions to counteract the unsustainability of contemporary urban development. This does not mean that we side with the few co-housing 'cynics' against the many co-housing 'believers', to use Tummers' (2016) labels. Rather, our approach is different in the sense that it is defined by a critical perspective, providing explanations and interpretations based on structural and contextual analyses. While critical analysis of the role of the sustainability agenda in contemporary urban governance is not uncommon anymore, it is less common in existing research on co-housing. Even if we as researchers, like many others, see great potential in co-housing, it is important not to idealize it by disregarding the problems and conflicts that can emerge from this housing form. For example, we will discuss the risk of co-housing being co-opted or used by local or national governments as a way to legitimize economically, socially and/or ecologically unsustainable large-scale urban restructuring. We will show how 'successful' co-housing can contribute to processes of gentrification, where groups that are relatively strong in economic, social and cultural capital displace weaker groups. If co-housing becomes middle-class enclaves, this form of housing loses much of its transformative potential.

Our contribution to the field of co-housing research thus consists in providing analytical tools to integrate empirical research on co-housing with a structural analysis of contemporary urban governance, particularly concerning the way that agency is structured by the economic and political logics that define this context. Conversely, we argue that an analysis of co-housing projects provides an excellent case for advancing our analytical understanding of how sustainable urban development is governed in urban restructuring processes. In the following section, we will present our contextual approach, starting with a discussion on the discourse of sustainable development, and then presenting two contextual dimensions of co-housing.

The discourse on sustainable urban development

On 25 September 2015, the United Nations adopted the 2030 Agenda for Sustainable Development, which centres around 17 sustainable development goals set up to end poverty, protect the planet and ensure prosperity for all. Goal number 11, 'sustainable cities and communities', in turn, includes both social and ecological sub-goals, such as access to 'adequate, safe and affordable housing', participatory planning and management, and reducing 'the adverse per capita environmental impact of cities' (UN 2017). Urban sustainability issues paradoxically position cities as both the nexus of ecological crises, and as arenas for socio-technical solutions (Brenner and Schmid 2015). The role cities play in sustainability transitions, including the importance of urban governance, is also increasingly examined in fields such as transition management and innovation studies (Geels 2011).

However, the discourse on sustainable urban development is not new. On the contrary, it has been a major concern for municipalities worldwide for around three decades. This focus within contemporary urban development has also been reflected in a number of critical analyses of the discourses on sustainable urban development. These have often been theoretically driven (e.g. Marcuse 1998), based on analyses of municipal policy declarations or statements by planners and policymakers (e.g. Davidson 2010a; 2010b), as well as more empirically driven in providing a snapshot of how 'frontline' sustainable urban development projects are framed by the various actors involved (Hagbert et al. 2013), and how urban sustainability practices and discourses are constructed and circulated globally (Hult 2015).

Peter Marcuse (1998) has argued that the discourse on sustainable urban development is inherently contradictory and constructs 'the social' in a manner that other scholars have termed 'post-political' or 'de-politicizing' (Mouffe 2005; Swyngedeouw 2007). This discourse tends to suppress social conflicts in favour of a supposed consensus surrounding sustainability, since it rests on the assumption 'that there are social policies of universal benefit, that everyone, every group, every interest will or should or must accept in their own best interests' (Marcuse 1998: 111).

Regarding economic sustainability, official discourses, such as underlined in the UN Sustainable Development Goals, include economic growth and even presuppose it as essential to sustainable development, in spite of the critiques associated with the 'degrowth' and 'post-growth' argument that there is a profound contradiction between growth and a socially just development within planetary boundaries (Martínez-Alier et al. 2010; Kallis 2018). In the context of advanced liberal urban governance (Scheller and Thörn 2018), the concept of 'smart growth' has been introduced as a new, market-based strategy for land and housing development that is supposed to be able to integrate economic, social and ecological sustainability (Krueger and Gibbs 2008). Following ideas of ecological modernization (Lidskog and Elander 2012), key notions are often the promotion of eco-efficient technology, coupled with policies to strengthen financial incentives for investors and developers. Empirical insights moreover indicate that interpretations of sustainability in new sustainable urban development and in housing in particular tend to be market-oriented, incremental and technology-centred (Hagbert et al. 2013; Jensen and Gram-Hanssen 2008; Lovell 2004).

Contrary to the original intentions of the Brundtland Commission, the three dimensions of sustainability (the economic, the social and the ecological) have increasingly been separated, with programmes often designed to address only one or at best two dimensions (Davidson 2010a). While environmental and technical dimensions have tended to dominate the agenda for decades, social dimensions have only recently received more attention (Vallance et al. 2011; Jensen et al. 2012). The meaning of sustainable urban development has also become increasingly ambiguous, and perhaps particularly so regarding its social dimension – often interpreted in terms of social capital (Bourdieu 1986) and/or social cohesion (Fonseca et al. 2019) rather than in terms of social justice and equality. Davidson (2010a), for example, discovered a multiplicity of definitions of social sustainability in his examination of both policy literature and municipal programmes: social equity issues relating to access to services, facilities and opportunities; issues to do with the sustainability of community itself; social mixing; liveability; affordable housing; tolerance; street life; or a more targeted concern with homelessness, the 'under-served' or 'under-represented', such as seniors, youth and children. The 'mixing' of housing of various types, sizes and tenure forms, has in particular become a widespread strategy for addressing social sustainability in urban policy and planning practice (Dempsey et al. 2011).

While we find it accurate to view sustainable urban development as an empty signifier (Davidson 2010b) with global reach (considering the UN Sustainability Development Goals and the transnational circulation of urban sustainability practices), it does not imply that the actual meaning ascribed to sustainable urban development in different contexts is irrelevant or of no consequence (Scheller and Thörn 2018). On the contrary, empirical studies are needed to understand how the discourse actually works in various local contexts. Along these lines, this book is intended as a contribution to an emerging body of in-depth analyses of how sustainable urban development is put into *practice* (e.g. Metzger and Rader Olsson 2013), linking up with the body of work on local and regional sustainability with both a critical and an empirical orientation (e.g. Gibbs and Krueger 2007; Krueger and Gibbs 2008; Agyeman et al. 2002). In particular, Chapters 5, 9 and the Conclusion examine to what extent co-housing projects address, contrast and/or meet the sustainability goals as defined in official discourses and/or by practitioners. To what 'sustainability problems' is co-housing perceived as a solution by the cities, or by residents themselves? How is 'sustainability' conceptualized?

Contextualizing co-housing: civil society and governance

Our contextualization of co-housing will be set in relation to an *analytical distinction* between two contextual dimensions: 1) *urban civil society*, referring to the construction of communities and collective and individual identities in connection with the articulation of, and struggle over, values, norms and ideologies that govern urban life; and 2) *urban governance*, in this context referring to political and economic governing of urban life by public and private institutions and actors including government agencies, private companies and housing markets; and civic actors, such as associations and social movement organizations. In contemporary urban governance we have seen an increasing significance of collaboration between different types of actors and institutions in public-private-civic partnerships, which we have also found to increasingly involve co-housing. Related to the two contextual dimensions, we have identified two key dimensions of co-housing: forms of community, and forms of autonomy (in the sense of self-governance). Within these interlinked dimensions, we have identified certain dilemmas and conflicts that concern co-housing practices. These may be the result of tensions between different key values that define co-housing culture in Europe today, or, more importantly, might constitute conflicts between these values and the structural conditions that provide both constraints and opportunities for the realization of co-housing projects. Throughout the chapters of this book, and returning to this discussion in the conclusion, we will demonstrate how different and sometimes even conflicting definitions that guide co-housing practices may be seen as distinct ways to approach the three dimensions of sustainable urban development and the dilemmas that they involve.

Co-housing in the context of civil society: forms of community

In research, co-housing has most often been theorized as an expression of civil society, with concepts such as 'social capital', 'intentional community', 'social cohesion' or 'solidarity' as key analytical tools. From this perspective, the 'co' in co-housing implies a collective dimension of housing, as opposed to an individual, or private, form of dwelling. In this sense, co-housing may be seen as a particular form of (intentional) community that involves the articulation of a collective identity. At the same time, and particularly so in the contemporary wave, co-housing projects and research emphasize how co-housing combines collectivity with space for individual or private autonomy. This is spatially expressed in the fact that co-housing involves both shared and private spaces. A dilemma associated with this dimension concerns how much space the co-housing project, in its spatial organization and activities, should allow for individual/private autonomy, without undermining the collective side and thus ceasing to be a co-housing project. While the tension between collectivity and individual autonomy has been a recurring theme in co-housing research (Lang et al. 2018), less attention has been paid to the fact that this relation is often mediated by family relations. A significant part of many co-housing projects' self-understanding as experiments in 'alternative ways of life', if not 'radical living' (ibid.), is exploring new ways of doing family relations. While far from all co-housing projects involve such practices, we argue that family practices are key to understanding relations between the individual and the collective in co-housing projects, which is why we examine this subject in particular in Chapter 7.

The relation between the individual, the family and the collective also needs to be contextualized in relation to different cultural traditions that exist in national civil societies. The World Value Survey has established that two of our case countries, Sweden and Denmark, belong to those where individualization has gone deeper than in most other countries in the world (World Value Survey 2019). Inglehart's cultural map emphasizes religious traditions, placing Scandinavia in the Protestant sphere, and the less individualized countries, such as Spain, in the Catholic sphere, while Germany is on the border between the Catholic and the Protestant. At the same time, we would also emphasize that the degree of individualization may be seen as a cultural effect of the different political models that transformed social life in the post-war era (Esping-Andersen 1990). Further, In Part I of the book (Chapters 1–4), we examine how contemporary forms of co-housing need to be understood in relation to the historical trajectories of twentieth-century national housing politics and struggles, which, while sometimes having a transnational dimension, have been shaped by the specific political cultures that define civil society in the respective countries.

However, co-housing is not only shaped by national civil society cultures. In fact, the two post-war waves of co-housing partly emerged as local articulations of transnational movements. For example, in Denmark and Sweden the first wave was an extension of the 1960s counterculture (Chapters 1 and 2), while co-housing in Hamburg and Barcelona are related to the transnational squatting movement (Chapter 6).

It is not just informal but also formal organizational forms that shape co-housing projects. This importantly involves the modes through which the self-governance of the co-housing project is exercised, which tend to be affected by the associational life of the wider civil society context of which co-housing is part. Further, a co-housing project is not only a community in itself, but also creates links to the wider community, including not only the neighbourhood, but also the city. These relations may partly depend on how the form of collective identity corresponds with the identities of the neighbourhood and the wider community. While most co-housing projects identify with the concept of 'alternatives', they typically have strategies to avoid becoming 'gated communities'. As will be demonstrated in Chapter 8, a dilemma associated with this is that a strong emphasis on strategies for opening up the co-housing project to the neighbourhood and/or the city may undermine the sense of internal community that is crucial to sustain the co-housing project – and vice versa. Further, different ways of dealing with this dilemma again depend on the civil society context of the co-housing project in the city, including both the characteristics of community and associational life in the neighbourhood and the city.

To sum up, in relation to the context of urban civil society and the dimension that we call forms of community, we ask the following questions in various ways and to different degrees:

- *Internal relations*: What forms of collective identity are articulated in co-housing projects? What relations between community, individual and family do they imply? What forms of self-organization are used and what modes of self-governance do they involve?
- *Alternative forms of housing and the organization of everyday life*: To what extent, and how, do actual co-housing practices provide alternatives to dominant forms of housing and the organization of everyday life? How do they relate to national and transnational cultures and movements? Do they practice alternatives to the nuclear family? To what extent, and how, are co-housing projects designed to challenge and/or reproduce power inequalities?
- *Architectural forms*: What is the relation between the spatial organization of co-housing projects and the social, and how do they interact with the wider context of contemporary urban development?
- *External relations*: What are the strategies for 'opening up', and linking, the co-housing project to the neighbourhood and the city?

Co-housing in the context of urban governance: forms of autonomy

Historically, the relation between co-housing and governments is multi-faceted and ambiguous. In Chapter 2 we will point to how the early-twentieth-century collective houses in Sweden were, if not initiated, then at least supported by the government as a way of addressing both a housing crisis and specific housing needs. However, as an expression of the transnational counter-culture, the first post-war co-housing wave emphasized autonomy, based on Left and Green ideas (with the important exception of Sweden, where co-housing projects espousing such Leftist or Green ideas still involved cooperation with local government through its housing companies, see Chapters 2 and 5). In the current co-housing wave, we see an even more diverse picture, involving a strong tendency among several European countries towards active involvement of both social movements and local government.

We will use the concept of 'governance' for our analysis of co-housing projects' relations, not just with local, regional and national government, but also with private housing companies, housing markets and social movements. Unlike 'government', 'governance' highlights not only relations between different levels of government, but also includes 'partnership relations' with private and civic actors. This 'partnership trend' in urban governance needs to be seen in relation to a wider context, not least in terms of what we call advanced liberal governance. This form of governance involves collaboration between local government and private capital in public-private partnerships, leading urban development through both de-regulation and re-regulation. While these processes can partly be characterized in terms of neoliberal urbanism, we also use the term 'advanced liberal' (Miller and Rose 2008; Thörn and Larsson 2012) to highlight that contemporary urban governance does not necessarily mean less politics, less regulation, or less government in the way that the neoliberal dogma stipulates. This is clearly seen in our four case countries, where de-regulation has been combined with re-regulation to support market mechanisms (Chapters 1–4).

There are five dimensions to this form of governance (Thörn and Larsson 2012), all relevant to understanding how co-housing relates to governance in this context: First, *marketization* involves both de-regulation and re-regulation to support privatization, and has supported gentrification of inner-city areas and commercialization of its public spaces (Lees et al. 2008). Second, partnerships between public, private and civic organizations are organized for *co-regulation*, a process conceptualized by David Harvey (1989) as a shift from managerialism to entrepreneurialism. Third, this mode of governance is performed according to a new form of *responsibilization*, emphasizing self-governance and active involvement by civil society and business in political responsibilities that were previously associated with state agencies (Burchell 1993: 275–276). Fourth, this mode of governance also involves new forms of *disciplinary power*, e.g. sanctions introduced when civil society agents do not perform the responsibilities imposed on them, such as the self-governance of housing. Fifth, ideologically, these strategies also involve a heavy *emphasis on sustainability* in policy documents and declarations. While cities' policy declarations emphasize all three pillars of sustainability, referring to the UN Agenda, they rarely recognize tensions or contradictions between them. Definitions of economic and ecological dimensions are often straightforward; goals of on-going urban re-structuring are defined in terms of sustaining the economic growth of cities and increasing their climate adaptation. Definitions of social sustainability are, in contrast, rather ambiguous. In our understanding, sustainable urban development functions as an empty signifier, and as such

> works to embrace a multiplicity of different articulations, to provide cohesion, to work as a point of identification for a heterogeneous array of actors, and to encompass diverse and sometimes contradictory strategies and policies.
>
> (Scheller and Thörn 2018: 917)

This provides a starting point for our analysis in Chapter 5 of the meaning of sustainability in relation to forms of governance as a dimension of co-housing.

Since its meaning is not fixed, it is instead necessary to examine empirically how the discourse actually works – and varies – when it is translated into governing strategies and co-housing practices in the local contexts of urban governance.

Urban governance and the housing needs and strategies expressed through co-housing are also to a significant degree shaped by housing market conditions. For example, the co-housing wave of the 1980s in Sweden intersected with a housing surplus on the national housing market (produced by the Swedish government's 'Million Programme') that made it possible for co-housing projects of significant size to take over and retrofit high-rise buildings with highly affordable apartments. In stark contrast, contemporary co-housing in Europe is faced with a housing shortage and a lack of affordable housing that need to be understood in relation to the conditions in the housing market, which are defined by a roll-back of housing policies in combination with increasing capital investment in housing property and urban land – a process involving commodification, speculation and financialization of housing.

Inflating property prices in cities and the deregulation of the housing sector have led to mounting housing costs. The 2008 financial crisis in Europe has contributed to making it even more difficult for low-income groups to access appropriate housing. In Spain, property speculation played an important role in the crisis. Urban competition between cities to attract capital, tourism and middle-class taxpayers involves urban development projects and rising property values that produce gentrification and deepen socio-economic segregation. In this context, one possibility for co-housing groups is to form self-build groups (see Chapter 5).

The relation of co-housing projects to the market is first and foremost expressed in their ownership and tenure forms, which consequently is a matter of great concern (Larsen 2019). As we will argue in the conclusion, this dimension of co-housing has the greatest impact on the extent to which sustainability goals can be realized. We will demonstrate how co-housing may involve a number of different tenure and ownership forms. This variation partly reflects differences in housing legislation and housing market conditions in different countries. Importantly, it is also the result of collective choices that reflect the ideological commitments and class backgrounds of the residents in the co-housing projects. This is particularly relevant for decisions concerning whether ownership should be non-speculative or speculative, which we regard as having profound consequences for a co-housing community, and have found to be an issue related to ideological tensions in co-housing activism.

To sum up, in relation to the context of urban governance and the dimension that we call forms of autonomy, we ask the following questions:

- *Relations with government and public-private partnerships*: How are co-housing projects affected by support from, interaction with and regulation by, political institutions? To what extent are they part of public-private partnerships and how are they affected by it? What conflicts or tensions have emerged between various forms of government (national, regional and local) and co-housing projects? Who is addressed and who is not addressed by the political programmes and which alternatives come to the fore?

- *Ownership and tenure forms*: Which ownership and tenure forms exist in co-housing and how do they relate to the housing market in the particular national context? How do ownership and tenure forms affect forms of community?
- *Social composition and gentrification*: How does the social composition of co-housing projects affect, and how is it affected by, different legally instituted tenure forms? To what extent, and how, does contemporary co-housing counteract and/or play a part in gentrification and, more generally, processes of social and geographical inclusion and exclusion?

Our research

As explored in the project and elaborated on in this book, the prevalence of co-housing differs significantly between the countries, which meant that the approach taken in our research also varied. Denmark and Sweden were selected as they are often lauded as co-housing pioneers. As post-war Scandinavian welfare states, the two countries have certain cultural, political and economic similarities. However, in Chapters 1 and 2 we will also demonstrate how and why, in spite of these similarities, co-housing developments in the two countries look quite different. In addition to specific studies of co-housing communities in Denmark and Sweden, the research provides an updated overview of co-housing in the respective countries to also capture more general developments. In Germany, the sheer number of co-housing projects renders a similar task unfeasible, motivating instead a focused exploration of co-housing in the particular urban context of Hamburg – currently leading co-housing developments in Germany, which in turn can be considered as a leading country for co-housing developments in Europe. Our analysis in Chapters 3, 5 and 6 demonstrates how this is a result of the interplay between a significant presence of urban movements in Hamburg, on the one hand, and an active response from the city on the other. Conversely, in the case of Spain, co-housing as an alternative housing form is new, and there are only a few completed projects. Focusing on the Barcelona area, we demonstrate in Chapters 4 and 6 how this development partly needs to be understood as a response to the 2008 economic crisis, which led to a housing crisis that hit Spain harder than any other European country, but also as a challenge to longer-term social, political and economic developments.

A note on method and material

Since it was not our aim to carry out a systematic comparative analysis of co-housing (for the reasons given above), our collection of empirical material in

Denmark, Germany, Spain and Sweden differed with respect to the prevalence of co-housing, as described, and with regard to the issues we came to recognize as particularly salient in the four contexts. Our field work consisted of two national surveys (in Denmark and Sweden), a large number of interviews, collection of policy documents and visits to co-housing projects. The Danish survey provides the basis for Chapter 1 in the book. As the survey in Sweden did not turn out to be as productive (as too many declined to answer) as that in Denmark, we relied more heavily on semi-structured qualitative interviews in the Swedish case – as we did in the cases of Barcelona and Hamburg.[1] The majority of our qualitative interviews were conducted with people living in or attempting to set up co-housing projects, focusing on 1) experiences of living in co-housing projects; 2) the values they ascribe to co-housing, the strategies used to realize them, and the possible tensions and conflicts in relation to this; and 3) interactions with governments, mostly at the local level. Our method involved triangulation in the sense that we also analysed documents produced by co-housing projects to find out about their values and strategies; we interviewed politicians, policy makers and architects; and we analysed policy documents, to identify interactions between co-housing projects and governments.

Structure of the book

The book is divided into two main parts. Part I analyses and presents co-housing developments in the four case countries. While the chapters on Denmark and Sweden provide an overall picture of national developments, the chapters on the larger countries of Germany and Spain particularly focus on Hamburg and Barcelona respectively. Throughout Chapters 1–4, however, we argue that contemporary co-housing should be seen in relation to historical developments specific to national contexts in the twentieth and twenty-first centuries.

Chapter 1 provides an overview of five decades of co-housing developments in Denmark. Danish co-housing (*bofællesskaber*) is often seen as pioneering and relatively successful. With a dose of hyperbole, McCamant & Durrett (2011: 37) characterize it as 'the gold standard for cohousing world-wide'. Danish co-housing has been relatively successful and we chart the history of this development. But we also show that Danish co-housing projects to a large extent are enclaves for the relatively privileged. We argue that this importantly relates to the prevalence of owner-occupied tenure in Danish co-housing. But the Danish case also points at more affordable and possibly more inclusive ways to organize ownership in co-housing – cooperative tenure and rental housing in non-profit housing associations.

Chapter 2 outlines the context of co-housing development in Sweden, anchored historically in the collective houses of the 1930s, often built as private initiatives with little public support. The chapter describes how the new generation of co-housing in the 1980s, with roots in the alternative movement, aimed to create a sense of community in a society that was understood to create isolation. Enabled by a surplus of empty flats in the wake of the 1970s' economic crisis, several co-housing projects of the time were established in remodelled rental apartment buildings owned by municipal housing companies. Conditioned by the marketization of Swedish housing since the 1990s, contemporary co-housing in Sweden nonetheless remains a marginal phenomenon, with little public support or interest from the mainstream housing market, and with high construction costs that make new co-housing accessible only to a relatively well-to-do middle class.

Chapter 3 discusses the dynamic relationship between housing movements and local government in Germany, and specifically Hamburg, from the historical starting point of the cooperative movement in the later nineteenth century up to the present day. The aim of the chapter is to extrapolate the historical sediments that constitute tenure forms and (co-)housing struggles today. On the one hand, bottom-up movements have been the driving force for putting housing needs and demands on the political agenda during various crises, and movements have thus initiated social and structural change. They have created new political opportunity spaces and eventually enabled changes in the legal system and provided the background for new forms of tenure. On the other hand, local government has at times been supportive of collaborative housing, making changes to the legal framework and providing financial support through subsidies and the non-profit provision of land. Against this background, movements for collaborative housing can be seen as crucial actors for pushing forward sustainable urban development discourses. The municipality, in turn, partly reacts to demands for more affordable housing and the integration of self-governance.

Chapter 4 addresses the Barcelona area, where co-housing is a recent and still only emerging phenomenon. Using the La Borda project as a recurring illustration, but also drawing on other examples and developments, the chapter seeks to contextualize this nascent but noticeable interest in co-housing. Starting at the scale of the crisis-ridden Spanish housing system, the chapter gradually zooms in on co-housing at the scale of Catalonia, Barcelona, neighbourhoods and, eventually, the La Borda project. While still only emerging, co-housing activism in the Barcelona area is characterized by a high degree of urban-political awareness and organization, and the chapter suggests that this can serve as inspiration for those who want co-housing to evolve into a more sustainable housing form.

Part II provides in-depth thematic analyses of co-housing. While Chapters 5–6 focus on relations between co-housing projects and their neighbourhood or wider urban context, chapters 7–8 mainly focus on how the internal relations of co-housing practices are articulated in everyday life, as well as in the socio-spatial organization. Chapter 9, finally, critically examines whether (and if so, in what ways) co-housing can be seen as part of fundamental socio-ecological sustainability transitions.

Chapter 5 explores the intersection of co-housing, governance and urban sustainable development by analysing six co-housing projects in Hamburg and Gothenburg. The two cities were selected because both have launched programmes to support self-build groups and co-housing as part of their emphasis on promoting urban sustainability. With regard to the relation between autonomy and the capacity to realize sustainability goals, we found an interesting paradox: among our cases, the co-housing group that was most exposed to government strategies that prioritize the sustainability agenda also seemed to be the least capable of fulfilling a comprehensive 'sustainability agenda', while the co-housing group with the highest degree of autonomy had the greatest capacity to realize both ecological and social sustainability goals. We suggest that this paradox may be seen as a function of the economic and political logics of contemporary urban development, in which one pillar of the sustainability agenda – economic sustainability – is defined and practised in terms of 'growth first'.

Chapter 6 investigates how co-housing in Hamburg and Barcelona is often directly or indirectly related to urban activism. With particular attention on squatting and related questions of post-autonomous urban activism, this investigation is structured according to three issues: relations to the state; whether to legalize or not; and intersections with broader movements. On this basis, the chapter discusses what is termed the dialectics of the politics of co-housing, an interplay of bottom-up organizing and top-down governance. This dialectic plays out differently in Hamburg and Barcelona, but the chapter suggests that the underlying possibilities and constraints for co-housing as a sustainable housing form remain the same.

Chapter 7 looks more deeply at everyday life in co-housing, analysing the emotional boundary work relating to 'family' in co-housing communities, with a focus on shared meals, children's relationships and care. Based on empirical material from visits to co-housing communities in Sweden and Denmark, the chapter specifically addresses what are often seen as cornerstones for a sense of collectivity in co-housing: the kitchen and practices of cooking and eating together; and the dream of a 'good childhood' in many multi-generational co-housing communities. The chapter contributes to a recurring theme in research on the relationship between the individual and the collective in co-housing, exploring the different ways of doing family among co-housing residents, and the frictions that emerge.

Chapter 8 argues that co-housing must also be understood, and analysed, as a spatial organization that has shown some important characteristics over a long period. The chapter explores the 'social logic of space' in co-housing, identifying two dialectic processes in the creation of 'commitment' in co-housing: on the one hand, 'detaching' from the surrounding context and, on the other hand, 'attaching' to the collective. Using some central concepts from Hillier and Hanson's space syntax, the chapter questions whether the two seemingly different models of co-housing that have emerged since the 1970s – the 'Danish' cluster of low-rise houses and the 'Swedish' high-rise multi-family building – are really that spatially different. Basing the analysis on early predecessors, the first and second waves of co-housing, as well as empirical insights from contemporary Swedish co-housing communities, the chapter discusses how co-housing can deal dialectically with the potentially vicious circle between 'internal' community and 'external' detachment.

Chapter 9 addresses the socio-ecological sustainability claims of co-housing more specifically. It provides a theoretically based analysis of whether co-housing can be seen as part of more fundamental sustainability transitions, or if it rather serves as an example of incremental, yet insufficient, change within prevalent discourses of ecological modernization and individual responsibilization in contemporary urban development and governance. While co-housing could be dismissed as being merely a slightly 'greener' middle-class lifestyle choice, the principles of anti-consumerist, collaborative, and low-impact everyday practices found in many co-housing communities also have the potential to offer a more radical alternative. In this sense, co-housing can function as an arena for pursuing far-reaching sustainability transitions, but the chapter argues that living in co-housing is not per se to be equated with a sustainable way of living.

In the Conclusion we argue that, while we have demonstrated in this book that definitions of co-housing as well as co-housing practices in different European countries vary, there are some general lessons to be learned for anyone interested in understanding or practising co-housing in the context of advanced capitalist societies. This conclusion has three parts: first, we address the questions asked in the introduction regarding the relation between contemporary co-housing ideas and practices and the discourse on sustainable urban development. Second, we address the questions asked in the introduction regarding the two key dimensions of co-housing, community and autonomy, as understood in relation to the broader contexts of civil society and urban governance. Third, we will conclude by paying particular attention to the constraints on co-housing produced by contemporary urban development regimes as well as the potential of co-housing to contribute towards more just and ecologically sustainable cities.

Note

1 In Denmark, we surveyed co-housing communities as well as co-housing residents. 72 communities and 436 residents replied to these surveys (for a detailed presentation of the methodology, see Jakobsen and Larsen 2018). In Sweden, the survey was sent to 33 co-housing projects, using a list produced by the national co-housing association called KOLLEKTIVHUS.NU, and 17 of them responded. The reason we did not conduct a survey in Germany was a lack of resources to conduct a survey that would be representative of the great number of co-housing projects (3,000). In Spain, the number of known co-housing projects are too few to make it meaningful. In Sweden we conducted 56 qualitative interviews with a total of 64 people; in Spain we conducted 20 interviews with a total of 30 people; in Germany 18 interviews with 24 people; and in Denmark four interviews with a total of six people. In Sweden, Denmark and Germany, the research team included native speakers. In Spain, the research was aided by a local scholar.

References

Aalbers, M. B. (2015) 'The Great Moderation, the Great Excess and the global housing crisis', *International Journal of Housing Policy*, vol. 15, no. 1, pp. 43–60.

Agyeman, J., Bullard, R. D. and Evans, B. (2002) 'Exploring the Nexus: Bringing Together Sustainability, Environmental Justice and Equity', *Space and Polity*, vol. 6, no. 1, pp. 77–90.

Bourdieu, P. (1986) 'The forms of capital', in J. G. Richardson (ed.) *Handbook of Theory and Research for the Sociology of Education*, pp. 241–258. New York: Greenwood Press.

Brenner, N. and Schmid, C. (2015) 'Towards a new epistemology of the urban?', *City*, vol. 19, no. 2–3, pp. 151–182.

Burchell, G. (1993) 'Liberal government and techniques of the self', *Economy and Society*, vol. 22, no. 3, pp. 267–282.

Chatterton, P. (2013) 'Towards an agenda for post-carbon cities: Lessons from Lilac, the UK's first ecological, affordable cohousing community', *International Journal of Urban and Regional Research*, vol. 37, no. 5, pp. 1654–1674.

Chiodellia, F. and Baglione, V. (2013) 'Living together privately: a cautious reading of cohousing', *Urban Research & Practice*, vol. 7, no. 1, pp. 20–34.

Davidson, M. (2010a) 'Social Sustainability and the city', *Geography Compass*, vol. 4, no. 7, pp. 872–880.

Davidson, M. (2010b) 'Sustainability as ideological praxis: The acting out of planning's master-signifier', *City*, vol. 14, no. 4, pp. 390–405.

Dempsey, N., Bramley, G., Power, S. and Brown, C. (2011) 'The social dimension of sustainable development: Defining urban social sustainability', *Sustainable Development*, vol. 19, no. 5, pp. 289–300.

Droste, C. (2015) 'German co-housing: An opportunity for municipalities to foster socially inclusive urban development?' *Urban Research & Practice*, vol. 8, no. 1, pp. 79–92.

Esping-Andersen, G. (1990) *The Three Worlds of Welfare Capitalism*. Cambridge: Polity Press.

Fonseca, X., Lukosch, S. and Brazier, F. (2019) 'Social cohesion revisited: A new definition and how to characterize it', *Innovation: The European Journal of Social Science Research*, vol. 32, no. 2, pp. 231–253.

Geels, F. (2011) 'The role of cities in technological transitions: analytical clarifications and historical examples', in H. Bulkeley, V. C. Broto, M. Hodson and S. Marvin (eds) *Cities and Low Carbon Transitions*, pp. 13–28. London: Routledge.

Gibbs, D. and Krueger, R. (2007) 'Containing the contradictions of rapid development? New economy spaces and sustainable urban development', in R. Krueger and D. Gibbs (eds) *The Sustainable Development Paradox: Urban Political Economy in the United States and Europe*, pp. 95–122. New York: Guilford Press.

Hagbert, P., Mangold, M. and Femenías, P. (2013) 'Paradoxes and possibilities for a "green" housing sector: A Swedish case', *Sustainability*, vol. 5, no. 5, pp. 2018–2035.

Harvey, D. (1989) 'From managerialism to entrepreneurialism: The transformations in urban governance in late capitalism', *Geografiska Annaler B*, vol. 7, no. 1, pp. 3–17.

Hult, A. (2015) 'The circulation of Swedish urban sustainability practices: to China and back', *Environment and Planning A*, vol. 47, no. 3, pp. 537–553.

Jakobsen, P. and Larsen, H. G. (2018) 'An alternative for whom? The evolution and socio-economy of Danish cohousing', *Urban Research & Practice*, doi:10.1080/17535069.2018.1465582

Jarvis, H. and Bonnett, A. (2013) 'Progressive nostalgia in novel living arrangements: a counterpoint to neo-traditional new urbanism?', *Urban Studies*, vol. 50, no. 11, pp. 2349–2370.

Jensen, J. O. and Gram-Hanssen, K. (2008) 'Ecological modernization of sustainable buildings: A Danish perspective', *Building Research & Information*, vol. 36, no. 2, pp. 146–158.

Jensen, J. O., Jørgensen, M. S., Elle, M. and Lauridsen, E. H. (2012) 'Has social sustainability left the building? The recent conceptualization of "sustainability" in Danish buildings', *Sustainability: Science, Practice, & Policy*, vol. 8, no. 1, pp. 94–105.

Kallis, G. (2018) *Degrowth*. Newcastle upon Tyne: Agenda Publishing.

Kehl, K. and Then V. (2013) 'Community and civil society returns of multigeneration cohousing in Germany', *Journal of Civil Society*, vol. 9, no. 1, pp. 41–57.

Kido, H. and Nnakajima, Y. (2012) 'Predicted energy conservation by use of common areas in cohousing', *International Journal of Sustainable Building Technology and Urban Development*, vol. 3, no. 3, pp. 177–184.

Krokfors, K. (2012) 'Co-housing in the making'. *Built Environment*, vol. 38, no. 2, pp. 309–314.

Krueger, R. and Gibbs, D. (2008) '"Third Wave" sustainability? Smart growth and regional development in the USA', *Regional Studies*, vol. 42, no. 9, pp. 1263–1274.

Lang, R., Carriou, C. and Czischke, D. (2018) 'Collaborative housing research (1990–2017): A systematic review and thematic analysis of the field', *Housing, Theory and Society*, doi:10.1080/14036096.2018.1536077

Larsen, H. G. (2019) 'Three phases of Danish cohousing: tenure and the development of an alternative housing form', *Housing Studies*, vol. 34, no. 8, pp. 1349–1371.

Lees, L., Slater, T. and Wyly, E. K. (2008) *Gentrification*. New York: Routledge.

Lidskog, R. and Elander, I. (2012) 'Ecological modernization in practice? The case of sustainable development in Sweden', *Journal of Environmental Policy & Planning*, vol. 14, no. 4, pp. 411–427.

Lovell, H. (2004) 'Framing sustainable housing as a solution to climate change', *Journal of Environmental Policy & Planning*, vol. 6, no. 1, pp. 35–55.

Madden, D. and Marcuse, P. (2016) *In Defense of Housing: The Politics of Crisis*. London: Verso.

Marcuse, P. (1998) 'Sustainability is not enough', *Environment and Urbanization*, vol. 10, no. 2, pp. 103–111.

Martínez-Alier, J., Kallis, G., Veuthey, S., Walter, M. and Temper, L. (2010) 'Social metabolism, ecological distribution conflicts, and valuation languages', *Ecological Economics*, vol. 70, no. 2, pp. 153–158.

Mayer, M. (2016) 'Neoliberal urbanism and uprisings across Europe', in M. Mayer, C. Thörn and H. Thörn (eds) *Urban Uprisings: Challenging Neoliberalism in Europe*, pp. 57–92. Basingstoke: Palgrave Macmillan.

McCamant, K. and Durrett, C. (1988) *Cohousing: A Contemporary Approach to Housing Ourselves*. Berkeley: Habitat Press.

McCamant, K. and Durrett, C. (2011) *Creating Cohousing: Building Sustainable Communities*. Gabriola Island: New Society Publishers.

Metzger, J. and Rader Olsson, A. (eds) (2013) *Sustainable Stockholm – Exploring urban sustainability through the lens of Europe's greenest city*. New York: Routledge.

Miller, P. and Rose, N. (2008) *Governing the Present: Administering Economic, Social and Personal Life*. Cambridge: Polity Press.

Mouffe, C. (2005) *On the Political: Thinking in Action*. London: Routledge.

Ruiu, M. L. (2016) 'The social capital of cohousing communities', *Sociology*, vol. 50, no. 2, pp. 400–415.

Sargisson, L. (2012) 'Second-wave cohousing: A modern utopia?', *Utopian Studies*, vol. 23, no. 1, pp. 28–56.

Scanlon, K. and Arrigoitia, M. F. (2015) 'Development of new cohousing: Lessons from a London scheme for the over-50s', *Urban Research & Practice*, vol. 8, no. 1, pp. 106–121.

Scheller, D. and Thörn, H. (2018) 'Governing "Sustainable urban development" through self-build groups and co-housing: The cases of Hamburg and Gothenburg', *International Journal for Urban and Regional Research*, vol. 42, no. 5, pp. 914–933.

Swyngedeouw, E. (2007) 'Impossible/undesirable sustainability and the post-political condition', in J. R. Krueger and D. Gibbs (eds) *The Sustainable Development Paradox*, pp. 13–40. New York: Guilford.

Thörn, H. and Larsson, B. (2012) 'Conclusions: re-engineering the Swedish welfare state', in B. Larsson, M. Letell and H. Thörn (eds) *Transformations of the Swedish Welfare State: From Social Engineering to Governance?* pp. 262–282. Basingstoke: Palgrave Macmillan.

Tummers, L. (2015) 'Introduction to the special issue: Towards a long-term perspective of self-managed collaborative housing initiatives', *Urban Research & Practice*, vol. 8, no. 1, pp. 1–4.

Tummers, L. (2016) 'The re-emergence of self-managed co-housing in Europe: A critical review of co-housing research', *Urban Studies*, vol. 53, no. 10, pp. 2023–2040.

UN (2017) 'Sustainable development goals'. https://sustainabledevelopment.un.org/topics/sustainabledevelopmentgoals (23 January 2017).

Vallance, S., Perkins, H. C. and Dixon, J. E. (2011) 'What is social sustainability? A clarification of concepts', *Geoforum*, vol. 42, no. 3, pp. 342–348.

Vestbro, D.-U. (1982) *Kollektivhus från enkökshus till bogemenskap*. Stockholm: Statens råd för byggnadsforskning.

Vestbro, D.-U. (2010a) 'Concepts and terminology', in D.-U. Vestbro (ed.) *Living Together – Cohousing Ideas and Realities Around the World*, pp. 21–29. Stockholm: Division of Urban and Regional Studies, Royal Institute of Technology.

Vestbro, D.-U. (ed.) (2010b) *Living Together – Cohousing Ideas and Realities around the World*. Stockholm: Royal Institute of Technology.

Vestbro, D.-U. and L. Horelli (2012) 'Design for gender equality: The history of co-housing ideas and realities', *Built Environment*, vol. 38, no. 3, pp. 315–335.

Williams, J. (2005) 'Designing neighbourhoods for social interaction: The case of cohousing', *Journal of Urban Design*, vol. 10, no. 2, pp. 195–227.

World Value Survey (2019) www.worldvaluessurvey.org/WVSContents.jsp?CMSID=Findings (3 June 2019).

Part I

Co-housing in context

1 Denmark

Anti-urbanism and segregation

Henrik Gutzon Larsen

Introduction

In a newspaper intervention from the late 1960s, the architect Jan Gudmand-Høyer (1968: 3) made a plea for probing the 'practical possibilities of realising "the missing link" between utopia and the outdated single-family house'. Gudmand-Høyer was somewhat vague on the nature of this 'missing link', but he suggested a vision of a housing form made up of several individual units devised to foster 'interplay between common and private spaces'. Moreover, he indicated that this vision emerged from a 'consciousness of the good that only can be realised through cooperation between families' and could have implications beyond the practicalities of everyday life: 'One is tempted to compare thoughts on a housing form of this sort with attitudes to kindergartens before and now', Gudmand-Høyer suggested: 'Kindergartens originally came into being as a social provision to meet practical needs of parents.... Today, most agree that the kindergarten is a very important character-building factor, which children for their own sake cannot do without.' Together with an earlier newspaper intervention by the psychologist Bodil Graae (1967), who with an eye for children's life similarly argued for a new housing form (also Graae 1969), Gudmand-Høyer's call is often seen as a key impetus for the rise of what eventually became known as *bofællesskaber* (approximately living or housing communities). In turn, these communities subsequently inspired the architects Kathryn McCamant and Charles Durrett (1988) to coin the term 'co-housing' (cf. Vedel-Petersen et al. 1988: 101).

This chapter analyses how Danish co-housing has developed over the five decades since Jan Gudmund-Høyer and Bodil Graae published their interventions. Often seen as pioneering and relatively successful, Danish co-housing is habitually mentioned in the literature on co-housing and collaborative housing more generally, and is the subject of several case studies (e.g. McCamant and Durrett 2011; Tornow 2015). As in the recent study by Beck (2019), these studies tend to focus on the 'internal' dimensions of co-housing communities. Whether concerned with architecture or social relations, such studies are important and necessary. In line with the other chapters in Part 1 of this book, however, this chapter approaches Danish co-housing in a perspective that emphasises longer historical trends and broader societal contexts. This entails that much of the richness and variation of co-housing is lost. But a wider perspective can help to situate case studies and to identify more general successes and challenges.

In Denmark, as in other countries, it could be said the co-housing has come in two 'waves' since the second world war. In the Danish context, this amounts to a pioneering wave during the 1970s and 1980s, and a more recent wave since some time in the late 1990s. But in comparison with the many communities that were established in the 1970s and the 1980s, the recent 'wave' is rather a ripple (Figure 1.1).[1] To a significant degree, I will argue, this is because Danish co-housing has evolved in three phases, which are closely tied to the dominant tenure form of new co-housing communities (also Larsen 2019). Rather than a singular 'wave', the rise of Danish co-housing during the 1970s and 1980s was in fact sustained by two distinct phases. While by not suggesting that tenure forms should be the essence of debates on co-housing, the chapter – like this book – emphasises the importance of property relations and is structured in three sections that roughly follow the three tenure-oriented phases of Danish co-housing: a first phase from about 1970 to 1981, a second phase from 1981 to 2004 (but effectively ending in the early 1990s), and a third phase from some time in the late 1990s until today.

Following from the issue of tenure forms, the underlying concern of this chapter is social sustainability in the sense of access to and affordability of co-housing. (For an analysis of environmental dimensions of Danish co-housing, see Marckmann et al. 2012.) It should in this respect be noted that the focus is placed on the 'traditional' intergenerational co-housing communities. In

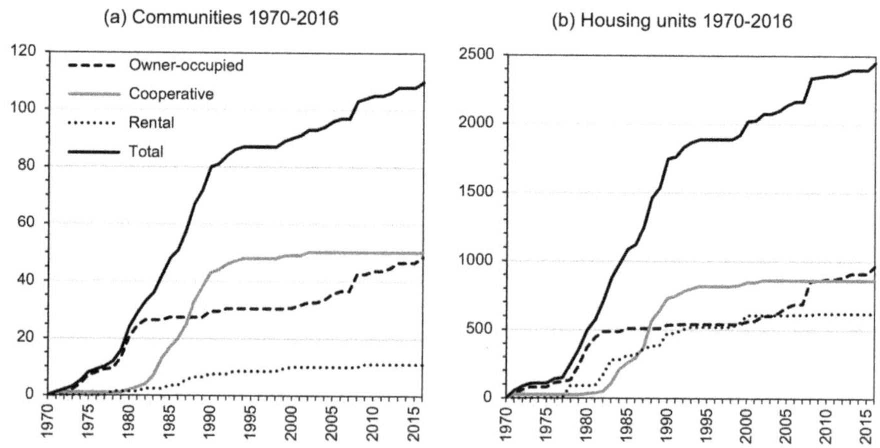

Figure 1.1 Danish intergenerational co-housing communities and housing units, 1970–2016 (cumulative count of 110 communities)
Source: Jakobsen and Larsen (2018)

some cases, it can be difficult to draw a line between these communities and kindred housing forms. But we have in our research identified 110 intergenerational co-housing communities (Figure 1.1), and a qualified estimate would be that there are some 150 intergenerational co-housing communities in Denmark today. Co-housing reserved for particular groups, notably the many senior co-housing that have been in Denmark established over the past three decades (Pedersen 2015), is only addressed in passing.

First phase

There was a history to Gudmand-Høyer's 1968 call for a new housing form. Already in 1964, he and a group of friends had begun discussing the possibilities of an alternative housing form. As Gudmand-Høyer (1984: 7) later put it, they were a 'group of second generation Copenhageners with peasant roots, who had grown weary of the large city'. The detached houses and high-rise blocks of the suburbs were not seen as inviting. Rather, the group wanted to reconstruct some of the qualities that had characterised Danish villages before the enclosure (*udskiftningen*), and with inspiration from More's *Utopia* and early philanthropic and cooperative housing projects, the aim was a community of some thirty families. The group found a plot of land near a forest on the outskirts of Copenhagen, but their plans were frustrated by the neighbours: 'their fear of this odd project was so pronounced that they ganged up and bought the piece of land that should have been our access road' (Gudmand-Høyer 1984: 7). It was against this background that Gudmand-Høyer in exasperation wrote his 1968 call for what became known as *bofællesskaber*, co-housing communities. By then, however, Danish society was in rapid change:

> [O]ver the next month we received almost a hundred letters and loads of calls from people, who believed in the idea and wanted to live in such a place. It was overwhelming, now there were suddenly possibilities for creating not one but three or four co-housing communities. Journalists poured in. Now they suddenly found the theme highly relevant. But by then, of course, we had reached the middle of the year of the youth rebellion.
>
> (Gudmand-Høyer 1984: 7)

As suggested by Gudmand-Høyer, Danish co-housing emerged as 'child' of the cultural, social and political changes associated with the 1960s and '1968' specifically. And while many co-housing projects soon were faced with the economic crises of the 1970s and 1980s, the ideas germinated in a context of mounting prosperity and the 'golden years' of the welfare state. Ideas about alternative housing forms were not new, of course. Since around 1900, Denmark had seen the development of housing cooperatives, which questioned conventional notions of housing as either privately owned or rented (Larsen and Lund Hansen 2015). Somewhat closer to the everyday-life concerns of the emerging co-housing communities, some 'collective houses' (*kollektivhuse*) had been built during the 1930s and 1950s (Langkilde 1970; Nielsen 1979; on collective houses, see also Chapter 2). But the aim of these houses was particularly to rationalise domestic work within traditional families. The co-housing ideas were closer to the generally small communes (*kollektiver*), which from the mid-1960s sought 'a rebellion against the isolation of the individual and the family' (Hansen 1979: 54). Christensen and Kristensen (1972) estimate that there by 1971 were more than 700 of these communes in Denmark. And at a larger scale, Denmark in the early 1970s saw collective experiments such as Thylejren (est. 1970) in Norther Jutland and the 'free city' of Christiania (est. 1971) in Copenhagen (Buus et al. 2010; Thörn et al. 2011).

There were clear connections between the emerging co-housing communities and the wider phenomenon of communes. Indeed, the first recorded use of '*bofællesskab*' appeared in a 1971 newspaper notice seeking people for a 'commune-like co-housing community' (*kollektivlignende bofællesskab*) (Anonymous 1971; Jarvad 1999). The word caught on. In the newspaper *Information*, which during the 1970s became a key channel for debates on all aspects of the new social movements, there were 78 entries using '*bofællesskab*' in 1976, and the number peaked with 274 entries in 1981. During the 1980s, annual entries settled around some 150 before falling to 50–100 from the early 1990s onwards (Dagbladet Information, no date). Not least during the 1970s and 1980s, many of these entries were notices by people seeking (or seeking to form) some kind of collaborative housing arrangement. Possibly because it is less susceptive to prejudice, '*bofællesskab*' was (and is) frequently used as a synonym for '*kollektiv*' (commune). And well into the 1980s, both scholarly and more popular texts often had to clarify a distinction between the more widely known communes and the emerging co-housing communities (e.g. Andersen and Lyager 1984; Reich and Bjerre 1984). In spite of some affinities with communes and other collective ventures, however, the Danish co-housing communities were more mainstream. We shall here take note of three features of Danish co-housing, which emerged during the 1970s.

First, and in a sense defining, the co-housing communities that emerged during the 1970s were generally a housing form that combines individual housing units with substantial common spaces and activities aimed at everyday life. As already noted, there were (and are) some ambiguities in the use of co-housing as '*bofællesskab*'. But by the late 1980s, the term had generally assumed this meaning. For Navne (1987: 11), for example, co-housing communities (as distinct from communes) are characterised by 'several, fundamentally independent housing units, which are inhabited by families, individuals or groups that cooperate on a range of activities in relation to their daily household work.' A similar characterisation was used in a study by the Danish Building Research Institute (Vedel-Petersen et al. 1988) – and internationalised by McCamant and Durrett (1988). The material cornerstone of commonality is generally the 'common house' (or a similar space), which typically includes a kitchen and a dining room for common meals. To make room for this, spatially and financially, the size of the individual dwellings is often somewhat smaller than in 'ordinary' housing. In line with the ideas of Bodil Graae (1967; 1969), pioneering co-housing communities like Sættedammen (est. 1972) originally expected children to become a key common concern, but somewhat surprisingly, it was common meals that became central (Bendixen et al. 1997; see also Chapter 7).[2] Reflecting a general trend in Danish co-housing, it is no coincidence that Overdrevet (est. 1980) made 'Do you really eat together every day?' the title of its silver jubilee publication (Ove R. Drevet 2005). (Many co-housing communities do not have common meals every day and participating is usually voluntary.) Reflecting on their spatial relationship to the surrounding society, a point to which we will turn next, Hansen (1979: 55) describes the early Danish co-housing communities as 'collective individualists'. But given their private-common characteristic, this notion could equally be applied to the internal community of Danish co-housing.

Second, and partly to enable the private-common feature, Danish co-housing communities have since the 1970s generally (but not exclusively) been purpose built and have assumed a rather distinct architectural form and geography. During the 1970s, the so-called dense-low (*tæt-lav*) architecture was particularly dominant (Jantzen and Kaaris 1984). This style is associated with a 1971 architecture competition by the Danish Building Research Institute, and, as Nygaard puts it, dense-low in Denmark became 'the architecture of the new Left' and aimed to 'build *low* to preserve relations to nature and *dense* to achieve social contact' (Nygaard 1984: 227, 230). Dense-low was not confined to the emerging co-housing communities, but this architecture became somewhat of a hallmark; in the words of Hansen (1984b: 17), 'a ring of dense and low buildings around some form of common space is the most general image of the contemporary Danish co-housing community' (see also Hansen 1984a; and Chapter 8). Additionally, Hansen notes, these communities generally have a 'somewhat solitary location' in the urban periphery, and it is a striking feature of Danish co-housing communities that they were (and are) located mainly in suburban or quasi-rural environments (for a map, see Jakobsen and Larsen 2018). In part, this geography is explained by the price of land, but there are also other forces at play. As we have already seen, co-housing pioneers like Gudmand-Høyer sought away from the city, and this feeds into a wider 'anti-urban' sentiment of the 1970s. This is illustrated by two much-debated visions for a radical different Denmark. On the Left, the 1972 *Langeland Manifesto* outlines a vision of the country separated into thousands of loosely federalised settlements of 200–1,000 individuals (Reich and Prins 1977), while from the political centre, the 1978 *Revolt from the Centre* includes a somewhat similar vision of society structured into small, mainly rural units based on participatory democracy (Meyer et al. 1978; 1981). Nygaard (1984) sees the anti-urban sentiments of the 1970s as a national-romantic reaction to Denmark's (hotly debated) 1973 entry into the European Economic Community (EEC). This is probably only a partial explanation, but it remains that Danish co-housing communities from the outset generally have assumed the form of village-like developments in suburban or quasi-rural settings. In the critical assessment of Lund (1981), this reflects longer-standing notions of the 'evil city' set against the 'good countryside', for which he sees Ebenezer Howard's garden city as an antecedent, and Lund castigates the early co-housing communities as 'escape-utopias' (*flugtutopier*) for the educated class.

Third, it is characterising for the co-housing communities that emerged during the 1970s that they with only a few exceptions were based on owner occupation (Figure 1.1). To a large extent, this was because owner occupation – often through imaginative constructions – was the only available way to organise (and finance) housing experiments. But it could also be argued that ownership structures were a secondary issue for many co-housing pioneers. In the words of one pioneer:

> [W]hether the state, credit institutions or the inhabitants themselves in the last instance own the co-housing communities is, for the time being, a secondary detail. The issue is first and foremost whether people *themselves* can shape and manage their housing environment. Put a little lavishly: It is about the right to everyday democracy.
>
> (Meyhoff 1984: 7)

An alternative option was to establish co-housing communities as rental housing in the existing sector of non-profit housing associations (*almennyttige boliger*, today *almene boliger*). This happened in a few instances, notably Tinggården (est. 1978), the winning project of the low-dense housing competition (Kragh 1979). But the non-profit housing sector did not leave room for the experimentation and self-management sought by co-housing pioneers (Byggeriets Udviklingsråd 1983; Gudmand-Høyer 1984), and Kløvedal (1981) was 'furious' when he saw the pragmatic results of the Tinggården project he had helped to conceive. When ownership structures in co-housing became a point of debate in the 1980s, a point to which we will return, Gudmand-Høyer (1984) found that the price of an owner-occupied dwelling in his own co-housing community – Skråplanet (est. 1973) – was 'quite reasonable' and that the community did not lived up to its media reputation of being a 'well-to-do project' (*velhaverprojekt*). Nonetheless, a report aimed at promoting co-housing concluded that 'the privately-owned co-housing communities will remain reserved for a rather small group of the better-off' (Byggeriets Udviklingsråd 1983: 20). Andersen (1985: 58) similarly notes that co-housing in the late 1970s was 'mostly restricted to higher income groups due mainly to the high housing costs of newly built owner-occupied housing.'

Second phase

The early 1980s saw a change in Danish politics, which was not aimed at the emerging co-housing communities but had a significant impact on their multiplication. The opportunity came with the introduction of state support for new-built housing cooperatives in 1981. Housing cooperatives in Denmark has a history that reaches back to the years around 1900, but from the 1930 onwards, most housing cooperativism was absorbed into the sector of non-profit housing associations. A few housing cooperatives (*andelsforeninger*) remained, however, and particularly in cities like Copenhagen, this tenure form got a boost when legislation in 1975 gave tenants a first option to form a cooperative and buy existing rental housing (with state support), should their landlord choose to sell (Larsen and Lund Hansen 2015). But in 1981, as aid to a slumping construction industry, it also became possible to apply cooperative tenure (with state support) to new-built housing. As McCamant and Durrett (1988: 142) aptly put it, this was a 'windfall' for Danish co-housing, which, as we have seen, is mostly purpose built.

Technically, the 1981 law made it possible for a housing cooperative to cover 80 per cent of construction costs through loans on which it had to pay index-linked instalments while the state covered accumulated interests. Practically, this had significant implications. In the first of a series of interventions in the newspaper *Information*, which sought to reenergise Danish co-housing, Reich and Bjerre (1984: 5) found that the 'in all its technical tedium', the 1981 law was 'the most epoch-making concession Danish legislation in time immemorial has bestowed on the self-management idea, the cooperative ideology [*andelstanken*], the commune movement or evolutionary, utopian socialism'. In essence, like several others at the time, Reich and Bjerre saw the law as an opportunity for people, who wanted to develop co-housing but who had little money for it. Cooperative tenure could, in other words, potentially rid Danish co-housing of the image of being 'well-to-do communes' (*velhaverkollektiver*) (Nygaard 1984: 251). And because cooperative tenure could make co-housing accessible to a larger group of people, some humorously nicknamed this model 'the Volkswagen of co-housing' (Bjerre and Sørensen 1984).

While not necessarily strictly as low-dense architecture, the spatial form of village-like settlements in the urban periphery continued to characterise Danish co-housing during the 1980s, and so did the mixing of individual dwellings with common facilities and activities. Reflecting broader trends in society, the 1980s involved a greater attention to environmental and ecological dimensions (Nygaard 1984), which eventually entailed that some co-housing communities were set up a eco-villages (Marckmann et al. 2012). In the perspective of this chapter, however, the most notable change during the 1980s was the virtual total shift from owner occupation to cooperative tenure as the basis for new co-housing communities (Figure 1.1). To a significant extent, this implied that new co-housing communities became more affordable. In the Danish context, a housing cooperative implies that the property is owned collectively and that members have a use-right to a housing unit. But apart from a monthly fee, members must buy a 'share' (*andel*) to gain access. The price of shares is regulated by law rather than the market, however, and during the 1980s and 1990s, shares in housing cooperatives were comparatively affordable. At least until the early 2000s (Bruun 2018; Larsen and Lund Hansen 2015), whether as co-housing or otherwise, Danish housing cooperatives were non-speculative limited-equity cooperatives. Comprehensive data are not available, but an inventory of one of the first co-housing communities based on cooperative tenure, Uldalen (est. 1983) in northern Jutland, suggests a relative wide and varied socio-economic composition (Bjerre and Sørensen 1984). A later study also confirms that cooperative-tenure co-housing communities were more diverse than owner-occupied ones with respect to age, income, occupation and family structure (Vedel-Petersen et al. 1988).

Even in its cooperative form, co-housing was the target of some criticism in the 1980s. For Petersen (1984), for example, true social change would emerge from labour relations rather than from alternative housing forms (for a reply, see Meyhoff 1984). This paralleled scepticism towards cooperativism in the early Danish labour movement (Grelle 2012; 2013), which again was rooted in classic Marxism (e.g. Engels 1979). Without the more affordable cooperative tenure, however, it is unlikely that Danish co-housing communities would have expanded as rapidly as they did during the 1980s. But state support for new-built housing cooperatives was governed by quota, and as economic conditions improved, quota for housing cooperatives dried out in the early 1990s and the legislation was eventually terminated in 2004. In some cases, although not for co-housing, state support for new-built housing cooperatives had also been used as a way to produce owner-occupied housing in all but name. Just as co-housing had been an unintended beneficiary of a state policy, the arguably most substantial boost to this housing form was similarly ended by wider changes.

Third phase

While other factors undoubtedly played a part, much suggests that gradual termination of state support for new-built housing cooperatives played an important part in slowing down the establishment of new co-housing communities during the 1990s (Figure 1.1). When new communities again began to be established, owner occupation was again the dominant tenure. Some co-housing communities based on (or including) rental housing in non-profit housing associations have been established over the years, and as these communities often are bigger than communities based on owner occupation or cooperative tenure, their share in terms of housing units is notable. But owner-occupied co-housing is now catching up on (or even surpassing) co-housing based on other tenure forms. In a sense, Danish co-housing has since the late 1990s returned to where it was in the 1970s. But the context has changed, of course. We shall here take note of two aspects.

First, it should be acknowledged that co-housing generally is highly valued by those who live in these communities. Of the 436 respondents to a survey among Danish co-housing residents in the winter 2016–2017, 34% replied that co-housing was 'strongly positive' for their general life satisfaction, 45%

replied 'generally positive' and 10% 'more positive than negative' (Jakobsen and Larsen 2018). But according to a recent analysis, motives for choosing co-housing have changed. Whereas the co-housing communities (and communes) of the 1970s in many ways were 'ideological experiments, which sought to challenge the norms and values of established society and to explore new gender roles and family forms', contemporary co-housing is 'a sort of practical "lifebelt" for the modern human and an attempt to recreate the meaningful social relations that are no longer automatically provided by the nuclear family' (Dansk Bygningsarv 2016: 15).

Second, the state – local as well as central – is starting to take notice of co-housing. This does not amount to what we see in cities like Barcelona, Hamburg or Gothenburg. But in comparison to the indifference by municipalities noted by Gudmand-Høyer (1984), for instance, there have been changes. Central government has commissioned a series of reports aimed at promoting co-housing (Dansk Bygningsarv 2016; Second City 2016; Urgent.Agency and LB Analyse 2016), and several municipalities are actively trying to promote this housing form. To a large extent, however, co-housing is in these efforts seen as an instrument of regional development, not least to attract people to the depopulating areas peripheral to the prospering metropolitan regions – what has become known as the 'outer Denmark' (*Udkantsdanmark*) (Carter et al. 2015). This is aided by the fact that most new co-housing communities continue to be located in suburban or quasi-rural locations. The price of land in this respect remains an important factor. But the non-urban character of most co-housing communities is probably also aided by the wish of many to settle outside urban centres (Aner 2016).

Changing motives and instrumental intentions do not diminish the value of living in co-housing, of course. But it should be noted that Danish co-housing in its current form is exclusive. Our survey of Danish co-housing residents shows that they in important respects differs from the country average (for a comprehensive presentation and discussion of the survey results, see Jakobsen and Larsen 2018). In terms of socio-economic status, the co-housing respondents are above the Danish average in the upper-level and particularly the medium-level categories of employees, while the number of unemployed and people receiving transfer payments is significantly below the average. Even more prominent, compared to the 25% Danish average, 83% of the co-housing respondents had a medium-long education (e.g. schoolteacher) or a university education. No less than 44% of the co-housing respondents had completed a master or a doctoral degree (compared to a little above 8% Danish average). Finally, 97% of the co-housing respondents were 'Danish' by ancestry, while the Danish average is 87%. We should be careful when drawing conclusions from a voluntary survey. That said, the survey clearly suggests that Danish co-housing residents are highly educated, belong socio-economically to the middle and upper strata of society, and that they predominantly are ethnic Danes. This is particularly pronounced for residents in owner-occupied co-housing. But residents in co-housing based on cooperative or rental tenure are also above the Danish average, if more towards the 'middle'.

Focused on Sweden, but equally applicable to Denmark, Berggren and Trägårdh (2015) argue that the Scandinavian countries have developed a social contract based on 'anti-social solidarity', a system where individuals through collective solidarity have obtained a radical autonomy from traditional communities, notably family and church (see also Introduction). This argument is centred on the Scandinavian welfare state. But twisting a notion from Hansen (1979), I have previously suggested that Danish co-housing communities internally as well as externally could be described as composed of 'collective individualists'. And one could speculate whether the relative success of co-housing in Denmark has to do with this housing form's adaptability to a society based on 'anti-social solidarity'.[3]

Conclusions

While still only a fraction of all housing, co-housing as *bofællesskab* has over the past five decades developed into a comparatively well-established and successful alternative housing form in Denmark. While the word has been and is used in various ways, co-housing as *bofællesskab* has generally come to imply a housing form that combines individual dwellings with substantial common facilities and activities aimed at everyday life. Regular common dinners, prepared and consumed in common facilities, have become somewhat of a hallmark of this in Danish co-housing (as similar to Sweden, see Chapter 2).

Broadly following this 'bottom line' understanding, a significant number of senior co-housing communities have emerged over the past three decades. In this chapter, however, the focus has been on intergenerational co-housing. There are considerably differences between these communities, of course. Seen as a group, however, two features stand out. First, and perhaps most striking, Danish co-housing is particularly located in suburban or quasi-rural settings. However, it would be wrong to deduce from this that Danish co-housing is outright 'anti-urban'. There are examples of communities in urban settings, and other urban co-housing projects are at various stages of completion. A key reason for the suburban and quasi-rural location of many co-housing communities is the cost of land, particularly when co-housing groups aim for a spatial form of detached or semidetached houses. Still, in the 1970s when co-housing emerged, influential ideas about small and geographically disbursed communities were circulating, and many continue to seek non-urban milieus for settlement. To a significant degree, the geography of Danish co-housing reflects these wider sentiments. Second, and arguably more profound, Danish co-housing communities are based on three of the four main tenure forms in Denmark: owner occupation, housing cooperatives (*andelsforeninger*) and non-profit rental housing (*almene boliger*).[4]

How did it come to look this way? To a significant degree, as I have argued in this chapter, this is because Danish co-housing has evolved in three phases, which are closely tied to shifts in the dominant tenure form of new co-housing communities (Figure 1.1). In the first phase, from round about 1970 to 1981, new co-housing communities were almost exclusively based on owner occupation. This was mainly because owner occupation was the only readily available tenure form for groups, which needed purpose-built housing to facilitate the housing form they were pursuing and wanted to be in control of both the production and maintenance of the resulting housing. However, this also implied that co-housing became relatively expensive. Rental housing in the non-profit housing associations sector was a more affordable alternative that was used in the establishment of some communities. But regulations governing this sector were not compatible with the wishes of most would-be co-housing groups. This changed during the second phase, starting in 1981 when it became possible to establish new-build housing cooperatives with state support. While not a policy aimed at co-housing, this greatly facilitated the establishment of new co-housing communities. On the one hand, cooperative tenure made co-housing more affordable; and, on the other hand, the tenure form made it possible for co-housing groups to retain autonomy. Much suggests that state support for new-build cooperative housing was a significant reason for the continued expansion of co-housing during the 1980s. In fact, it could be argued that the pioneering 'wave' of Danish co-housing would have been less remarkable and sustained without state-supported cooperative tenure. However, state support for new-build cooperative housing was regulated by quota, and as the wider economic issues that had prompted the policy changed, the possibility of state support dried out from the early 1990s and was finally terminated in 2004. Therefore, during the third phase from sometime in the late 1990s, new co-housing communities are again predominantly based on owner occupation.

What does this historical development imply for contemporary Danish co-housing in relation to sustainability issues? Ecological sustainability has not figured large in this chapter. It is reasonably clear, however, that Danish co-housing in many cases is a contribution rather than challenge to this aspect of sustainability. The challenges for Danish co-housing is mainly in the realm of social sustainability. Again, it should be underlined that co-housing generally is highly important and beneficial to people living in these communities. For this reason alone, co-housing is an alternative housing form that is worthwhile to pursue. But if social sustainability is considered to include issues such as equality and social justice, notably in the form of affordable housing, Danish co-housing faces a challenge. There are notable examples of co-housing communities based on (or including) the most affordable tenure, rental housing in non-profit housing associations, and many communities are still based on (or include) the comparatively affordable cooperative tenure. But the return of owner occupation as the dominant tenure of new co-housing communities excludes low- and lower-income groups. It is in this respect indicative that our research shows that the inhabitants of Danish co-housing communities are significantly better educated than the Danish average, have a high socio-economic status and are overwhelmingly of Danish ancestry.

It has been debated whether co-housing is a form of gated community (Chiodelli 2015; Chiodelli and Baglione 2014; Ruiu 2014). Little suggests that Danish co-housing communities are, or likely to become, gated communities in a literal sense. Rather, the risk is that co-housing communities will become (if not remain) enclaves for the relatively privileged. As most Danish co-housing communities are purpose-build, these communities generally do not displace people directly (on forms of displacement, see Marcuse 1986). Nonetheless, this may amount to new-build gentrification (Davidson and Lees 2010). More importantly, co-housing based on owner occupation is likely to contribute to the commodification of housing and land (cf. Clark 2005), which, in Denmark as elsewhere, is a root cause of social and spatial inequalities (Olsen et al. 2014). Co-housing communities formed during the second phase moved somewhat away from this path. But during the current third phase, Danish co-housing has largely – if not necessarily enthusiastically – returned to the path of commodification. If co-housing is to depart 'from the often "middle-class" character attributed to these initiatives' (Czischke 2018: 58), it will in the Danish context as a minimum require a critical engagement with tenure forms and ownership structures. A greater involvement with the sector of non-profit housing associations is in this respect an obvious option, which would bring Danish co-housing somewhat closer to the situation of co-housing in Sweden. However, there are other possibilities. Denmark (like Sweden) may have been pioneer country in developing what today is seen as 'co-housing'. However, if co-housing is to evolve into an inclusive housing alternative, there is much to be learned from German and emerging Spanish experiences.

Notes

1 Danish co-housing communities are not systematically registered by any public or private entity. Figure 1.1 is based on a list compiled from the Internet page bofællesskab.dk and other sources, including inputs from co-housing residents. The list is not exhaustive, but it is the most complete registration of Danish co-housing communities. Tenure status is mainly based on a survey completed by 72 communities. For the remaining communities, tenure status and number of housing units has been established using Internet sources, primarily community homepages. This analysis only captures communities that still exist, but there are few examples of co-housing communities that have been dissolved – once they have negotiated the thorny establishment process. For a full discussion of the methodology and date of Figure 1.1, see Jakobsen and Larsen (2018).

2 In this chapter, including Figure 1.1, the year the first members of a co-housing community took up residence is used as the year of establishment. The group behind the community is usually several years older.

3 Somewhat similar, Sandstedt and Westin (2015) suggest that co-housing in Sweden is a late-modern phenomenon that is beyond *Gesellschaft* and *Gemeinschaft*.

4 The fourth tenure form, private rental housing, is in some instances offered for a few housing units of co-housing communities, for example as dwellings for young adults.

References

Andersen, H. S. (1985) 'Danish low-rise housing co-operatives (bofællesskaber) as an example of a local community organization', *Scandinavian Housing and Planning Research*, vol. 2, no. 2, pp. 49–66.

Andersen, H. S. and Lyager, P. (1984) 'Tæt-lave bofællesskaber – erfaringer, problemer og perspektiver', *Arkitekten*, vol. 86, no. 4, pp. 78–81.

Aner, L. G. (2016) 'Dwelling habitus and urban out-migration in Denmark', *European Urban and Regional Studies*, vol. 23, no. 4, pp. 662–676.

Anonymous (1971) 'Kan dit barn heller ikke klare alm. skole?', *Dagbladet Information*, Copenhagen, 19 November 1971, p. 5.

Beck, A. F. (2019) 'What is co-housing? Developing a conceptual framework from the studies of Danish intergenerational co-housing', *Housing, Theory and Society,* doi: 10.1080/14036096.2019.1633398.

Bendixen, E. L., Dilling, L., Holten, C., Illeris, S., Illeris, G., Bjerre, B. and Rasmussen, B. (1997) *Sættedammen i 25 år.* Hillerød: Sættedammen.

Berggren, H. and Trägårdh, L. (2015) *Är svenskan människa? Gemenskap och oberoende i det moderna Sverige* (second edn). Stockholm: Norstedts.

Bjerre, L. and Sørensen, E. M. (1984) 'Bofællesskabernes folkevogn', *Blød By*, no. 29, pp. 41–43.

Bruun, M. H. (2018) 'The financialization of Danish cooperatives and the debasement of a collective housing good', *Critique of Anthropology*, vol. 38, no. 2, pp. 140–155.

Buus, M., Knudsen, P. Ø., Poulsen, O., Skipper, F. and Sørensen, S. (2010) *Thylejren.* Thisted: Museet for Thy og Vester Hanherred.

Byggeriets Udviklingsråd (1983) *Veje til bofællesskab.* Copenhagen: Byggeriets Udviklingsråd.

Carter, H., Larsen, H. G. and Olesen, K. (2015) 'A planning palimpsest: neoliberal planning in a welfare state tradition', *European Journal of Spatial Development*, no. 58, pp. 1–20.

Chiodelli, F. (2015) 'What is really different between cohousing and gated communities?', *European Planning Studies*, vol. 23, no. 12, pp. 2566–2581.

Chiodelli, F. and Baglione, V. (2014) 'Living together privately: for a cautious reading of cohousing', *Urban Research & Practice*, vol. 7, no. 1, pp. 20–34.

Christensen, S. K. and Kristensen, T. S. (1972) *Kollektiver i Danmark.* Copenhagen: Borgen/Basis.

Clark, E. (2005) 'The order and simplicity of gentrification – a political challenge', in R. Atkinson and G. Bridge (eds) *Gentrification in a Global Context: The New Urban Colonialism*, pp. 256–264. London: Routledge.

Czischke, D. (2018) 'Collaborative housing and housing providers: towards an analytical framework of multi-stakeholder collaboration in housing co-production', *International Journal of Housing Policy*, vol. 18, no. 1, pp. 55–81.

Dagbladet Information (no date) Digitalised archives of *Dagbladet Information.* www.information.dk (7 June 2016)

Dansk Bygningsarv (2016) *Fremtidens bofællesskaber.* Copenhagen: Udlændinge-, Integrations- og Boligministeriet.

Davidson, M. and Lees, L. (2010) 'New-build gentrification: its histories, trajectories, and critical geographies', *Population, Space and Place*, vol. 16, no. 5, pp. 395–411.

Engels, F. (1979) *The Housing Question.* Moscow: Progress Publishers.

Graae, B. (1967) 'Børn skal have hundrede forældre', *Politiken*, Copenhagen, 9 April 1967, pp. 49–50.

Graae, B. (1969) 'Den store familje', *Politiken*, Copenhagen, 16 March 1969, pp. 49–50.

Grelle, H. (2012) *Det kooperative alternativ: Arbejderkooperationen i Danmark 1852–2012*. Copenhagen: Arbejdermuseet & Arbejderbevægelsens Bibliotek og Arkiv.

Grelle, H. (2013) *The cooperative alternative: worker cooperation in Denmark 1852–2012*. Copenhagen: Arbejdermuseet & Arbejderbevægelsens Bibliotek og Arkiv.

Gudmand-Høyer, J. (1968) 'Det manglende led mellem utopi og det forældede enfamiliehus', *Dagbladet Information*, Copenhagen, 26 June 1968, p. 3.

Gudmand-Høyer, J. (1984) 'Ikke kun huse for folk – også huse af folk', *Dagbladet Information*, Copenhagen, 4 April 1984, p. 7.

Hansen, J. W. (1979) 'Sættedammen – 60'ernes sociale opbrud og kollektiverne', *Blød By*, no. 3, pp. 54–55.

Hansen, J. W. (1984a) 'Den nye type: Tæt-lav bofællesskaberne i Danmark', *Arkitektur*, vol. 28, no. 6, pp. 239–247.

Hansen, J. W. (1984b) 'Made in Denmark: De danske bofællesskaber', *Blød By*, no. 31, pp. 15–19.

Jakobsen, P. and Larsen, H. G. (2018) 'An alternative for whom? The evolution and socio-economy of Danish cohousing', *Urban Research & Practice*, doi:10.1080/17535069.2018.1465582

Jantzen, E. B. and Kaaris, H. (1984) 'Danish low-rise housing', *Scandinavian Housing and Planning Research*, vol. 1, no. 1, pp. 27–42.

Jarvad, P. (1999) *Nye Ord: Ordbog over nye ord i dansk 1955–98*. Copenhagen: Gyldendal.

Kløvedal, H. J. (1981) 'Hvad var det nu vi ville? Et rasende indlæg i jubilæumsdebatten', *Blød By*, no. 13, pp. 16–21.

Kragh, S. (1979) 'Tinggården i Herfølge', *Blød By*, no. 3, pp. 37–40.

Langkilde, H. E. (1970) *Kollektivhuset – en boligforms udvikling i dansk arkitektur*. Copenhagen: Dansk Videnskabs Forlag.

Larsen, H. G. (2019) 'Three phases of Danish cohousing: tenure and the development of an alternative housing form', *Housing Studies*, vol. 34, no. 8, pp. 1349–1371.

Larsen, H. G. and Lund Hansen, A. (2015) 'Commodifying Danish housing commons', *Geografiska Annaler: Series B, Human Geography*, vol. 97, no. 3, pp. 263–274.

Lund, N.-O. (1981) 'Den onde by og det gode land', *Blød By*, no. 13, pp. 35–37.

Marckmann, B., Gram-Hanssen, K. and Christensen, T. H. (2012) 'Sustainable living and co-housing: evidence from a case study of eco-villages', *Built Environment*, vol. 38, no. 3, pp. 413–429.

Marcuse, P. (1986) 'Abandonment, gentrification, and displacement: the linkages in New York City', in N. Smith and P. Williams (eds) *Gentrification of the City*, pp. 153–177. Boston: Allen & Unwin.

McCamant, K. and Durrett, C. (1988) *Cohousing: A Contemporary Approach to Housing Ourselves*. Berkeley: Habitat Press.

McCamant, K. and Durrett, C. (2011) *Creating Cohousing: Building Sustainable Communities*. Gabriola Island: New Society Publishers.

Meyer, N. I., Helveg Petersen, K. and Sørensen, V. (1978) *Oprør fra midten*. Copenhagen: Gyldendal.

Meyer, N. I., Helveg Petersen, K. and Sørensen, V. (1981) *Revolt from the Center*. London: Boyars.

Meyhoff, P. (1984) 'Bofællesskaber, huspriser og samfundsforandringer', *Dagbladet Information*, Copenhagen, 4 April 1984, p. 7.

Navne, A.-D. (1987) *At bo i fællesskab: En bog om kollektiver og bofællesskaber*. Copenhagen: Arkitektes Forlag.

Nielsen, E. S. (1979) 'Klintgården – 30'ernes danske kollektivbebyggelse', *Blød By*, no. 3, p. 24.

Nygaard, E. (1984) *Tag over hovedet: Dansk boliggyggeri fra 1945 til 1982*. Copenhagen: Arkitektens Forlag.

Olsen, L., Ploug, N., Andersen, L., Sabiers, S. E. and Andersen, J. G. (2014) *Klassekamp fra oven: Den danske model under pres*. Copenhagen: Gyldendal.

Ove R. Drevet (2005) *Spiser I virkelig sammen hver dag? Et bofællesskab i 25 år*. Hinnerup: Bofællesskabet Overdrevet/SøftenDal.

Pedersen, M. (2015) 'Senior co-housing communities in Denmark', *Journal of Housing for the Elderly*, vol. 29, no. 1–2, pp. 126–145.

Petersen, H. (1984) 'Det store parcelhus', *Dagbladet Information*, Copenhagen, 27 March 1984, p. 9.

Reich, E. K. and Bjerre, P. (1984) 'Fællesskabets ubrugte kræfter', *Dagbladet Information*, Copenhagen, 28 February 1984, p. 5.

Reich, E. K. and Prins, H. K. (1977) *Langelands-manifestet – en skitse til Danmark* (second edn). Copenhagen: Imladris.

Ruiu, M. L. (2014) 'Differences between cohousing and gated communities: a literature review', *Sociological Inquiry*, vol. 84, no. 2, pp. 316–335.

Sandstedt, E. and Westin, S. (2015) 'Beyond Gemeinschaft and Gesellschaft: cohousing life in contemporary Sweden', *Housing, Theory and Society*, vol. 32, no. 2, pp. 131–150.

Second City (2016) *Fire byer på jagt efter nye fællesskaber*. Copenhagen: Udlændinge-, Integrations- og Boligministeriet.

Thörn, H., Wasshede, C. and Nilson, T. (eds) (2011) *Space for Urban Alternatives? Christiania 1971–2011*. Möklinta: Gidlunds förlag.

Tornow, B. (2015) 'Dänemark, Pionierland für Cohousing/Denmark, pioneer country for cohousing', in wohnbund e.V. (ed.) *Europa: Gemeinsam Wohnen/Europe: Cooperative Housing*, pp. 80–91. Berlin: jovis Verlag GmbH.

Urgent.Agency and LB Analyse (2016) *Deleby: Bofællesskaber som drivkraft for regional udvikling*. Copenhagen: Udlændinge-, Integrations- og Boligministeriet.

Vedel-Petersen, F., Jantzen, E. B. and Ranten, K. (1988) *Bofællesskaber: En eksempelsamling*. Hørsholm: Statens Byggeforskningsinstitut.

2 Sweden

In between co-housing and public housing

Claes Caldenby

Introduction

In a Gothenburg suburb dating from the 1960s, at the end of a row of similar eight-storey point-block apartment buildings clad with concrete panels, lies what was once another house of the same sort, but now stands out as a shining example of an energy-efficient building, covered with dark blue solar cells. This is Stacken, which in the 1970s was a pioneer of the small *kollektivhus* (collective house), an alternative Swedish co-housing model based on the sharing of household work. The story of Stacken illustrates the typical Swedish co-housing project, as a concentrated multi-family dwelling, with a strong emphasis on autonomy and community, but at the same time deeply entangled with Swedish housing policy of the post-war decades. A recent Italian survey of co-housing projects from all over the world, in which Stacken is one of the cases discussed, describes the Swedish model as different:

> Unlike other countries in the world, for example the USA, Swedish co-housing projects are usually rented and managed autonomously by the residents in association, but still in municipally owned facilities.
>
> (Gresleri 2015: 160, author's translation from Italian)

Even if things are a bit more complex than that when one looks closer, especially before and after the post-war heyday of the 'Swedish model', this points at some important characteristics of Swedish co-housing. We will come back to Stacken and its almost 40-year-long history, but before that we need a background in the early Swedish co-housing projects of the *kollektivhus* as large multi-family dwellings, and in Swedish housing policy as it developed during the twentieth century.

Together with Denmark, Sweden has been seen as a model for the international development of co-housing in recent decades, but even as far back as the 1930s. The change in terminology in Sweden in the 1980s from *kollektivhus* to *bogemenskap* (co-housing) reflects a change in the scale of the buildings from large institution-like buildings to smaller units (20–50 households). It also, importantly, reflects a change in the organization of household work, from the division of labour to collaboration in cooking, taking care of children and house maintenance as a basis for community (see Caldenby 1992).

Elaborating on the distinction between the two post-war waves of co-housing (see Introduction) it will be argued that in Sweden it is important to identify an important predecessor of the *kollektivhus* (from the 1930s until the 1970s) that was largely intended to provide middle-class women with opportunities to enter the workforce and pursue a professional life. These were often built as private initiatives with relatively little interest or support from the state or municipalities. Later, as part of the first post-war co-housing wave, a new *co-housing* generation (in the 1980s) aimed to create a sense of community in a society that was understood to create isolation. Gender equality and ecological awareness are other aspects of this co-housing generation's roots in the 1970s alternative movement. Flats left empty in the wake of the 1970s economic crisis also offered an opportunity to remodel houses owned by municipal housing companies, thus organizing co-housing in the type of property that dominated in Sweden at the time: rented flats built by municipal housing companies (*allmännyttan*). During this period there was some interest and support from the public sector for co-housing.

More recently however, contemporary co-housing in Sweden (being part of the second post-war international wave) is conditioned by the marketization of Swedish housing since the 1990s, leading to a variety of tenure forms, from sub-letting to cooperatives and tenant-ownership models. The present housing shortage and oligopoly in the Swedish construction sector also means high construction costs for new buildings, especially in central locations in larger cities. All this tends to make new co-housing accessible only to a relatively well-to-do middle class, while public support is somewhat hesitant. The formulated aims of Swedish co-housing are nonetheless still community, gender equality and ecological awareness. In addition, co-housing for older people (55+) is a new form, and has been lauded internationally, with Swedish cases gaining interest from for example South Korea.

The number of officially listed projects (according to the national co-housing association, Kollektivhus NU) is no more than around 40, raising the question whether Sweden can still be considered a forerunner in co-housing development. Nevertheless, it is worth noting that typical Swedish multi-family houses traditionally have common facilities such as a shared laundry room, meeting room and guest room, and in some cases even shared saunas or workshops, which would fall under the definition of co-housing in many other countries. But taking a stricter definition that requires a higher level of collaboration between tenants, co-housing in Sweden is still a marginal phenomenon, with little public support and little interest from the mainstream housing market, even if there are some signs of change. In the following section, this chapter will take a look at the early *kollektivhus* in Sweden, an important predecessor of contemporary co-housing. This will be followed by a brief account of the most important features of the housing policy that was one of the pillars of the Swedish model, an important contextual dimension in the analysis of the first post-war wave of co-housing. Finally, in a similar manner, it will be argued that the roll-back of Swedish housing policy provides a significant context for the second post-war wave of co-housing. The chapter is centred around certain examples in Gothenburg, but in the highly centralized culture of Sweden, these cases should constantly be seen against a larger national context.

The early collective houses

Where to start the history of co-housing in Sweden is not so much a question of terminology as of typology. The word '*kollektivhus*' came into widespread use in the 1930s with the first modernist projects. But the type of housing that consists of a multi-family dwelling with certain common facilities, not least for cooking, which has dominated Swedish co-housing ever since, can be traced back to the early twentieth century. The form of housing has remained surprisingly constant, while the problems it was supposed to solve have changed.

Proposals to build large *kollektivhus* around 1930 were intended to solve two problems at the time: a shortage of housemaids and the right of married middle-class women to work (Caldenby and Walldén 1979: 145). Complaints from middle-class women about the high costs of housemaids and the difficulties of finding them first surfaced in the early 1900s. Collective solutions to cooking and child care were proposed and architects were asked to rationalize the design of the kitchens. For young women, a position as a housemaid living with the family and with little chance of an independent life was not very attractive. At the same time, middle-class women had been struggling for the right to work for quite some time. Usually women lost their job when they got married and especially if they had children. With the economic crisis of the early 1930s, the recently achieved right for middle-class women to work was in question.

In parallel with these developments there was interest among radical circles in Sweden in developments in the Soviet Union, even though information about what was happening there was quite fragmentary. In the book *Acceptera!* from 1931, which was a sort of architects' manifesto defending the modernist breakthrough at the Stockholm exhibition in 1930, the term 'family hotels' is used to describe a type of housing already being built in 'capitalist America and communist Russia'. Aleksandra Kollontaj was a radical feminist in the early Soviet Union and minister for the care of children and women. As such she was soon politically marginalized and 'expelled' to Sweden as ambassador in 1930, where she developed influential relations with women's groups.

Various more or less left-wing publications generally printed quite sympathetic articles on developments in the Soviet Union (Caldenby and Walldén 1979: 173). In 1931, *Morgonbris*, the magazine of the Social Democratic women's organization, published an article with the headline 'There will be a kollektivhus in Sweden: Gothenburg women want to build in the style of Russia's new housing' (*Morgonbris* 1931). The initiative came from a local 'women's council', connected to the Swedish Union of Tenants. Their policy was to try to convince the municipality and state to lower rents and limit profits, but also to develop appropriate apartments for families in which both men and women worked, as well as for single mothers. For the working-class women on the women's council, *kollektivhus* were a solution to an acute problem, but not the ideal. If possible, they would have preferred an arrangement where the woman, as mother, could afford to stay at home. In the end, nothing came of the women's council's *kollektivhus* project.

Soon after, an initiative in Stockholm, by a different sort of group, led to the construction of the first modern *kollektivhus* in Sweden (Caldenby and Walldén 1979: 176). In December 1932, a meeting was held at a 'professional women's club' (*Yrkeskvinnors klubb*), at which the architect Sven Markelius, one of the leading Swedish modernist architects, presented a project for a *kollektivhus* – a term they claimed, without any support, was borrowed from the Soviet Union – which had been readapted to suit the Swedish situation. However, the proposed site belonged to the city, who were not willing to lease it for such a daring project. Instead the *kollektivhus* at John Ericssongatan 6 was built on a smaller plot and was finished in 1935 (Caldenby and Walldén 1979). It had 57 apartments, a restaurant that was open to the public and also provided food to the apartments, and a day nursery. After closing (at 9 pm), the restaurant could be used by the residents for meetings or reading. One argument behind the project was that a lot of women *need* to work to contribute to the family economy, and many more *want* to work out of interest or the will for independence. But with houses organized in the traditional way there was a perceived conflict between women's work and their role at home, a conflict which could be solved by the *kollektivhus,* where the central kitchen relieves women of household work and day nurseries give children 'rational care'. This gives women free time to spend with the family and on personal development.

Women's equal right to work and to rest was a key argument. The fact that it meant having other (working-class) women do the household work was never really discussed. Individual housemaids were effectively replaced by collective housemaids. At John Ericssongatan, 22 people, almost exclusively women, were employed to serve the 57 apartments. They did not live in the house, but only worked there. The reason was of course economic, they simply could not afford to live there. Calculations for the 1932 project showed that a family with two parents and two children would need a yearly income of 7,000–8,000 Swedish krona to live there. At the time an average male worker earned 3,000 krona per year and a female worker 50–70% of that. The house on John Ericssongatan was not cheaper. Even living in a small flat in a co-housing project was out of the question for the average worker's family. The champions of co-housing were not unaware of this problem. Alva Myrdal, later Social Democratic minister, ambassador and Nobel peace prize winner, was perhaps the most frequently interviewed among them. In 1933 she answered that 'at present' they could not reach those most in need of co-housing, working-class women. 'But we have argued that it is better to start somewhere and sooner or later the development will get going' (Caldenby and Walldén 1979: 187).

In Stockholm, half a dozen *kollektivhus* were built in the late 1930s and early 1940s (Vestbro 1982). They were all relatively large houses with 60 to 280 mainly small apartments. Half of them were aimed at single women. They all had restaurants and half of them had day nurseries. The initiative to build came from private developers or in two cases from foundations, and the form of tenure was cooperative or rented apartments. In the above-mentioned study (Waagensen and Rubin 1949) of four of these houses, two-thirds of the inhabitants said their main reason for moving into the house was as a way of combining work and household chores. The remaining third had come there by chance, with no special purpose. Nobody mentioned a need for community as a reason.

The neighbourhood unit was a town planning idea of the 1940s, intended to highlight the democratic importance of the 'group society', with certain collective facilities in the neighbourhood. The background was the perceived need for a counter-force to the mass societies in Nazi Germany and the Soviet Union. The first example built in Sweden was Norra Guldheden in Gothenburg, which opened with an exhibition in the summer of 1945. It included a collective house with 70 small apartments, intended only for single people. Directly adjacent to the collective house, by the central square in the area, was a restaurant, open to the public, but especially aimed at residents of the collective house. Next to the square there were also small apartments for housemaids, who could help the families in the area without having to live with them, thus preserving their own independence. At the same time the independence of the families was secured by 'normal' apartments with access to some collective services in the neighbourhood. *Kollektivhus* became a marginal solution for single households.

In a comprehensive plan for Stockholm drawn up in 1946, Markelius, then town planning director, mentioned *kollektivhus* as a solution for small households, but as being too expensive for families, who would prefer 'collectively organized housing groups', that is services in the neighbourhood (Vestbro 1982: 124). In a 1947 study of four collective houses in Stockholm (Waagensen and Rubin 1949), it was showed that few of the households living there consisted of families with working women and children, and that there was a heavy over-representation of middle-class families. It was against this background that, during the rapid post-war boom in housing construction, there was little state interest in supporting *kollektivhus*. It was seen as a marginal solution for certain groups, while the broader problem was an acute lack of decent, affordable housing. This was to remain the official line of the central authorities in Sweden during the heyday of the so-called 'Million Programme' in Sweden in 1965–74 (see further below), when one million flats were built in ten years.

Still, the idea was not completely abandoned, as *kollektivhus*, while few in number, continued to be built. Hässelby family hotel, opened in 1955 in

Stockholm's north-western suburbs, was the last and largest of a series of *kollektivhus* built by a private builder (Vestbro 1982). It consisted of four ten-storey tower blocks connected by lower buildings and corridors. It had 328 rented apartments of various sizes, two-thirds of them with two rooms and a kitchen or larger, and was therefore intended as a collective house for families. The residents were clearly middle class. Apartments had normal-size kitchens but there was also a restaurant serving dinners, for which the residents were obliged to buy coupons. There was a cafeteria, a grocery shop open in the evenings, laundry, barber shop, a doctor and a dentist, sports facilities and a municipal day nursery where residents' children were given priority. A number of *servicehus* (service houses) were also built, with enhanced access to certain commercial and public collective services, as well as 'service districts', an experiment launched by a state service committee in operation in 1968–1973 (Vestbro 1982).

Finally, Stolplyckan in Linköping, finished as late as 1980, shows that there were local initiatives that took the traditional ideas of the large *kollektivhus* further. This initiative was taken by a local group of women in 1977, who wanted to stimulate a sense of community and save resources (Vestbro 1982: 273; Pedersen 1991). It was met with some interest from the social authorities in the municipality, who wanted to develop new, more integrated types of housing for elderly and disabled people. Architects with experience from living in Hässelby family hotel helped to develop the programme for the building. The engagement of key individuals in the municipality was crucial for the project to go ahead. Like Hässelby, it consists of a number of tall apartment buildings connected by corridors and lower buildings with a dining hall, library and rooms for sport and hobbies. There are 186 rented apartments of different sizes, of which 44 are for elderly and disabled residents. The restaurant was used by elderly people at lunch and was planned to be open to all inhabitants in the evenings. Apartments are around 10% smaller than normal, to keep costs down. Stolplyckan was an ambitious project, but it was to remain an exception. With the emergence of co-housing in the two Swedish waves that took place in the 1980s and the 2010s, the ideas that had materialized in the *kollektivhus* instead found a different expression, which importantly should be seen in relation to the housing policy of the Swedish welfare state.

Swedish housing policies

Housing policy is a complex phenomenon consisting of legal, economic, organizational and cultural aspects. Because of this, forms of housing tenure are not easily translated from one country to another. The Nordic countries have much in common, as welfare states with relatively small differences in income standard and housing standard. The state and municipalities have had a strong role to play in financing and planning. At the same time, there are important differences between the Nordic countries in forms of tenure, the types of houses and the size of apartments in the housing stock. In Sweden, the post-war welfare model has included a long and strong tradition of financial state support and a universal housing policy, with no special social housing for lower income groups. It also means an internationally very high percentage of multi-family dwellings (~50%) as well as a large percentage of rented (~40%) or cooperative tenant-owned (~20%) flats. All this has a historical explanation.

'Good housing for everyone'

The roots of post-war housing policies in Sweden go back to the dire housing situation during the First World War. An already difficult situation, with a lower housing standard than in most other European countries, was aggravated by the war (Ramberg 2000). Local unions of tenants were formed in the 1910s to defend the rights of tenants, and merged into a Swedish Union of Tenants in 1923. Rent tribunals were founded, at which disputes could be resolved. State inquiries showed the gravity of the situation. The first municipal housing companies were formed. But soon the cooperative organization HSB, set up in 1923 by the Union of Tenants, became the main alternative to private builders. Meanwhile, construction workers started production cooperatives to build houses. In Gothenburg they had a clear socialist ideological background, and some of the protagonists would later become influential figures in the development of Swedish housing policy (Ramberg 2000). Ernst Wigforss, later Social Democratic minister of finance, was one of its ideologists, inspired by British Fabianism, and formulated his ideas in a 'Gothenburg programme'. In 1940 an important second national cooperative organization, Riksbyggen, was established by construction workers' trade unions in Gothenburg. HSB, Riksbyggen and the early municipal companies all focused on multi-family dwellings.

In 1933 the Social Housing Investigation (*Bostadssociala utredningen*) was initiated by the new Social Democratic government. This lasted until 1947 and formulated the basis for a new housing policy, which was introduced after the Second World War and would endure until the 1990s. The resulting housing policy formulated in 1945–1947 was not to give special support to the poor but provide 'good housing for everyone'. A clearly stated central argument of the Social Democratic government was to resist private speculation in housing (Ramberg 2000: 110). The means for this were the establishment of state loans and housing standards, and support for a rationalization of housing production and large-scale municipal housing companies. The state temporarily regulated rents, introduced means-tested housing allowances for households that could not afford rents and put in place certain housing regulations in the form of 'building standards' to secure a 'minimum standard' and prevent over-crowding. Most importantly however, the municipalities were given primary responsibility for handling the housing question through control of land use and planning. Further, municipal housing companies were set up to lead the construction of affordable housing on a large scale, facilitated by the state through a guarantee of favourable loans. The state made sure that municipalities were prevented from exploiting these to fund other expenditures through housing legislation which stipulated that these companies must be non-profit. Two forms of loans were introduced: for multi-family dwellings and for one-family houses. Municipal housing companies were given loans for 100% of the costs, cooperatives 95%, and private builders 85% .

The most important material manifestation of the Swedish welfare state's housing policies was the 'Million Programme' in the 1960s. In response to the housing shortage, a million apartments were built between 1965 and 1974 in order to realize the goal of 'good housing for all' – through large-scale industrialized production by private builders, with guaranteed state loans for a period of ten years. The programme was also linked to a project of large-scale demolition of old working-class districts in the central parts of the cities, through the major national 'Sanitation Programme'. As a consequence, the majority of working-class inhabitants moved from city centres to 'Million Programme' multi-family dwellings located in the urban periphery.

Marketization and speculation

Cooperative housing was formally constituted in 1930, based on the early housing production cooperatives already mentioned, and supported by the strong organizations of HSB and Riksbyggen. But the more idealistic early form changed substantially over time, as analysed by Svensson (1998). Inflation during the early 1950s put pressure on the Tenant-Ownership Control Act (*bostadsrättskontrollagen*). Finally, in 1971 a new act was passed which prohibited 'repurchase clauses' and freed the way for market pricing. Svensson summarizes the consequences of this as follows:

> In affirming and adapting to the legislative de-regulation the 'idealistic' part of cooperative ideology must be said to have failed, both at the elite level of the national leadership, and among the tenant-owning members. Cooperative ideology and practice transformed, from having been established as a corrective to the market, to become just another market-adapted, though still cooperatively organized, form of tenure.
>
> (Svensson 1998: 93–94)

Co-housing in the 1980s

The closing down of the restaurant in Hässelby family hotel in 1976 marked a generation shift in Swedish co-housing from large-scale projects to smaller ones, and from cooking by employed staff to cooking in collaboration, or from the division of labour to shared labour. It can also be understood as part of larger changes in society during the 1970s.

The 'boom years' of the 1960s and the Million Programme in housing, with a belief in technology and large-scale solutions, had addressed the Swedish post-war housing shortage, but it also ended in a critique of the social consequences. The radical sociologist Rita Liljeström gave her view at a seminar on co-housing in the late 1970s:

> We are now in a position where we can see the social costs of economic development. We have an enormous concentration and centralization of power.... On the other hand we also got something we could describe as social atomization.
>
> (Caldenby and Walldén 1984: 27, author's translation)

The lack of community in society became a focus of the co-housing movement. This was combined with an interest in management of resources and gender equality. The arguments were formulated by a number of leading social researchers such as Liljeström and Lars Ingelstam. Critics called their point of view 'romantic pessimism' or 'social democratic utopianism'.

There were also practical experiences of different forms of solutions to these problems. Small groups of young people shared large central apartments, older villas or small former institution buildings, sometimes referred to as 'extended families'. Lukas Moodysson's film *Tillsammans* (*Together*), released in 2000, dramatizes the life of such a collective. In Sweden it never reached the numbers found in Denmark or Germany, but estimates indicate that around 1980 there were at least 200 small collectives with an average of six to seven members (Palm Lindén 1982). Other forms in the 1970s included 'cooking teams' of friends or neighbours, taking turns to cook for each other at home, or cooperative day nurseries, started by parents in need of a day nursery for their children and with a mix of employees and shared work.

These different tendencies were combined in the idea of 'the small collective house' formulated by a group of ten women in Stockholm, many of them architects or journalists. Somewhat paradoxically they called themselves BIG, which stands for 'live in community' (*bo i gemenskap*). They started in 1977 with the aim of building a collective house for themselves, but soon became more involved in launching the idea. A book with the title *The small collective house* (*Det lilla kollektivhuset*), summing up their ideas, was published in 1982 (Berg et al. 1982). Four principles were fundamental to the idea: a size of 20–50 households shared work with daily activities coupled to living (such as cooking and house maintenance), freedom from economic speculation and the right to decide on common matters, and finally a varied group of residents. Among the arguments for the relatively small size are direct democracy and adaptability to existing buildings. Shared work promotes gender equality and makes household work more fun and socially developing. The existing forms of tenure could be developed, argued BIG: cooperative flats would be better if the market speculation that began in the early 1970s was abolished. Rental flats, in turn, needed greater influence from tenants. The means to achieve a varied group of residents was never very clearly formulated, apart from having flats of different sizes.

Stacken

The ideas outlined by BIG influenced the first Swedish co-housing project of the new generation, called Stacken ['the Ant-Hill'] in Gothenburg, opened in 1980 (Caldenby and Walldén 1984; see also Chapters 5 and 8 in this volume). A series of seminars with the title '*Bo i gemenskap*' were organized at Chalmers University of Technology by the professor in architecture, Lars Ågren, in the spring of 1978. Ågren also had a background as a social democratic politician. Several researchers involved in the 'vision' of new forms of living together gave speeches, including two members of BIG. The state was also involved in the discussion, presenting a 1977 publication from the National Board of Housing, *God Bostad 5: Kollektivhus.* In this, co-housing was seen as an interesting housing alternative for elderly people. In the audience were representatives from the municipal housing companies in Gothenburg. During the autumn semester, architecture students at Chalmers worked on a project to remodel an early 1960s tower block, originally designed by Lars Ågren, into co-housing. As a result, the municipal housing company proposed an experiment to remodel a similar building of 40 apartments in a poor suburb, Bergsjön, in north-eastern Gothenburg. The housing company Göteborgshem would finance the remodelling while Chalmers was assigned to do the planning and find tenants interested in living in co-housing – tasks not usually handled by academic institutions.

The special shape of this daring experiment needs to be understood in relation to the context of particular developments in Swedish housing policy and the housing market. First, since the first-generation co-housing activists wished to avoid a speculative ownership and tenure form, they were critical of the Swedish form of cooperative housing because of its marketization. Second, the 'Million Programme' had created a housing surplus in the late 1970s; newly built flats owned by municipal housing companies stood increasingly empty, because of the 'shrinking city' phenomenon. Those who could, left the rented apartments for one-family houses in the 'sprawl' that developed around larger cities. In Gothenburg, the crisis was aggravated by the closing down of the shipyards, which had been a major industry in the city. Municipal housing companies were bleeding economically and searched for all kinds of solutions, including co-housing. These developments laid the foundation for the two early co-housing projects in Gothenburg, Stacken and Trädet, which both moved in to pre-Million Programme high-rise buildings as a result of collaboration with municipal housing companies.

The search for tenants for Stacken started in the summer of 1979, with help from the municipal housing agency and advertisements in local newspapers. At the first meeting in the autumn, 100 people turned up and 44 of them signed a list stating their interest. In a single year, the planning process organized by Chalmers held 18 meetings. Twenty-five out of the 35 households that had been part of the first allocation of apartments moved in in the summer of 1980. The organization of the house was very close to the ideas of BIG. Residents nevertheless had the feeling that they had had the opportunity to influence the project as much as they wanted. And without doubt the planning process meant that the residents already knew each other by the time they moved in. The name Stacken (the Ant-Hill), was unanimously accepted.

Between 1975 and 1978 the building had been used as an office by the housing company. At the start of the planning process it was empty. It was a nine-storey building with a ground floor with storage rooms and laundry, and eight storeys with five similar three-room apartments each. After the remodelling the house had storage, a laundry, a youth room, carpentry workshop, sauna, photo laboratory and music room on the ground floor. The main common rooms – kitchen and dining room, day nursery and sewing workshop – had to be placed on the fifth floor for technical reasons, which was not an ideal solution. The precisely engineered structure prevented the free creation of openings in the load-bearing concrete walls lower down. Apartments were made a bit more varied in size, including one two-apartment collective within the house.

One special problem was the form of tenure. This was negotiated between three parties: the tenants, the landlord Göteborgshem and the tenants' association. Three possible solutions were proposed. One option was a rental contract between Göteborgshem and Stacken, the association of residents, which then would sublet apartments to tenants, that would give tenants a subletting contract with less rights. This was not accepted by the tenants' association. The second option was a 'tenants' influence contract' (*boinflytandeavtal*), giving tenants full control over the administration of the building, while each tenant would still have a contract for the apartment with the housing company. This was not accepted by Göteborgshem, who thought they would lose control. The third option was a cooperative tenant-owned form of tenure (*bostadsrätt*). This was not accepted by the residents, who wanted to avoid economic speculation. After long discussions the first option was chosen: subletting (*blockhyra*), a form that was on the margins of established procedures.

What all this shows is that on one hand there was official interest and support for the alternative form proposed by co-housing in certain circles. On the other hand, there were many obstacles and much doubt about the feasibility of this marginal form of housing. Co-housing remained an outsider in the thoroughly organized Swedish housing policy, even if tolerated with some curiosity and wonder, especially at a time when so many flats stood empty.

The 55 adults who moved into Stacken were a relatively homogenous group of people (Caldenby and Walldén 1984). Many of them worked in the public sector in schools, healthcare and social care. Few had working-class jobs. Salaries were lower than the average in Gothenburg, especially for the men. A clear majority were between 25 and 35 years old with young children. The most common household type was single adults (13 of 34). The second most common was man, woman and two children (8 of 34). Single mothers with one or two children were also common (8 of 34). Forty percent of the residents had moved more than 200 kilometres from their home town to Gothenburg, which is twice the average for low-income people, and meant that parents who needed help with baby-sitting had relatives far away. Politically and culturally, the Stacken residents were left-leaning and anti-establishment. When asked about their dreams of a home, two-thirds answered that they would prefer to live in a village or in the countryside with some friends, if only they could support themselves economically. This is the 'back to the village' dream of the 1970s green wave (Caldenby and Walldén 1984: 198).

Stacken was the pioneer, but it was soon followed by other examples. One of those was Trädet in a neighbouring poor suburb.

Trädet

The relative success of Stacken (it was after all possible) and the persistent problem of empty flats at the beginning of the 1980s soon led the municipal housing company to propose a follow-up along similar principles. An announcement searching for interested residents was sent out in the summer of 1983. Residents could choose between a few possible projects. Unfortunately, the one they chose and started to plan for, built in the late 1960s suburb of Hjällbo, was soon selected for reuse as offices for municipal companies. They were then offered an older tower block, built in 1956 in the suburb of Kortedala, two tram stops closer to the city centre than Stacken. This building was almost but not completely empty, but some of the old tenants agreed to join the co-housing project. The name given to the house was Trädet ['the Tree'] and tenants moved in in 1985.

Trädet was organized on much the same principles as Stacken, and the remodelling was designed by some young architects, one of whom had participated in the Stacken project. The building was however technically more easy to retrofit. The restaurant and other common facilities could be placed on the second floor with direct access from the outside. Like in Stacken, the building has one central staircase and a total of 39 apartments, on average slightly smaller than those in Stacken. The form of tenure was initially the same as in Stacken, subletting. No detailed interviews with residents were conducted in this sequel to Stacken. Maybe the impression was that researchers already knew what they could expect.

Notwithstanding considerable differences, the two pioneering projects in the first wave of co-housing in Gothenburg are clearly of the same type. They have now been working for more than 30 years, certainly not without problems and conflicts, but in principle according to the ideas of BIG in the early 1980s about 'the small collective house' with shared household work (for their further developments, see Chapter 5). The rents are very low, due both to the sharing of work and the low-end location. Residents work mainly in the public sector. Many have low incomes or are on long-term sick leave. As one resident of Stacken explained: 'This is a way of having a decent life even if you are poor'. At the same time, it is necessary to underline once again that the condition for starting these two projects in the 1980s was very special, with many empty flats in certain suburbs. The situation today in Gothenburg, as in most Swedish municipalities, is very different.

Second wave of co-housing

There was a 'gap' in the interest in new co-housing in Sweden in the 1990s. One sign of this is that the association Kollektivhus NU did not hold any board meetings between 1992 and 2005 (kollektivhus.nu). It seems to have become a mostly dormant organization by the mid-1980s, remaining so for some 20 years (William-Olsson 1994: 3). An explanation for this is given by Bertil Egerö, one of the long-term activists for co-housing: 'In Sweden, the co-housing movement of the 1980s virtually died out when most of its members had found themselves new homes in the co-housing projects. Only a few have found their way back to activism with a purpose beyond their own house' (Vestbro 2010: 20). In a recent booklet on co-housing Vestbro himself points at a broader context to explain the dip: 'Individualism and consumption thinking came to dominate development' (Grip et al. 2014: 86). In a longer historical perspective it is possible to identify a fairly regular oscillation in both debate about and the building of co-housing in Sweden (Caldenby 1992: 66–69). There are waves of interest in the 1930s, early 1950s, around 1968 and in the early 1980s. One could, like Egerö, put forward an 'internal' explanation of this as a 'saturation process'. But one could also, like Vestbro, search for an 'external' explanation in societal changes.

Most importantly, beginning in the 1990s and continuing in the 2000s, Swedish housing policy clearly shifted towards a marketized model, albeit with some remainders of the old system. When the Ministry of Housing was abolished in 1991, it signalled a dramatic roll-back of key features of the housing policies launched as part of the Swedish model (Clark and Johnson 2009; Christophers 2013). This included abolishing concessions to the municipal housing companies and subsidies for investment in rental housing; removing restrictions on profit-making by municipal housing companies and the selling-on of municipal housing. Means-tested housing allowances were slashed; between 1995 and 2009 there was a 70% fall in households entitled to and claiming allowances (Christophers 2013: 895). Further, home ownership was supported by tax reforms that included a highly regressive property tax; state credit guarantees for first-time buyers and owner-occupation in multi-dwelling buildings as a new form of tenure. This roll-back of housing policies was more or less completed with the 2011 housing law, which stipulated that municipal housing companies were no longer allowed to be non-profit, instead they had to be managed according to 'business principles'. A previously introduced law stating that municipal housing companies also set the cap for rents in privately owned housing was abolished. As a result of the abolishing of subsidies to municipal housing companies to invest in new housing, the number of new apartments built in Sweden was very low between the early 1990s and early 2010s, with a high share of tenant-ownership apartments. A shortage of housing was reported by 243 out of 290 Swedish municipalities in 2018. The situation is especially difficult for those who cannot afford to buy a new apartment.

As a result of these developments the housing question has become increasingly politicized in Sweden during the past decade, as a new housing movement has criticized marketization and the rising costs of housing, making it unaffordable for young people as well as other socio-economically weaker groups. New organizations and networks have been established locally to influence politicians to build more, and in particular, cheaper housing, that is adapted to the needs of young people. In 2014 some 30 housing organizations joined forces in Bostadsvrålet (the housing roar). At their conferences, co-housing has been a recurring theme as one possible solution to the housing crisis. While many of the activists of the first post-war co-housing generation were people who had been part of the 68 movement and had reached a new phase in their lives (building family while still looking for alternative ways of living), the second wave of co-housing recruited some of its key activists from the new activism movement of the early 2000s, connected to Global Justice and Reclaim the Streets. Activists from the first wave of co-housing are however still highly visible and active; in this context driving co-housing for elderly people as well as intergenerational projects.

One co-housing project that was completed in 1993, after a six-year planning period, is Färdknäppen in Stockholm (William-Olsson 1994). In many ways it is a typical Swedish *kollektivhus*, a multi-family dwelling built by a municipal housing company, but in another way it is a sign of a new tendency dating from the 1990s: co-housing specifically built for people 'in the second half of life', without children. It was an initiative by an active group searching for a housing solution for middle-aged and elderly people, making them less dependent on municipal services as they grow old and leaving the 'empty nest' of one-family houses or larger apartments to a younger generation with children. This group gave their house the name 'Undantag' (Exception), reflecting a tradition of elderly people moving into a small house to allow the younger generation to take over a farm. After a long search for an interested developer, preferably a municipal housing company, it was built by Familjebostäder in Stockholm, the municipal housing company that currently has the most co-housing projects in Sweden: five, of which four are for elderly people. The building has a central location in Stockholm and has 43 apartments, ranging in sizes between 37 and 75 square metres, plus 350 square metres of common spaces, including a kitchen, dining room, library/living room, sauna, hobby rooms and laundry. Meals are cooked by residents five days a week. The rent is 'normal' for the central location, which is fairly high, SEK 8,437 per month for 55 m^2 + 8 m^2 of shared spaces in 2019.

An analysis of the process by one of the initiators points at some problematic aspects of the relationship between initiators/residents and developer/housing policy/politics (William-Olsson 1994: 21–26). The situation with initiators who are also future residents was unusual for the municipal housing company as developer and caused disturbances in the process. It takes time for initiators to grasp that building costs do not have a direct relation to future rent. It was difficult to work to a different standard than usual, and especially to get a lower standard, since rents in the Swedish system are set in relation to a 'utility value rent' ('*bruksvärdeshyra*') that is decided centrally and in advance. The developer had to consider the co-housing project as a temporary user and construct the building as if it would be used 'normally' in the long term. The initiators, in turn, had the familiar problem of being a small active group, who did not necessarily represent other future residents, but only themselves. The Tenants' Union as well as the left-wing parties and some of the public authorities in the municipality were slightly sceptical towards the group of initiators, who they saw as well-educated, high-income people (some members of the planning group had to leave during the process because the rents would be too high). William-Olsson's conclusion of this analysis is that for more co-housing projects to be built it is important not to rely on time-consuming bottom-up initiatives, which demand both economic and cultural resources from the initiators. If Färdknäppen is to be anything more than an exception, more initiatives must come from interested and ambitious housing companies and developers, but with an invitation to the future users to be part of the process from the beginning. It could also be added that this demand for, and trust in, public support for co-housing is related to the history of the Swedish model. But such initiatives from public or private developers are still uncommon. Co-housing projects usually start with an initiative by a group of interested people.

One such group is BoIHOP ('Live together') in Gothenburg, founded in 1988 at a weekend course called '*Bo på kvinnors villkor*' ('Live on women's terms'). In 2003, BoIHOP organized a meeting for the municipal housing companies, leading to a discussion between BoIHOP and the municipal company Familjebostäder in Gothenburg. Majbacken, a care home for older people, which already had a dedicated space for a restaurant, was offered by the company to be converted into co-housing. Because of this the process was very quick. Within little more than a year the first residents could move in, in late 2004. The house was then gradually taken over by co-housing residents. It is rented by the association and apartments are sublet to residents.

The co-housing project Kornet, in Mölndal, just south of Gothenburg, also has its roots in BoIHOP. A local association in Mölndal was set up in 2003, inspired by Färdknäppen in Stockholm. They managed to raise the interest of politicians with the argument that a sense of community and support from neighbours can ultimately be measured in decreasing healthcare costs. As early as 2006, residents were able to move into a newly built point block with 44 apartments rented in the new form of cooperative tenancy. The website clearly states the importance of the initiators: 'That the house stands here today mostly depends on the tireless work of the driving spirits to reach the goal' (boigemenskap.nu/historien-om-huset).

'Under samma tak' ('Under the same roof') (presented in detail in Chapter 5) is a group of initiators in Gothenburg who had to go through a different and much longer process to get their house (undersammatak.org). The group was formed in 2009 by eight people with a wish to live in co-housing. The house is a newly built six-storey building located in a 1950s suburb and will be finished in 2020. In collaboration with the municipality it will contain seven apartments for people in need of supported living services. A ten-year process is quite strenuous and demanding, both for older people and for young families with children. During the long planning process '*Under samma tak*' visited several other co-housing projects and also used a book published by SABO, the Swedish Association of Municipal Housing Companies, called *Gemenskap och samarbete: Att bygga upp och bo i kollektivhus* (Community and collaboration: Building and living in a collective house), first published in 2007. In a later version from 2014 the title was changed slightly to *Kollektivhus och Bogemenskap* (*Collective Houses and Co-housing*). The book is a practical guide to the planning and building of co-housing projects. The fact that the book is published by SABO, the central organization of municipally owned public housing companies in Sweden, which manages 800,000 apartments, again shows the typical, even somewhat contradictory, Swedish entanglement of private initiators and public authorities.

The first ever international conference on co-housing was held in Stockholm in 2010. Kerstin Kärnekull, an architect and a long-term activist, who herself lives in Färdknäppen and was an initiator of the conference, wrote the foreword to the proceedings (Vestbro 2010: 7). Her experience from more than three decades of work with co-housing is that residents are generally very satisfied with this way of living, which is however combined with what she describes as a 'general lack of interest and ignorance surrounding the developments, e.g. among neighbours, planners, architects, politicians and developers'. The lack of public interest puzzles her, given 'the advantages of such living; a sense of community, the potential for economizing on resources, the value of resident cooperation and of learning together'. At the same time the sponsors of the conference form a long list of public organizations within the housing sector (Vestbro 2010: 4).

Still a marginal phenomenon

It is no wonder that Sweden hosted the first co-housing conference. Co-housing activists and residents are well organized. One hub of this activism is the association Kollektivhus NU, which is again very active today. They describe it as part of a trend 'in favour of collaborative housing'. The association's aim is: 'to promote collaborative housing and other alternative ways of living'. The association supports existing co-housing as well as groups intending to create new projects, and it also wants to 'inform the public' and 'influence authorities'. In 2019 it represents some 50 co-housing communities and around 2,000 residents are registered as full members (www.kollektivhus.nu), which is far less than in Denmark, a country with half the population of Sweden. It is worth noting that Kollektivhus NU still uses the term *kollektivhus* (collective house). There is an interesting difference here to Denmark, partly in terminology but not least in the very existence of such an organization (some attempts notwithstanding there is no Danish counterpart).

The long history of co-housing in Sweden shows us its complex relation to housing policies, housing markets and social movements. The housing system has changed from market-led until the 1930s, to being characterized by a strong public policy from the 1940s until the 1990s and then a more market-driven development again. But some characteristics of the relationship between the co-housing movement, the state and Swedish society in general seem to have remained surprisingly constant, which could help explain the expected but still missing breakthrough:

1 Co-housing projects are almost always initiated by 'groups of socially interested' people with social and cultural resources who are able to get support from research and to influence politicians and authorities.
2 These groups expect and, when successful, also get support from politicians and (mostly) municipal housing companies. But politicians and companies do not themselves take initiatives to start projects.
3 The planning of co-housing projects in collaboration with public housing companies often runs into conflicts between their alternative ideas, the general principles of the housing sector and the market principles of the companies. These conflicts take time and demand resources from initiators.

In his critical reflections on the international conference in 2010, Guillermo Delgado formulates an activist perspective on 'Cohousing as a tool to address challenges in contemporary cities', published in the conference proceedings (Delgado 2010). He sees co-housing as 'a way of resistance' in the face of contemporary housing production and ways to live, and he proposes an open definition of co-housing, not as for example offering community, but as 'housing with the possibility of sharing'. He underlines the risk of excluding those who cannot afford to buy an apartment. And finally, he claims that 'the potential of co-housing to be a feasible alternative on the current housing market relies on municipal ownership and the possibility it offers of sharing'.

Co-housing in Sweden has an entangled relation to the complex history of Swedish housing policy. The role of the public housing sector has in many ways been restricted since the 1990s. At the same time its roots in the idea of 'Good housing for everyone' make municipal housing companies sceptical of special types of housing for privileged groups. There is potential somewhere between co-housing and public housing, but this will require an opening up from both sides.

References

BIG-gruppen (1982) *Det lilla kollektivhuset* [The small collective house]. Stockholm: Byggforskningsrådet.

Caldenby, C. and Walldén, Å. (1979) *Kollektivhus: Sovjet och Sverige omkring 1930* [Collective houses: The Soviet Union and Sweden around 1930]. Stockholm: Byggforskningsrådet.

Caldenby, C. and Walldén, Å. (1984) *Kollektivhuset Stacken* [The Ant-Hill collective house]. Göteborg: Bokförlaget Korpen.

Caldenby, C. (1992) *Vad är ett kollektivhus?* [What is a collective house?]. Göteborg: Arkitekturens teori och historia, Chalmers Tekniska Högskola.

Christophers, B. (2013) 'A monstrous hybrid: the political economy of housing in early twenty-first century Sweden', *New Political Economy*, vol. 18, no. 6, pp. 885–911.

Clark, E. and Johnson, K. (2009), 'Circumventing Circumscribed Neoliberalism: The "System Switch" in Swedish Housing', in S. Glynn (ed.), *Where the Other Half Lives: Lower Income Housing in a Neoliberal World*, pp. 173–194. London: Pluto Press.

Delgado, G. (2010) 'Collaborative Housing at a Crossroad: Critical Reflections from the International Collaborative Housing Conference', in D.-U. Vestbro, *Living Together: Cohousing Ideas and Realities Around the World*, pp. 212–223. Stockholm: Division of Urban and Regional Studies, Royal Institute of Technology.

Gresleri, J. (2015) *Cohousing: Esperienze internazionali di abitare condiviso.* Busalla: plug_in.

Grip, E., Kärnekull, K. and Sillén, I. (eds) (2014) *Gemenskap och samarbete i kollektivhus och bogemenskap* [Community and collaboration in collective houses and cohousing]. Stockholm: Migra Förlag.

Kollektivhus NU (2019) Protokoll från årsmöte med, lördag 3 december 2005 [Protocol from yearly meeting]. www.kollektivhus.nu (11 April 2019).

Kornet (2019) www.boigemenskap.nu/historien-om-huset (11 April 2019).

Lujanen, M. (2001). *Boende och bostadspolitik i Norden* [Housing and housing policy in the Nordic countries]. København: Nordisk Ministerråd.

Morgonbris (1931, May) 'Det blir kollektivhus i Sverige: Göteborgskorna vilja bygga i stil med Rysslands nya bostäder' [There will be a collective house in Sweden: Gothenburg women want to build in the style of Russia's new housing].

Palm Lindén, K. (1982) *Att bo i storfamilj* [Living in an extended family]. Lund: Byggnadsfunktionslära.

Pedersen, B. (1991) *Kollektivhuset Stolplyckan: Från idé till verklighet* [Stolplyckan collective house: From idea to reality]. Stockholm: Byggforskningsrådet.

Ramberg, K. (2000) *Välfärdsbygge 1850–2000* [Welfare construction 1850–2000]. Stockholm: Byggförlaget.

Svensson, S. (1998) *Transformations of a Tenure: The Evolution of Tenant-Ownership in Sweden.* Uppsala: Institutet för bostadsforskning.

Turner, B. and Vedung, E. (1997) *Bostadspolitik för tjugohundratalet: Återtåg och nya värden* [Housing policy for the 21st century: Retreat and new values]. Gävle: Meyers.

undersammatak.org www.undersammatak.org (11 April 2019).

Waagensen, B. and Rubin, J. (1949) *Kollektivhuset og dets forudsætninger* [The collective house and its preconditions]. København: Nyt Nordisk Forlag Arnold Busck.

Vestbro, D.-U. (1982) *Kollektivhus från enkökshus till bogemenskap* [Collective houses from one-kitchen houses to co-housing]. Stockholm: Byggforskningsrådet.
Vestbro, D.-U. (2010) *Living Together: Cohousing Ideas and Realities Around the World*. Stockholm: Division of Urban and Regional Studies, Royal Institute of Technology.
William-Olsson, M. (1994). *Vi gjorde ett undantag: Färdknäppen* [We made an exception: Färdknäppen]. Stockholm: SABO.

3 Hamburg

Housing movements and local government

David Scheller

Introduction

In June 2018, more than 8,000 people hit the streets of Hamburg for the 'MietenMove' – a festival-like demonstration against rising rents and the housing crisis. Affordable housing has become one of the burning topics in many German cities in recent years. Hamburg is one of the most expensive cities in Germany and movements in the city have been at the forefront of resistance to urban neoliberalism (Birke 2016; Füllner and Templin 2011; Rinn 2016; Twickel 2011). When we talked to a spokesperson for the Hamburger Netzwerk Recht-auf-Stadt (Hamburg right to the city network), he explained the motivation behind the movement:

> When we fight for the right to the city, we don't want to fight only for the right of the … more privileged people, we want to fight together with people who organize themselves and fight for their right to stay and for the right to dignified living, and so on.
>
> (RaS interview 2015)

Referring to the broader discussion of co-housing and sustainable urban development in this book, this chapter focuses on the historical interrelation between housing movements and local urban government regarding collaborative housing, or co-housing. Today, we find more than 3,000 co-housing projects in Germany, and notions and practices of collectively shared houses and communities have a long history. Since the early 2000s, the leading city in this development has been Hamburg, which also harbours many traces of past housing movements. The aim of this chapter is to analyse the historical context for contemporary co-housing developments, particularly focusing on relevant structural and political conditions that have provided both opportunities and constraints.

To this end, the chapter presents a historical analysis of the crises and challenges that have engendered housing movements, on the one hand, and the political interactions and reactions by government actors, on the other hand. This starts in industrializing Prussia and the German Empire, spans the

Weimar Republic, National Socialism, post-Second-World-War East and West Germany, and ends with the neoliberal urbanism of reunited Germany. The overall aim of this endeavour is to shed light on the intersection of housing movements and local governments that have structured 'collaborative housing' (see Introduction) leading up to the co-housing projects we are dealing with today. Housing movements have changed and policies have shifted, but the role of decent and affordable housing has always been an existential one. Collaborative housing has developed from housing cooperatives into co-housing as attempts to achieve affordable housing and self-governance in specific historical contexts. At the same time, it becomes clear that the bottom-up efforts of different housing struggles and movements have been accompanied by top-down politics.

I argue that the roles of both *the state* and *the actors* involved in collaborative housing and co-housing have shifted over the last century. A strong state that regulated the Fordist model of welfare has been replaced by a post-Fordist neoliberal governance of workfare. At the same time, housing cooperatives originally driven by the working class have been accompanied by predominantly middle-class-driven co-housing projects. These shifts are tied to socio-political transformations and, furthermore, to the rise of the sustainable development discourse in recent decades. Moreover, the various ownership forms of contemporary co-housing projects – such as associations, cooperatives and limited liability companies – can be seen as historical sediments of political dynamics between housing movements and (local) government. In order to discuss such political dynamics between civil society actors and the state, I follow the hypothesis that (urban) social and structural change should be understood as a result of (urban) social movements.

First phase: from Prussia to National Socialism

Historically, housing cooperatives were closely connected to the emerging workers' movement, functioning as its 'third pillar' beside unions and parties (Notz 2014). Starting with claims for better living conditions in late nineteenth-century capitalism, both from bottom-up struggles and top-down policies, the movement boomed during the Weimar Republic, facing suppression during National Socialism until the end of the Second World War.

Legal groundwork and first cooperatives (1867–1918)

The emerging industrialization and urbanization were the driving forces behind housing struggles in the late nineteenth century. Dramatically growing metropolises, such as Hamburg, Berlin or Cologne, faced major challenges in providing housing for the rapidly expanding working class,[1] and a massive lack of affordable housing caused miserable living conditions. Overcrowded and dark one-room flats with desperately poor sanitation were a serious problem for the new class of urban-poor factory workers. The political organization of the working class coincides with the first attempts to set up housing cooperatives as instances of collective self-help. Ideas of collective and cooperative living were promoted and financially supported by conservative bourgeois intellectuals. As a top-down approach, cooperatives were seen as a way to prevent epidemics and to defuse the social revolutionary potential of the impoverished working class, in what has been called the 'inner colonialization of the poor' (Huber 1983/1846).

In 1862, the first housing cooperative – *Häuserbau Genossenschaft zu Hamburg* – was founded by shipbuilders. This did not come as a surprise, since Hamburg from the very beginning was a stronghold of the workers' movement as well as the social democratic and communist parties. The aims of (housing) cooperatives were 1) collective self-help, 2) democratic self-organization through their members, 3) self-liability of members, 4) a non-profit orientation of housing provision and 5) members as users and shareholders of the cooperative.

When the first cooperative law was passed in Prussia in 1868, it became easier to form a cooperative. The number of cooperatives increased with an amendment of the cooperative law in 1889 that introduced a limited liability membership.[2] Small cooperatives were the predominant ownership form during the early years. Most of the time these cooperatives were founded with organizational help and money from bourgeois donors (Crome 2007: 212). But this would not have been possible without the pressure on the streets and bottom-up mobilization and organizing (Novy 1983: 83).

In the first 50 years, cooperatives were predominantly founded with the goal of providing living space for workers. But at the same time, cooperatives of officials and civil servants emerged. At the end of the First World War there were about 1,400 cooperatives in the German Empire (FMTBH 2004: 117). In Hamburg, workers and employees in particular founded small housing cooperatives for their professions. One example of this development is the *Wohnungsgenossenschaft von 1904 e.G.* (referred to as W1904 from here on), which was founded by four postmen with the aim of providing decent housing for their colleagues. Ever since then, W1904 has followed these principles: a) housing as a common good rather than a commodity; b) self-government; c) mutual support and solidarity (W1904 interview 2016). Today, 1904 is a large cooperative with about 5,000 members and is also owner of the multi-generational co-housing project *Heimspiel* (see also Chapter 5).

Legal support and cooperative boom (1919–1933)

After the 1918 Revolution and the end of World War One, the social situation in Hamburg was still very tense and there was a great need for affordable and dignified housing for workers. The structural poverty resulted in a strong movement of workers and poor people, which together with unions took a political stand in Hamburg. In spite of attempted coups by radical groups from the left and the right, the social democrats, together with left-liberal parties, had the majority in the Hamburg Senate until 1933 (Büttner 2019).

During the early 1920s, reforms of the legal system, state funding, financial support (*Hauszinssteuer*) and a growing economy led to a boom in small and large housing cooperatives founded by workers and civil servants. These cooperatives can be described as homogeneous, based on the jobs and the socio-cultural and political backgrounds of their members (FMTBH 2004: 119). This was clearly a bottom-up movement for the construction of large-scale affordable housing combined with a sense of community, aims that we find in the current co-housing projects. Moreover, as also found today, self-labour became a key instrument in keeping down building costs (Crome 2007: 213). As a result of this movement, the Weimar Republic provided land and the legal framework to enable alternative ownership forms. By 1928, there were more than 4,000 housing cooperatives in Germany. This can be seen as the culmination of cooperativism as a driving force in housing provision (ibid.).

Prohibition and caesura (1933–1945)

During the period of National Socialism, cooperatives and unions were seen as beacons of radical left and socialist movements, and as such they were considered a threat to the state (Notz 2014). The Nazi state opposed and attacked the internal structures and foundations of the movements and cooperatives through numerous repressive actions and laws. In 1933, the foundation of (housing) cooperatives was prohibited, and following the 1934 Cooperative Amendment (*Genossenschaftsnovelle*), all existing cooperatives had to join an umbrella organization and had to accept obligatory checks. Moreover, with the enforced conformity law (*Gleichschaltungsgesetz*), board members of existing cooperatives were replaced by NSDAP officials. Smaller cooperatives were forced to merge with large cooperatives. The process culminated in the complete assimilation of all types of cooperatives into the German Labour Front (*Deutsche Arbeitsfront*) (Weyerer 2013). Since 1938, Jews had not been allowed to become members of cooperatives. The period of National Socialism was a caesura in the cooperativist movement that has shaped housing cooperatives right up until the present, since the enforced merges were never reversed. At the end of the war, only 1,600 cooperatives remained in Germany, with a significantly reduced number of members and size of housing stock (Crome 2007: 213).[3]

Second phase: after the Second World War

With the end of the war and the reconstruction works in divided East and West Germany, housing cooperatives became important in the provision of affordable housing and were strongly supported by the state in both countries. In the West, the rebellion of 1968 and the economic crisis of the 1970s marked a drastic socio-political demarcation, not just with emerging new social movements, such as the squatting movement, but also as a renaissance of housing cooperatives and the establishment of the first co-housing projects in Germany. Starting in the early 1980s, this can be described as a reaction to the urban crisis in the rise of neoliberal urbanism.

Fordist hegemony and backbone of the reconstruction (1945–1967)

In East and West Germany, the years following 1945 were dominated by state efforts. For both countries, cooperatives became the backbone of the large-scale reconstruction of housing. Most of the cooperatives merged by the Nazi regime were not separated and just a few new cooperatives were founded. The driving members of the cooperatives during this period continued to be workers.

West Germany realized the reconstruction with a bundle of subsidy laws and special loans for social housing in order to (re)build the rental apartment sector. The Housing Act was accordingly introduced with the goal to build 1.8 million flats in six years, predominantly with fixed rents and occupancy rights. This became the basic path for funding for the coming decades until the decline in new constructions in the early 1980s (Crome 2007: 213). Cooperatives played a major part in that process, encouraged by tax reductions for public benefit (*Gemeinnützigkeit*) controlled by the *Wohnungsgemeinnützigkeitsgesetz* (Housing Act) until 1989.

In East Germany, the state took a strong position in the constitution of cooperatives. Starting in 1954, *Arbeiterwohnungsgenossenschaften* (AWG) were founded with the goal to provide housing for industrial workers, and this housing was realized with significant levels of personal contribution during the building process. The state supported the cooperatives by providing free land for permanent use and special loans at zero interest. The AWGs were the driving force for building apartments. Existing 'old' cooperatives remained, but were restructured into public benefit cooperatives in 1957. However, they received less support than the AWGs (Crome 2007: 214). As a result, it was mainly the larger cooperatives that survived.

During the late 1960s the student movement emerged in Hamburg, as in other West German cities. A new era of protest movements driven by a much wider spectrum of issues and actors emerged, which fundamentally challenged the status quo, including the housing sector.

Fordist crisis and first renaissance of collaborative housing (1968–1980)

The first wave of co-housing in Germany needs to be understood in the context of the large-scale social housing projects that were built to quickly create a housing surplus during the decades following the war. The so-called new social movements emerged as part of the struggle against the establishment in the context of the emerging crisis of a paternalistic Fordist state. For the first time, autonomous squatters occupied abandoned buildings and started alternative co-housing projects, and communes were established as part of a counter-movement (Fedrowitz 2016: 10). The famous slogan 'The houses for those who live in them!' (*Die Häuser denen, die drin wohnen!*) was coined. The housing question again became the basis for a shift to a more general political question about how social life should be organized. The counter movements of students, squatters, communes and collectives created experimental spaces to overcome the hegemony of the nuclear family. A collaborative approach to deal with the social question again came to the fore. In the light of the economic crisis, vacancies, segregation and brutal restructuring of the city, a rather fragmented protest milieu of different subcultures and workers became a driving force for political change in the segregated cities. Autonomy from the state and market-based self-determination were the driving factors for these movements (Mayer and Künkel 2012: 65). Such urban social movements turned out strongly in public in West Germany. In East Germany, where the regime was much more repressive, squatters were more discreet in their actions.[4] Whereas cooperative movements were generally supported and subsidized by the state in both countries, the new alternative co-housing movement was viewed with more scepticism and primarily considered a youth-related niche phenomenon.

Hamburg was one of the main sites of the first wave of the squatter movement in West Germany (see Chapter 6). In many parts of the city, numerous citizen initiatives and small district groups emerged and reclaimed participation in political decision-making processes. As in other cities, the early squatting movement was driven by young workers, marginalized and unemployed people, ex-inmates of correction institutions and students, as well as migrant workers (Amantine 2012: 12ff). In 1973, a squatting attempt took place in central Hamburg in order to create a home for students, apprentices and migrant workers (ibid.: 17). The occupation of the house in Ekhofstraße 39 was widely supported by the neighbours, who opposed severe restructuring plans. After six weeks the squatters were violently evicted by heavily armed police and, for the first time, with support from special police forces. This illustrates the draconian political course of these years, following an anti-communist agenda and a perceived link between the Red Army Faction (RAF) and the squatting scene (Heinsohn 2019). The house was immediately demolished by a city-owned housing company, which instead built luxury condominiums. Almost half of the evicted residents were sentenced on charges of building or supporting a criminal organization. This strategy of criminalization, supported by the Yellow Press, expressed the tense relations between the local government and the housing movements.

At the same time the city experienced a strong suburbanization movement. As a result, the inner city was depopulated and became predominantly a space of workplaces, and again became the object of heavy restructuring. The residential structure of the inner city districts changed, with migrant workers moving into less attractive buildings. A decrease in the number of middle-class taxpayers caused a fiscal crisis, and this resulted in severe financial cuts after 1975, mainly in the social and administrative sector.

In his famous speech 'The ungovernability of the cities' (*Die Unregierbarkeit der Städte*), the mayor of Hamburg at the time addressed democratization and civil society (Klose 1975). He argued for necessary political adjustments towards less top-down decisions and stronger instruments of citizen participation in planning processes and in economic and social development in the city. This was a precursor to the introduction of an entrepreneurial approach to city governance, in which 'Enterprise Hamburg' (*Unternehmen Hamburg*) (Dohnanyi 1984) marked a major neoliberal shift towards service-oriented sectors and city marketing. The crisis in the city and the discursive shift of the local state actors mark a significant step towards the neoliberalization of urban restructuring in Hamburg.

Roll-back neoliberalism and the second squatting wave (1981–1989)

Suburbanization, fiscal crisis, recession and austerity politics, on the one hand, and large-scale vacancies, dilapidation of buildings, housing speculation and segregation on the other hand, were the major frontiers that many West-German cities had to deal with. Old houses were demolished and new owner-occupied apartment buildings were built in order to attract capital and bring back the (upper-)middle-class taxpayers. Against this background, urban movements boomed in the early 1980s, focusing on efforts to put a stop to the deconstruction and gentrification of inner-city neighbourhoods, for example by occupying empty buildings and flats. The term '*Instandbesetzung*' (renovation/preservation squatting) described the motivation and the political method for collective occupation and autonomous self-maintenance of alternative lifestyles and economies. All over West Germany, more than 400 houses in 74 cities were squatted (Amantine 2012: 18).

The co-housing movement became more heterogeneous during this period, involving a variety of different so-called subcultures – Punks, Autonomous, Feminist, LGBTQ, Ecos, Hobos, etc. Even though the first feminist co-housing projects emerged back in the early 1970s in Frankfurt am Main and other West-German cities, the numbers of such projects increased all over West Germany. Most importantly, the squatter movement also gained support from a wider public of neighbours, university professors and even federal judges, who actively supported the movement to preserve and renovate old buildings as well as the creation of alternative collaborative experimental spaces. These can be seen as forerunners of the co-housing projects two decades later.

The state's reaction was violent and repressive, spearheaded by the zero-tolerance course of evicting squatters within 24 hours, which the Berlin mayor in 1981 termed '*Berliner Line der Verknuft*' (Berlin line of reason). This strategy was adopted by many other cities. The repressive political attitude towards the movement led to discussions in the occupied houses about how to deal with the constant threats. Debates about legalization divided the movement. On the one hand, there were those who considered it an anti-capitalist political statement and saw mass squatting as the answer to zero-tolerance politics. Violent evictions caused more and more violent street fights in Berlin, Frankfurt am Main, Hamburg and other cities (see Chapter 6). On the other hand, a wave of legalization of projects took off and brought in a variety of different ownership forms, such as housing associations and cooperatives. This also marked the beginning of the so-called new cooperative movement in the mid-1980s (Fedrowitz 2016: 11).

In processes of accelerating deindustrialization and suburbanization, Hamburg became a shrinking city.[5] As a result, many inner-city neighbourhoods became the object of large-scale restructuring programmes. Starting in 1981, empty flats in the houses at Hafenstraße were occupied by youth, Punks and apprentices, who joined forces with the remaining residents. The houses near the harbour, owned at the time by the municipal housing company SAGA, were planned for demolition, and the conflict over the houses in Hafenstraße became one of the most famous examples of anti-authoritarian resistance against restrictive city policies. Furthermore, Hafenstraße became an international symbol of anti-imperialist politics, transnational solidarity, and alternative collaborative housing. At the same time, it was the object of massive criminalization and defamation by officials and the Yellow Press. It was argued that Hafenstraße would be a hub of violence and even the RAF (Amantine 2012: 21). The residents were constantly harassed by state institutions. The electricity company cut off power to the houses, welfare recipients were denied payments, and the police made rigorous attempts to enter the buildings and evict the residents. Nevertheless, after violent struggles the residents signed individual contracts for flats with SAGA in 1983. During this time the houses got 'a lot of money' to fix the roof (Hafenstraße interview 2015). But the individual contracts were terminated after a few years, and by 1985 the situation had already deteriorated again (ibid.). The residents mobilized support with flyers and a pirate radio station, 'Radio Hafenstraße'. Only by making the police plans to demolish public via radio could they prevent further attempts. A long-term resident since the occupation pointed out: 'A very frightening situation. But we also had friends coming in, the houses were full of people' (Hafenstraße interview 2015).

In 1987, formerly evicted flats were squatted again and an explicit 'women's house' was set up as a safe space for up to 20 women in one of the houses (Amantine 2011: 106–114). The living conditions were described as hard, since the buildings were in poor shape, structurally and hygienically, and there were anti-eviction barriers everywhere. But the more repression the houses faced, the more support they got from neighbours in St. Pauli. This solidarity was widespread, and included school pupils, students, professors, churches, unions, political parties, neighbourhood centres, artists, celebrities, left-wing initiatives and, last but not least, FC St.-Pauli fans (Amantine 2012: 21). More than 1,000 supporters held a rally in 1987. In the end, all houses were given a lease contract and the residents were not evicted. But the contracts were terminated again in 1993 until eventually in 1996 the houses were transformed into a small cooperative.

> People understood; if we don't do anything against this, this will become normal. We cannot accept it. A really solid kind of alliance was built.

> There were a lot of political discussions as well, about political struggle, militants, all these kinds of things. There were people even from the social democratic party.
>
> (Hafenstraße interview 2015)

As a result of the struggles around Hafenstraße, construction supervisors such as *Stattbau* and the *Lawaetz foundation* were established, acting as intermediaries between the state and the (former) squats, as well as trustees for subsidies. *Stattbau* was founded in 1985 by a radical left initiative, first and foremost to give legal advice on the projects with the aim of mediating conflicts, and later to provide support and coordination on building and renovation issues (MHM interview 2016). The Lawaetz foundation was established by the city in 1986, with the aim of pacifying the conflict between the city and the autonomous co-housing projects through a top-down approach. Today both Stattbau and Lawaetz work as redevelopment agencies (*Sanierungsträger*) and general developers for co-housing projects in cooperation with the Hamburg Agency (see also Chapter 5).

In the following years the urban social movements became splintered between alternative subcultures and workers' initiatives, although they did join forces around Hafenstraße. Affordability was contextualized in an anti-capitalist and anti-authoritarian political discourse. The aim of the movement was to protect the collective status of the co-houses. Permanent squat status seemed logical to the autonomous movement as an anti-commodification strategy. One building that was closely associated with this idea is *Rote Flora*, which was squatted in 1989 as a social centre (see also Chapter 6). Again and again the squatters refused to buy the house or to sign a contract with the city – as a constant symbol of refusal to integrate with the commodified system. Instead, Rote Flora would remain an ongoing source of friction to the political system (Rote Flora 2012).

Third phase: post-reunification (1990–today)

The reunification of the two German states marks a new period of political interaction between the (co-)housing movement and the local governments. Cities in the east were 'colonized' and became objects of privatization and capitalization processes, with a massive influx of capital, first from national and later from international companies and investors. In the west, entrepreneurial city policies became the dominant political tool kit, which resulted in mega projects and large-scale restructuring – like the construction of the new borough *HafenCity* in Hamburg since 2001. Urban social movements arose in opposition to these political courses, again with Hamburg as a forerunner. The 'right to stay put' in a squatted building developed further and extended the scope to a much wider spectrum of urban struggles, as part of the claim for a 'right to the city'. At the same time, this process also illustrates how alternative ideas and concepts were at risk of being integrated and co-opted by neoliberal urbanism. Co-housing projects became ambiguous. On the one hand, they often manifest a strategy in opposition to gentrification. On the other hand, co-housing projects can also be conceived as potential pioneers of gentrification, whose cultural capital is commodified and capitalized by private and public housing developers.

Countering roll-out neoliberalism: struggles and legalization (1990–2000)

The third wave of squatting came right after the reunification of East and West Germany. Again, this led to massive confrontations in the early 1990s. The internal discussions on whether the legalization of squatted houses was a better option than keeping an uncertain status of constant occupation was at the core of each group, and continued throughout the decade (and is still ongoing). One political result of these struggles was the so-called 'careful urban development' (*Behutsame Stadtentwicklung*), which became hegemonic for the next decade and included neighbours as 'active' participants in development decisions.

In Hamburg, the conflict around Hafenstraße escalated again in the early 1990s. This time a political campaign was run by the city government suggesting direct connections between Hafenstraße activists and the RAF (Hafenstraße interview 2015). In the end, these efforts failed juridically. The solidarity was not undermined and the houses had strong support in the neighbourhood. Eventually, in 1996, the Hafenstraße houses gained a secure status when they were transformed into a small cooperative called *Schanze e.G.* To allow for the financial status of the residents and make them eligible for special bank loans, the houses were all declared social housing.[6]

Neoliberal crisis and second renaissance of collaborative housing (since 2001)

An ongoing and widespread shortage of affordable housing, combined with neoliberal urbanism as the dominant strategy for (sustainable) urban development, can be seen as the socio-economic and political roots of the boom in social urban movements since the early 2000s. Housing has again become one of the most urgent social questions of our time. It has also been declared a human right in the United Nations (urban) agenda. In this context, the 'right to the city' has been described as having a holistic perspective on the city, a counter hegemonic approach, an empty signifier for reform politics as well as a horizontal approach for mobilization (Holm and Gebhardt 2011: 13).

Today, inner-city gentrification has led to evictions of many autonomous co-housing projects from the 1970s, 80s and 90s. In some cases, however, squatted houses have undergone a process of legalization, a development that forms a significant part of the second post-war wave of co-housing in Germany. But there is also a new wave of co-housing taking shape, predominantly made up of actors with middle-class backgrounds that are trying to establish co-housing projects the legal way, for example with the *Mietshäuser Syndikat*[7] (Apartment-house Syndicate) or as a cooperative (see Chapters 5 and 6). These political-economic developments have led to a new wave of cooperatives and self-owned building communities that realize some form of collective housing. The number of housing cooperatives have increased slightly over the last decade. Today, there are more than 2,000 housing cooperatives, managing over two million flats and with more than three million members (Wikipedia 2019). Membership structures have also become heterogeneous. More and more people are considering joining an existing large cooperative with the aim of securing relatively affordable and stable rents. People are also searching for a sense of community and solidarity in a highly individualized, segregated social environment that fosters isolation (Thomas et al. 2020). About 3,000 co-housing projects exist all over Germany (Fedrowitz 2016). Besides Hamburg, local city governments substantially support self-build co-housing groups in cities such as Freiburg and Tübingen (see Chapter 5).

In Hamburg, there are plans to build 10,000 flats per year, but they are not all affordable (Green Party interview 2016; MHM interview 2016). Only 3,000 are planned to be social housing and thus subsidized by the city (Hamburg 2017). Cooperatives are again considered a driving actor in this plan. However, the basic problem for cooperatives is the need for starting capital and cooperative shares. The amounts required are simply out of reach for many potential residents, and this constitutes a financial barrier for low-income families. In some cases, this financial burden is compensated for by other project members.

2009 became a very important year for urban social movements in Hamburg, with the release of the iconic documentary 'Empire St. Pauli'. The manifesto 'Not in our name' was also published in the same year, right after the occupation of the *Gängeviertel*. The Hamburg Recht auf Stadt-Netzwerk (Hamburg-Right-to-the-City-Network) was set up as a city-wide association, with the following agenda:

> affordable housing, non-commercial spaces, socialization of property, a new democratic urban planning and the preservation of public greens; for the right to the city for all inhabitants – with or without papers. Against gentrification, repression, neoliberal urbanism and closed borders.
>
> (RAS website 2019)

The Hamburg Recht auf Stadt-Netzwerk consists of more than sixty city-wide initiatives from diverse backgrounds and thematic fields – a cohesion of alternative subcultures, middle-class and working-class actors, as well as refugees (see Chapter 6). It combines artistic and social critique (Boltanski and Chiapello 2003) with creative direct actions of civil disobedience, large rallies and events that challenge the status quo of neoliberal urbanism (Twickel 2010). City planning from below became the central demand for the different thematic fields of conflict that emerged in opposition to the ongoing entrepreneurial course of the Hamburg senate (Füllner and Templin 2011:

79). This development is deeply rooted in the history of housing movements and drastic segregation due to social divides and polarization. In Hamburg, the highest density of millionaires in Germany contrasts with the everyday deprivation of many residents (Pohl and Wicher 2011: 7). From the grassroot perspective it is still necessary to keep pressuring the city government to achieve non-speculative spaces and projects within the entrepreneurial city:

> it's important for us as a social movement to keep the pressure that when there's a plot for sale, that the city doesn't sell the plot to Baugemeinschaften who, or to investors who pay, who can pay the most.
>
> (RAS interview 2015)

The Hamburg Agency for Self-build Communities (*Agentur für Baugemeinschaften*)[8] picked up on these developments, especially the new co-housing movement and the political awakening of the middle class. Since 2003, the Hamburg Agency has been providing land and support for co-housing groups through its programme. In contrast to the squatting movement, questions about lifestyle and multigenerational support became driving factors during this period. The new ownership forms that emerged with the self-owned building communities differ from the non-profit cooperative idea with their explicit option to resell flats for a profit. Private and communal housing companies adapted the idea of co-housing, especially in a multigenerational context.

At the same time, because of the shortage of land, the Hamburg Agency's programme is designed to be very competitive. As the head of the city building department (*Baustadtrat*) – which is a member of the Green Party faction in the city council – points out:

> And they have, I think, eight times more people applying for land than they actually have available. Even if it takes time and work to create a building community in the beginning, and it may take you five or six years from your first ideas to the finished house, a lot of people are doing it, because they like this way of living.
>
> (Green Party interview 2016)

Building communities are, first and foremost, a self-empowerment option for left-wing intellectuals, who have the cultural and social capital needed, if not the financial capital, to realize such a project successfully (MHM interview 2016). However, there is also potential for emancipative politics and to push the boundaries further for affordable and self-maintained forms of housing in the city. One example is the *Weg damit Projekt* (Away-with-it project), which is similar to the idea of the Mietshäuser Syndikat but focuses on individual flats. The aim is to collectivize flats under an umbrella association to enable residents to step out of the speculative market and self-organize their housing. An example of this is the initiative *Yes, in my backyard* (YIMBY), a neighbourhood project that is trying to integrate low-income residents and refugees in a co-housing project in Hamburg-St-Pauli (MHM interview 2016). Beyond this, in recent years a new squatting movement with a different composition of actors has emerged in Hamburg and other German cities. *Gängeviertel* stands as an emblem of this movement, with its collaboration of artists, precarious workers and political activists (see also Chapter 6). Besides a noticeable tendency to co-optation and commodification by 'new urban governance' (Kuhn 2014; Mayer and Künkel 2012), a shift in city policies towards more radical democratic approaches is thus visible today (Scheller 2019).

Conclusion

The different co-housing projects, as well as related ownership forms and political programmes that we find today in Germany can be understood as a historical sedimentation of historical phases. As such, co-housing projects cannot simply be considered reactions to socio-demographic and socio-political circumstances of their specific time. Rather, they have to be seen as results of constant and ongoing struggles from the bottom up for self-determined, affordable and dignified housing beyond the basic capitalist principles. Even today, when co-housing has become a lucrative market segment, for example for collectives that build owner-occupied housing (*Baugruppen*), the majority of co-housing groups choose a non-speculative ownership form for their projects. The emphasis on *use value* rather than *exchange value* is written into the statutes of many cooperatives, associations and, in the case of the Mietshäuser Syndikat, even in the core entity of the capitalist system, a limited liability company (LLC). This illustrates the historical achievements of the cooperative and co-housing movements as well as the creative and subversive potential of co-housing. As a consequence, movements for collaborative housing in general and co-housing projects in particular, create not only a socially, financially and ecologically sustainable environment for their residents; they also have political effects on the discourse and practices of sustainability itself. Again and again, these movements provide experimental spaces for new forms of sustainable collaborative housing and, not least, new tenure forms.

Starting as a niche phenomenon, the increasing number of co-housing projects in Germany illustrate a new trend that might become a boom (again) or at least shift the discourse in the direction of collaboration, mutual help and solidarity, rather than the neoliberal atomization of the profit-oriented citizen. As the historical examples have illustrated, such a development, first and foremost, strongly depends on the provision of legal and financial support by the state and, furthermore, on unrestricted autonomy and self-organization of the projects. The non-profit provision of land for collaborative democratic use seems to be a particularly promising tool for that purpose.

Today, as a result of dealing with the housing crisis, Hamburg has taken a leading role regarding the intersection of urban social movements and urban

Table 3.1 Types of collaborative housing in Germany

Types	*Ownership*	*Specialty*	*Government*
Small cooperative	Collective	High share rates	Supported and subsidized
Large cooperative	Collective	Moderate share rates Can act like company and expand	Supported and subsidized
Private building group	Private	Profit-oriented resell option	Supported and subsidized
Mietshäuser Syndikat	Collective Non-profit LLC	No private capital necessary	Supported and subsidized
Squats	Collective No fixed status	Very low rents Only operational costs	Zero-tolerance to toleration

governance of co-housing. The Hamburg Recht auf Stadt-Netzwerk, YIMBY and Weg damit emphasize the need for alternative forms to deal with the housing crisis, to counter entrepreneurial approaches to neoliberal urban development. As a result, municipal programmes are partly a reaction to the claims from the movements for more affordable housing and aspects of self-governance beyond the usual co-housing context. Alternative approaches are integrated in participatory planning projects, such as the plan for the Esso Houses. Nevertheless, such grassroot collaborations in the city remain the exception rather than the rule.

As argued in this chapter, the increased interest in co-housing can be seen as result of constant pressure from grassroot housing movements at different periods of time. The Hamburg Agency and the intermediaries Stattbau and Lawaetz Foundation are historically rooted in the intense and long-term struggles around the houses at Hafenstraße. But against this wider historical background, it also becomes clearer how co-housing has shifted from a counter-culture niche phenomenon to a predominantly middle-class-dominated movement. In that sense, the emphasis on social sustainability among co-housing projects today is a result of specific political deficiencies of neoliberal urbanism, but is also rooted in the struggle of the traditional housing movements (see also Chapter 6). Moreover, co-housing could also turn into a political instrument organized along principles of neoliberal urbanism, manoeuvring between responsibilization and self-determination (see Chapter 5). The political pressure channelled by grassroot movements is necessary to achieve small pockets of non-speculative spaces and collaborative projects that experiment with sustainable forms of co-housing in the entrepreneurial city, which could also lead to wider political shifts towards alternative and socially just housing policies. However, financial and cultural barriers need to be broken down in order to extend this option to working-class actors, who are in need of affordable and fixed rents in the long run. For the municipality, it should be a central aim for sustainable urban development to provide tools and programmes that not only cater to the middle class but especially empower those with less cultural capital (see also Droste 2015).

Referenced interviews

Hafenstraße interview, Hamburg, 20 October 2015.
Green Party interview, Hamburg, 11 May 2016.
Lawaetz foundation interview, Hamburg, 13 May 2016.
Mieter helfen Mieter (MHM) interview, Hamburg, 30 June 2016.
Hamburg Agency interview, Hamburg, 19 October 2015.
Hamburg Recht auf Stadt-Netzwerk (RAS) interview, Hamburg, 20 October 2015.
Wohnungsbaugenossenschaft von 1904 e.G. interview, Hamburg, 30 June 2016.

Notes

1 Between 1870 and 1910, Hamburg's population grew from 327,000 to about 1,100,000 and manufacturing grew from 685 factories employing 18,400 workers in 1880, to 6,715 factories employing 109,200 workers in 1913 (Brietzke 2019).
2 In contrast to full liability, where all an individual's possessions and savings are at risk, a limited liability membership means that a member's personal liability is limited to the fixed sum of the cooperative shares.
3 In Hamburg about 10,000 people (Jews, political activists, people with disabilities) were deported and killed, including members of housing cooperatives (Schmidt 2019).
4 Even if there are no exact figures for East Germany, it can be assumed that there were 1,200 registered cases in Berlin alone for 1979 due to large-scale vacancies of old apartment buildings (Amantine 2012: 81).
5 Between 1967 and 1987 there was a decrease of 400,000, from 1.87 million to 1.59 million inhabitants.
6 In Hamburg, social housing in general means that its units are subsidized by the government to support people with low to moderate income. The aim is to provide a certain level of rent for these individuals according to a certain defined standard income level. Moreover, there are special subsidies in the form of low-interest loans for housing cooperatives.
7 The Mietshäuser Syndikat was founded in 1990 in Freiburg to collectivize squats and protect the houses from commodification. Today it is a solidarity network of 144 established collectively owned and self-organized houses, as well as 17 upcoming projects. The tenure form is a limited liability company that is owned by two shareholders – the housing association of all residents in the house and the association of all members of the Syndikat. In contrast to cooperatives, no individual financial shares are necessary. With this legal model it is possible to create affordable housing and, moreover, prevent the collectivized houses from being resold (MHS website 2019).
8 We refer to the institution as the 'Hamburg Agency' throughout this chapter and also in the rest of the book.

References

Amantine (2011) *Gender und Häuserkampf.* Münster: Unrast Verlag.

Amantine (2012) *Die Häuser denen, die drin wohnen!*Münster: Unrast Verlag.

Birke, P. (2016) 'Right to the City – and Beyond: The Topographies of Urban Social Movements in Hamburg', in M. Mayer, C. Thörn and H. Thörn (eds) *Urban Uprisings: Challenging Neoliberal Urbanism in Europe*, pp. 203–232, New York: Palgrave Macmillan.

Brietzke, D. (2019) 'Industrialisierung, soziale Frage und Arbeiterbewegung in Hamburg'. https://geschichtsbuch.hamburg.de/epochen/industrialisierung/ (12 June 2019).

Büttner, U. (2019) 'Das demokratische Intermezzo: Not und Aufbruchsstimmung 1918–1933'. https://geschichtsbuch.hamburg.de/epochen/weimarer-republik/ (15 February 2019).

Chrome, B. (2007) 'Entwicklung und Situation der Wohnungsgenossenschaften in Deutschland', *Informationen zur Raumentwicklung*, 4, pp. 211–222.

Dohnanyi, K. von (1983) 'Unternehmen Hamburg'. Talk November 29, 2011Übersee-Club, Hamburg, http://uebersee-club.de/resources/Server/pdf-Dateien/1980-1984/vortrag-1983-11-29Dr.%20Klaus%20von%20Dohnanyi.pdf (21 August 2019).

Droste, C. (2015) 'German co-housing: an opportunity for municipalities to foster socially inclusive urban development?', *Urban Research & Practice* vol. 8, no. 1, pp. 79–92.

Federal Ministry for Traffic, Building and Housing (FMTBH) (2004) *Wohnungsgenossenschaften – Potentiale und Perspektiven. Bericht der Expertenkommission Wohnungsgenossenschaften.* Berlin.

Fedrowitz, M. (2016) 'Gemeinschaftliches Wohnen – Stand und Entwicklung in Deutschland', in *Wohnprojekte – Von der Nische zum Trend?*, in *Nachrichten der ARL 1/2016*, pp. 9–12. https://shop.arl-net.de/media/direct/pdf/nachrichten/2016-1/Nachr_1-2016_Fedrowitz_S9-12_online.pdf (15 February 2019).

Füllner, J. and Templin, D. (2011) 'Stadtplanung von Unten. Die »Recht auf Stadt«-Bewegung in Hamburg', in A. Holm and D. Gebhardt (eds) *Initiativen Für Ein Recht Auf Stadt. Theorie und Praxis städtischer Aneignung*, pp. 74–104, Hamburg: VSA-Verlag.

Hamburg (2017) 'Wohnen in Hamburg 2030. Eine Stadt für Alle – Strategien für Bezahlbares Wohnen', *Fachkonferenz*, 3 April 2017, Behörden für Stadtentwicklung und Wohnen. www.hamburg.de/contentblob/9466960/.../d-wohnen-in-hamburg-2030.pdf (13 June 2019).

Heinsohn, K. (2019) *Die Hafenstraße – Hausbesetzungen und neues Zusammenleben*, https://geschichtsbuch.hamburg.de/epochen/siebziger-und-achtziger/die-hafenstrasse-hausbesetzungen-und-neues-zusammenlebenhausbesetzer-und-hafenstrassenaktivisten/ (12 June 2019).

Holm, A. and Gebhardt D. (2011) 'Initiativen für ein Recht auf Stadt', in A. Holm and D. Gebhardt (eds) *Initiativen für ein Recht auf Stadt. Theorie und Praxis städtischer Aneignung*, pp. 7–23, Hamburg: VSA Verlag.

Huber, V. A. (1983/1846) 'Über innere Kolonisation', in H. Frank and D. Schubert (eds) *Lesebuch zur Wohnungsfrage*, pp. 122–126, Cologne: Pahl-Rugenstein.

Institute for Creative Sustainability (2012) *CoHousing Cultures: Handbuch für selbstorganisiertes, gemeinschaftliches und nachhaltiges Wohnen*, Berlin: Jovis Berlin.

Klose, H.-U. (1975) 'Die Unregierbarkeit der Städte, Vortrag in der Evangelischen Akademie Tutzingen', *Berichte und Dokumente aus der Freien und Hansestadt Hamburg*, 450.

Kuhn, A. (2014) *Vom Häuserkampf zur neoliberalen Stadt: Besetzungsbewegungen in Berlin und Barcelona.* Münster: Westfälisches Dampfboot.

Mayer, M. and Künkel, J. (eds) (2012) *Neoliberal Urbanism and its Contestations.* London: Palgrave Macmillan.

Mayer, M. (2016) 'Neoliberal Urbanism and Uprisings Across Europe', in M. Mayer, C. Thörn and H. Thörn (eds) *Urban Uprisings: Challenging Neoliberal Urbanism in Europe*, pp. 57–92, London: Palgrave Macmillan.

Margit, M. (2012) 'The right to the city in urban social movements', in N. Brenner, P. Marcuse and M. Mayer (eds) *Cities for People, not for Profit. Critical Urban Theory and the Right to the City*, pp. 63–85, London/New York: Routledge.

MHS (Mietshäuser Syndikat) (2019) 'Der Projekteverbund'. www.syndikat.org/de/unternehmensverbund/ (23 April 2019).

Notz, G. (2014) 'Die sozialistische Genossenschaftsbewegung als die dritte Säule der Arbeiterbewegung – Geschichte und Perspektiven', in A. Weipert (ed.) *Demokratisierung von Wirtschaft und Staat – Studien zum Verhältnis von Ökonomie, Staat und Demokratie vom 19. Jahrhundert bis heute*, pp. 100–118. Berlin: NoRa Verlag.

Novy, K. (1983) *Genossenschafts-Bewegung. Zur Geschichte und Zukunft der Wohnreform*, Berlin: Transit Verlag.

Pohl, G. and Wicher K. (2011) *Armes Reiches Hamburg: Metropole Zwischen Wohlstand Und Armut*. Hamburg: VSA-Verlag.

RAS (Hamburg Recht auf die Stadt Netzwerk) (2019) *Über uns [About]*. www.rechtaufstadt.net/ueber-about/ (18 May 2019)

Rinn, M. (2016) *Konflikte um die Stadt für alle: Das Machtfeld der Stadtentwicklungspolitik in Hamburg*. Münster: Westfälisches Dampfboot.

Rote Flora (2012) *Flora bleibt unverträglich – Zu den kommenden Kämpfen um die Rote Flora*. https://rote-flora.de/flora-bleibt-unvertraeglich-zu-den-kommenden-kaempfen-um-die-rote-flora/ (23 April 2019).

Scheller, D. (2019) *Demokratisierung der Postdemokratie. Städtische soziale Bewegungen im Vergleich*, Bielefeld: transcript.

Schmidt, S. (2019) *Nationalsozialismus 1933–1945. Teil 1: Von der Machtübernahme der Nationalsozialisten bis zum Kriegsbeginn*. https://geschichtsbuch.hamburg.de/epochen/nationalsozialismus/#NS-Teil1 (15 February 2019).

Thomas, S., Scheller, D. and T. Ehmann (2020) *Substanzielle Gemeinschaften - Selbstorganisation und Gemeinwohl in Mehrgenerationenwohnprojekten, Wiesbaden:* Springer VS.

Twickel, C. (2011) *Gentrifidingsbums oder eine Stadt für alle*. Hamburg: Ed. Nautilus.

Weyerer, G. (2013) *Den Nazis ein Dorn im Auge – Tagung über die Genossenschaften in der NS-Zeit an der Universität Hamburg*. www.deutschlandfunk.de/den-nazis-ein-dorn-im-auge.1148.de.html?dram:article_id=268134 (15 February 2019).

Wikipedia (2019) *Wohnungsbaugenossenschaft*. https://de.wikipedia.org/wiki/Wohnungsbaugenossenschaft (15 February 2019).

4 Barcelona

Housing crisis and urban activism

Henrik Gutzon Larsen

Introduction

'*Construïm habitatge per construir comunitat*' (We build housing to build community) read a banner over the building site when the La Borda group in early 2017 celebrated that construction of their building had started, some five years after the idea of an alternative housing community in the Can Batlló area of Barcelona's La Bordeta neighbourhood emerged. In an early version of its website, the La Borda group presented its project in these words:

> We … aim to meet the need to access socially, economically and environmentally sustainable living spaces, while bypassing the conventional real estate market. For us it is essential to generate forms of collective property that put the focus on the effective use of living space, rather than its exchange value in the capitalist market. At the same time we want to promote more communal forms of living, that facilitate the interrelationship between neighbours and the division of housework and care needs through communal spaces.
>
> (La Borda, no date)

In late 2018, the building was ready for the members to move in. By then, however, La Borda already had inspired other groups in the city and become somewhat of a flagship for Barcelona Municipality's nascent policy of promoting alternative housing forms.

Co-housing as an alternative housing form is a new concept in Spain.[1] In fact, in a country where the housing system is overwhelmingly based on owner occupation and private rental, everything but that could seem 'alternative'. But co-housing and kindred housing forms are now actively explored as a way of challenging dominant structures of housing provision as well as addressing wider social, economic, political and ecological concerns. Nevertheless, co-housing is still a highly marginal housing form in Spain, and while some projects and initiatives are emerging elsewhere, it is in Catalonia and the Barcelona area in particular that co-housing is becoming a noticeable phenomenon. In the words of the Barcelona councillor for housing, who during the local government of Barcelona en Comú (2015–2019) helped to make co-housing a municipality policy, 'We are at the beginning of a new tradition' (Interview A). The La Borda project figures prominently in this endeavour.

Using La Borda as a recurring example, this chapter analyses emerging co-housing projects in the Barcelona area. La Borda has been examined by others (Brysch 2018; Cabré and Andrés 2018; Garcia i Mateu 2015), and the purpose is not to analyse this or other projects in detail. Rather, the chapter focuses on how and why co-housing projects emerge and are seen to contribute to wider struggles and projects in the context of Spain, Catalonia and, particularly, the Barcelona area. As we will see, the history and politics of the Can Batlló area is key to the emergence of La Borda, but the project is not confined to this particular context. Summing-up some of the influences and concerns he found to be at work in the project, a member says: 'La Borda within Can Batlló, Can Batlló within the sovereignty movement in Catalonia, the sovereignty movement within the global crisis of – what the fuck are we doing with the Planet; that is, I would say, the contextualisation' (Interview B). Despite the obvious simplification, the member here effectively inserts La Borda into wider historical-geographical contexts interacting at many scales. This chapter takes a similar approach of situating the recent emergence of co-housing in the Barcelona area in a context of interrelated scales. While not suggesting a hierarchy of importance, we will start with the Spanish housing system – and housing crisis. From this, the chapter continues to an overviews of co-housing developments in Catalonia before zooming in on this issue in Barcelona through the scales of city, neighbourhood and, finally, the material La Borda project.

The Spanish housing system: Thatcherism *avant la lettre*

As 'Thatcherism *avant la lettre*', in the pithy formulation of López and Rodríguez (2011: 6), the seeds of the current Spanish housing system were sown during the Francoist regime. Unable to furnish a competitive industrial economy, the dictatorship founded Spain's post-war economic modernisation on mass tourism and the construction sector. Already from the late 1950s, this entailed an aggressive promotion of private home ownership, which also served as a disciplinary mechanism and as a way to circumvent potential conflicts between state and tenants in a state-led housing system. By 1970, more than 60% of Spanish housing was privately owned. This trend did not end with the fall of the dictatorship. Embedded in policies aimed at converging the Spanish economy with other European economies and partly related policies of market liberalisation ('globalisation'), construction and private home-ownership continued to be a main driver of the Spanish economy. And following the long and in important respects real-estate driven boom in the Spanish economy between 1997 and 2007, which subsequently turned out to be a credit inflated 'bubble', private home-ownership had in 2007 reached a staggering 87% of Spanish housing (Di Feliciantonio and Aalbers 2018;

García 2010; López and Rodríguez 2011). Private home-ownership has fallen a little in the wake of the 2007 crisis but remains high. The Spanish housing system has in this way come to epitomise the 'ownership model' (Singer 2000), which 'identifies property as essentially private, with state property as the anomalous exception' (Blomley 2004: xix).

The details of the Spanish crisis (or crises) are not important in the present context. It is sufficient to note that the boom and eventual bust between 1997 and 2007 in important respects was pushed by real-estate speculation and housing. In the analysis of García-Lamarca and Kaika (2016), for example, the process was partly driven by macro-economic and political changes, which led to a financialisation of the housing market. But this process was in important respects sustained by an aggressive mobilisation of mortgage contracts, which was driven by a narrative of housing as a prudent and safe investment for individuals. Lives became mortgaged, as Colau and Alemany (2012) put it. Financial institutions used this to push predatory subprime loans to low- and middle-income groups, which were particularly affected when the financial crisis and unemployment forced many hyper-indebted households to default on mortgages based on inflated property values (Palomera 2014). Not for anything, '*no es un crisis, es una estafa*' (it is not a crisis, it is a fraud) is a main motto of the Plataforma de Afectados por la Hipoteca (PAH, Platform for People Affected by Mortgages), the initially Barcelona-based housing movement (Chapter 6; García-Lamarca 2017). But beyond those hit directly by foreclosure or eviction, many are faced with persistent housing precarity. Because of the ever-increasing prices of housing, one member of La Borda has over a ten-years period lived in 16–17 different flats, for example (Interview C).

While also other factors and motivations are in play, the dominant housing system and the protracted housing crisis is an important backdrop for many alternative housing projects in the Barcelona area. This has already been suggested by the 'mission statement' of La Borda quoted in the introduction; still, although initially describing the group as 'left wing or extreme left wing', a La Borda member recalls: 'We all decided not to build an anti-capitalist project, not a real confrontational project, just try to propose new things: can we relate with our house in a different way?' (Interview D). Starting with an overview of alternative housing initiatives in Catalonia, the following sections will gradually zoom in on Barcelona generally and the La Borda project particularly.

Catalonia

While still modest in comparison with co-housing in Northern Europe, Spanish alternative housing initiatives are primarily located in Catalonia and the Barcelona area in particular. In his pioneering study, Pointelin (2016) identifies 25 (legal) alternative housing initiatives in Catalonia, three of which he records as either arrested in development or abandoned. The COPHAB project on collaborative housing has since catalogued 41 initiatives in Catalonia. That these are initiatives should be stressed. Only 16 projects are functioning and seven projects are in the process of being constructed, while a group has been formed for ten initiatives. The remaining eight registered initiatives have either stalled or are uncategorisable. Moreover, most of these alternative housing initiatives have emerged since 2011 (COPHAB 2019; Ferreri et al. 2019). Alternative housing projects is thus an emerging but noticeable phenomenon, which could seem to have some relation to the interrelated financial and housing crises – and the 15M protests. It should be noted, however, that many of these projects differ somewhat from conceptions of co-housing in other countries. A brief look at the pioneering Cal Cases community may help to introduce this issue – and nuance a causal understanding of links between co-housing and the financial crisis. Furthermore, Cal Cases was a source of inspiration for the La Borda project.

After three years of preparation, the Cal Cases community was established in 2007 by a group of people from an anti-capitalist *ateneu*, a social centre, which ran a food cooperative and various other social-transformative activities in Barcelona's Gràcia neighbourhood.[2] But in their private lives, a member recalls, 'our home [had] the renting price of the market or [we had to] buy home in this neighbourhood, which is quite expensive. So, the first idea was to also put in practice in our homes a collective way to live.' It took the group a long time to find a location, not least because it was initially decided that the project should not be located in the countryside. In the end, however, the group opted for a former farmstead that had been used and developed by a drug rehabilitation project in the rural hills near the village of Santa Maria d'Oló, more than an hour by car from Barcelona (and not accessible by public transport). This was essentially due to the fact that the group looked for a suitable site in midst of the real estate boom and could not afford properties in a more urban setting. In 2015, the Cal Cases community consisted of some 30 people (two-thirds of them adults) living in a total of 12 living units of 35 to 40 square meters. Eight of these units are in retrofitted buildings from the rehabilitation project and four are in a self-build straw-bale house. The old farmhouse serves as common house with dining room, kitchen and various common rooms and workshops. The housing units have a kitchenette, and the members take turns in preparing common lunches and dinners.

Cal Cases is legally organised as a housing cooperative, which was – and to some extent still is – an unfamiliar model in Spain. With help from Sostre Cívic, an organisation promoting cooperative projects and acting as an 'umbrella' cooperative in and around Barcelona, the Cal Cases group helped to pioneer the notion of housing cooperatives, which has become a characteristic of alternative housing projects in Catalonia (see below). Yet, a member emphasises, 'The cooperative is like [an] umbrella for the community project; it is our legal personality, but it is not our finality.' Another member concurs: 'I think the general feeling is that we are a community; the other is the legal form, but it is not the main basis for us.' Decisions in the Cal Cases community are reached by consensus at weekly general assemblies.

As for all alternative housing initiatives in Catalonia, financing was the major problem, because banks – unaccustomed with housing cooperatives – were only willing to provide individual loans to finance the project. This would entail individual property rights (and individual responsibilities for servicing loans), which is against the ideology of the group. In the end, the financing of Cal Cases was organised though a credit cooperative from the social and solidarity economy movement that was about to establish itself in Catalonia and was looking for a 'big' project to finance. The credit cooperative made the necessary loan available and provided guarantees: 'It was a magic moment', a member says; 'they [the credit cooperative] were looking for people and a project, and we were looking for a bank'. New members must buy a EUR 15,000 share in the Cal Cases cooperative, which, if a member leaves, is payed back by the cooperative in instalments over five years. When Cal Cases was established, most members were working at universities and could afford the share price. But in 2015, when the community sought new members in a situation of crisis, the share price was beyond what many could afford.

Cal Cases initially operated a system in which all had to contribute the same amount of work and money in monthly contribution, which pays for all running costs of the community, including food (with no extra monthly contribution for children). This proved difficult, however, because some did not have sufficient time for common work, while others could not afford the monetary contribution. Therefore, since around 2012, Cal Cases has operated according to a model in which the monthly contribution corresponds to 80 hours of work. This can be paid as a combination of 1) regular money, translated into hours depending on individual wage levels, 2) common work for Cal Cases, and 3) social currency (*monedas sociales*). This entails that individual monetary monthly contributions can range from EUR 100 to 400. However, nobody can only 'pay' or 'work'. All must work a minimum, as there are tasks which the community find all should do, for example care of children and sick people, cleaning and cooking. On the one hand, a member points out, this is because 'we don't want a system of someone working for the others, so that they are, in a way, employed by the others'. On the other hand, 'some people have more precarious work than others in the capitalist system, and we wanted to find a way to mitigate this, because we cannot change it completely'.

While Cal Cases in terms of participation and self-management would fit virtually any characterisation of co-housing (e.g. McCamant and Durrett 2011; Tummers 2015), the community's negotiation of the private and the common in many respects goes further than most understandings of co-housing. In Denmark, for example, a community like Cal Cases would probably be seen as a commune rather than a co-housing community (see Chapter 1; Larsen 2019). More generally, however, the (planned) element of common everyday life in alternative Catalan housing initiatives often fall short of what would be expected of co-housing practices elsewhere.

As suggested by the example of Cal Cases, but not surprising in a society where private ownership of housing is paramount, a key challenge for alternative housing initiatives is unfamiliarity with housing cooperatives and collective property rights. This applies to people as well as institutions. A member of La Borda recounts his mother's difficulties in understanding his housing choice, for example (Interview F). But the challenge is acute when it comes to authorities and financial institutions. Lack of applicable legislation is in this respect a problem, which is further complicated by the quasi-federal structure of Spain, which gives the regions considerable but often partial jurisdiction over some matters. Nonetheless, Pointelin (2016) points out, the comparatively many alternative housing initiatives in Catalonia is in part explained by the fact that the regional government of Catalonia (Generalitat de Catalunya) in recent years has passed legislation that makes it easier (but not easy) to form housing cooperatives.

Barcelona

In the wake of the recent housing-rooted crisis in Spain, the occupation of housing and related housing movements like the PAH have become highly notable (Di Feliciantonio 2017; García-Lamarca 2017; Martínez 2019). Not least in Barcelona, this wave of crisis-induced occupations and activism feeds into longer histories of squatting and housing struggles (see Chapter 6; Debelle et al. 2018). In terms of people as well as political aims, there are many overlaps and parallels between these developments and the emerging alternative housing initiatives. But I will here focus on the initiatives and projects in Barcelona that most clearly relate to international understandings of co-housing.

The La Borda project is based on a long-term lease of municipality-owned land. This was negotiated while Barcelona Municipality was led by conservative Catalan nationalists. That was also the political constellation under which the squatters' initiative by 6 Claus was legalised in the neighbouring Municipality of Sant Cugat (see Chapter 6). This suggests that alternative housing initiatives are not necessarily blocked by conservative politicians. Indeed, when describing relations with the municipality as 'not very easy', a La Borda member distinguishes between the fundamental conditions for the project and the more practical issues arising during its realisation: 'On the one hand, of course, we have this lease on this piece of land. Without this condition we could never have done such a project in Barcelona, because [land] is very, very expensive. But on the other hand, we have to deal with different bureaucrats' (Interview D). Yet, when the citizen platform Barcelona en Comú (Barcelona in Common) became the governing minority of Barcelona in 2015 (Blanco et al. 2019), alternative housing initiatives were integrated into policy.

Considering the manifest housing crisis in the city and Barcelona en Comú's origins in the 15M protests and housing activism, it is hardly surprising that housing became political priority of Barcelona Municipality. A clear example is the municipality's accentuation of the 'right to housing' and a ten-year plan for addressing these rights (Barcelona City Council 2018). One point in this plan is 'promoting the assignment-for-use cooperative model: cohousing'. More specifically, in the words of the municipality housing manager, this entails:

> Housing that is affordable, non-speculative, social (but not public), environmentally sound and community-oriented. That which elsewhere in the EU is called co-housing and which we call cohabitatge should play an important role in the sophistication of local public action in housing, along with the involvement of civil society in solving collective problems. To do this, the public should help, facilitate and accompany. But the key is for civil society to generate power in terms of housing with its ability to be independent of government and politics.
>
> (Burón 2016: 7)

As housing falls mainly under the jurisdiction of the Catalan regional government and the Spanish state, Barcelona Municipality is limited in what it can independently accomplish. In important respects, this entails that the aim is political, to promote a tenure form that is new to Spain, and Barcelona en Comú's councillor for housing recognised that 'co-housing' (*covivienda/cohabitatge*) to some degree is used as a convenient label for this (Interview A). The municipality supports alternative housing initiatives in three ways: (very modest) economic assistance; changes to planning regulations that inhibit experimentation (the bureaucracy La Borda encountered as 'not very easy'); and, most substantially, by making municipality-owned land available for alternative housing initiatives. The first example of this was the Princesa 49 project from 2014 (Sostre Cívic, no date).

Regarding the last point, the municipality in October 2016 made seven plots of municipality-owned land available for co-housing projects (Ajuntament de Barcelona 2016a). A total of nineteen projects were submitted, and, in May 2017, five projects (with a total of 110 housing units) were selected for further development. (Two plots were disregarded, either because the proposed project did not meet the criteria or because there were no proposals for the plot.) In the selection process, particular emphasis was placed on environmental and social criteria as well as on promotion of community spaces, shared infrastructure and co-management (Ajuntament de Barcelona 2017). Shortly before the 2019 municipality elections, the Barcelona city council approved a second round of tenders for right-of-use housing cooperatives on municipality-owned land (see also below). This round includes three plots, one of them in Can Batlló – the area where La Borda is located (Ajuntament de Barcelona 2019). Only the conservative PP (Partido Popular) voted against, while the centrist Catalan ERC (Esquerra Republicana de Catalunya) abstained (Font 2019). While minuscular in the overall housing of the city, the councillor for housing stresses that these initiatives 'symbolically it is very important, because it is very visible; it is experimental, it is a kind of innovation. As a number, as a quantity, it is very little, but socially it means a lot' (Interview A).

In the tenders by the Barcelona Municipality, as also the case for La Borda, municipality-owned land is made available to housing cooperatives by 75-year leases for a relatively modest annual rent. As a condition, the municipality requires that entry to the housing cooperative is governed by the same income and wealth ceilings as admission to social housing. This entailed that some original participants in the La Borda project had to leave – they were too rich (Interview F). By separating ownership of land from ownership of the housing, this model has *some* similarities to a community land trust (cf. Aernouts and Ryckewaert 2018). On the one hand, this makes otherwise prohibitively expensive land available for relatively low-cost housing. Recall that the pioneering Cal Cases community without this model was forced to locate on inexpensive land, far from its initially preferred location. On the other hand, by making social housing income and wealth ceilings a condition for entry, the municipality ensures that the housing remains affordable – for the time being, at least. For, as Balmer and Bernet (2015: 186) note more generally, 'Arrangements primarily regulated through government policies are subject to the political *zeitgeist*.' Regulations can, in other words, be changed or lifted. In the case of the Barcelona housing cooperatives, a future municipal government could lift the socio-economic requirements, for example. As it has happened or is happening for housing cooperatives in Scandinavia (Larsen and Lund Hansen 2015; Sørvoll and Bengtsson 2018), this could lead to capitalisation and large windfalls for existing members. But spearheaded by people in and around the La Borda project, housing activists in Barcelona are trying to safeguard against such developments in three ways, which also point at other key aspects of alternative housing initiatives in Barcelona.

First, La Borda (and the organisation Sostre Cívic) has helped to pioneer a model for cooperative housing called 'right of use' (*cessió d'ús/cesión de uso*) (Cabré and Andrés 2018; Etxezarreta et al. 2018; Lacol and La Ciutat Invisible 2018).[3] Inspired by housing cooperative experiences in countries like Denmark and Uruguay (Vidal 2018; 2019), this model entails that the property – for La Borda the building on the municipality-owned land – is owned collectively and that members of the cooperative cannot individually sell or rent the housing unit to which they have a use right: 'This model eliminates property speculation and profiteering on a fundamental right like housing', La Borda (no date-b) points out: 'It is an alternative model of housing access to the traditional ownership and rent, with a strong commitment [to] use value above exchange value.' This could be termed a limited equity housing cooperative. But in Spain, many associate housing cooperatives with housing *production* cooperatives, which is to say cooperatives formed for the limited task of constructing what becomes privately owned housing. Particularly in the 1980s, housing production cooperatives was a noticeable phenomenon in Spain, often involving neighbourhood associations, local government and trade unions. But apart from not breaking with private ownership, which is at the heart of initiatives like La Borda, several housing production cooperatives were rocked by corruption scandals. There was, in other words, a need to clearly distinguish the new form of housing cooperatives from the older notion. The term 'right of use' (like Barcelona Municipality's use of 'co-housing') serves this end. It should be noted, however, that this model is a tenure form, which not necessarily amounts to co-housing. But as Etxezarreta et al. (2018: 63) point out in a study of emerging right-of-use housing initiatives in Spain,

> housing cooperatives generally, but not necessarily, entail a cohousing or collaborative housing project. Collaborative or cohousing initiatives involve living with other people and assignment of use cooperatives are a legal tool which can serve to carry out that purpose. They can occur together, and, in fact, this legal formula represents for most of the people interviewed the most adequate formula for being able to launch a collaborative housing initiative in Spain.

While generally aimed at providing affordable and non-speculative housing, right-of-use housing cooperatives in most cases still require that members buy a share in the cooperative. For La Borda, where substantial efforts have been made to secure alternative financing, shares eventually amounted to EUR 18,500. 'It is not a big amount of money,' a member reflects, 'but I know that there are people who cannot afford that' (Interview C). And already in the early phases of the project, some left because they for practical or political reasons found the share price unaffordable (Interview F).

Second, people in and around the La Borda project are playing important roles in developing and promoting the right-of-use model of housing cooperatives, most distinctly through the La Dinamo foundation, which one of the activists describes as a 'spin-off of La Borda' (Interview G). La Dinamo was established in 2016 and aims to 'promote and normalise the right-of-use housing cooperative model as an alternative to conventional housing models.' This is seen in relation to the social and solidarity economy (see below), and through cooperation and networking, La Dinamo hopes 'to collectively build an alternative model of non-speculative, inclusive, sustainable and collective property' (La Dinamo, no date). Recognising that costs is the main obstacle to housing cooperatives in Catalonia, the La Dinamo activist emphasises: 'We try to make the cooperative housing model more inclusive, more affordable.' But this is not just about economy; it is also about empowerment: 'We are interested not just to create cooperatives but also cooperative people' (Interview G). Solidarity mechanisms were, for example, the single most important criteria for selecting the group for the first La Dinamo project. This project is located in an existing residential building in the La Bordeta neighbourhood. Half of the building was donated to La Dinamo by a private person, the other half was acquired by the foundation. This has made the project significantly more affordable than new-build projects on municipality owned land, and while La Dinamo cannot expect similar donation in the future, the foundation is working to establish further projects. While currently smaller than even the limited initiatives begun by the Barcelona en Comú local government, ventures such as La Dinamo could point a way to affordable alternative housing initiatives that are independent of the ebbs and flows of formal political structures. The system La Dinamo is pioneering could become the basis for a genuine community land trust.

Third, while by no means spearheaded only by the 'extended family' of La Borda, the project is part of the wider efforts to promote and develop cooperativism as an alternative to both the capitalist market economy and the state, be it local, regional or central. This is an important component in the social and solidarity economy, which currently is receiving much attention in Barcelona and was actively promoted by the Barcelona en Comú local government (Ajuntament de Barcelona 2016b; Wahlund 2019). Still, while highly supportive of cooperatives ventures, a La Borda member voices some concern as to whether housing cooperatives is *the* solution to Barcelona's housing crisis:

> I am not sure if housing coops are the most important or the most universal tool to get social justice in the frame of housing. I think we have to fight for a law that doesn't allow [owners] to put huge prices for housing. And I think cooperativism is a tool regarding to that, but maybe the city that is completely build up, there are not a lot of empty terrain to build a lot of cooperatives, maybe the point is to get a more fair law. And I think La Borda is a contribution, but is maybe not *the* contribution but one of them.
>
> (Interview C; emphasis added)

Barcelona en Comú's policies on co-housing have been met with opposition in Barcelona politics. In the summary of the councillor for housing, the Right and even some parts of the Left commonly criticise cohousing for being a 'privilege for middle-class people with culture and capabilities' (Interview A). That the Right is critical of policies aimed at exploring collective alternatives to private ownership is hardly surprising. But in public debate, criticism has in several instances been framed in terms of cronyism. For Adell (2018), for example, the municipal government of Barcelona en Comú has 'rewarded' the 'radicals' of the Sants neighbourhood with 'juicy grants' of EUR 209.000, and in his mapping of this relationship, Adell includes La Borda, La Dinamo and several related cooperatives (for a similar critique, see González 2018). Not surprisingly, then, the conservative PP is the party most clearly opposed to the policies on co-housing implemented by Barcelona en Comú. But the centrist ERC, which weighs heavier in Barcelona politics, also has some reservations. ERC, like to some extent the left-wing CUP (Candidatura d'Unitat Popular), favours the expansion of the highly limited mass of public housing.[4] Still, based on a survey of positions on right-of-use housing cooperatives among parties in Barcelona politics, Font (2019) cautiously concludes that 'most of parties do not close their doors when it comes to promoting this model'.

Neighbourhood – and beyond

In the present, as in the revolutionary past (Ealham 2010), the neighbourhood plays an important role as a scale of social mobilisation for many Barcelonans. As we have already seen in relation to the Cal Cases community, where the members knew each other from an *ateneu* in the Gràcia neighbourhood, the neighbourhood connection is relevant to several co-housing and alternative housing initiatives, not least the La Borda project. Referring to the area in which the project is situated, a member says: 'La Borda cannot be understood without Can Batlló. La Borda is a flower of a fertile soil, that was Can Batlló' (Interview B).

Can Batlló is an abandoned industrial estate that was established during the early industrialisation of Barcelona. (The area is named after the Batlló family, which is perhaps better known from having procured what became Casa Batlló, the iconic 1877 building by Antoni Gaudí.) Although originally developed for textile industries, Can Batlló became a site for small workshops and businesses. However, as part of the 1976 General Metropolitan Plan for Barcelona that sought to remove industrial activities from urban areas, the workshops and businesses of Can Batlló were gradually abandoned. The municipality planned to demolish the buildings and to replace them with high-end housing and a park. This clashed with demands by activists in and beyond the La Bordeta neighbourhood, who saw the vacant industrial area as a space for creating various self-managed functions and activities. But the municipality kept postponing its plans, and in 2009 neighbours and social groups in the platform Recuperem Can Batlló: Can Batlló és per el barri (Reclaiming Can Batlló: Can Batlló is for the neighbourhood) fixed 1 June 2011 as a deadline for the municipality to open and transform the area. Otherwise, the activists would occupy and themselves open the area. Eventually, only days before the deadline (and heavily influenced by the 15M atmosphere and mobilisation), the municipality and the campaign reached a compromise that allowed neighbourhood activists to take over and use one of the abandoned industrial buildings (BlocOnze). Other buildings and spaces in Can Batlló have been added, but in a *quid pro quo* with the municipality (and between the municipality and private owners of parts of the area), some parts of the area have been reserved for commercial development. Since then, the Platform Can Batlló movement has developed its activities through self-management (Eizaguirre and Parés 2019). Can Batlló shifted from being an 'industrial factory' to being a 'social factory', as a member of La Borda puts it; for him, Can Batlló is an 'urban space in which the common, projects started by people not the public or the private, [become] concrete … like the idea of David Harvey, this is a space of hope' (Interview C).

Shortly after the opening of the area, in January 2012, a group of 10–15 activists within Can Batlló began to discuss ideas for alternative housing. In the words of one of the initiators, 'the main goal was to promote another way to understand housing, not connected with value in the real estate market; and also, like this collective community that we have started in other projects, another way of relating inside Can Batlló' (Interview D). The group initially hoped to retrofit an existing building in Can Batlló. The municipality was not opposed to the idea of an alternative housing project in the area, but as the building was not planned for housing, the municipality offered the group a municipality-owned plot of land. As previously discussed, the social provisions that came with the offer meant that some had to (or chose to) leave the project. But by accepting the municipality's offer, the group also committed itself to a larger project than first envisioned. Therefore, in January 2014, the informally organised pioneers made a public presentation of their visions in Can Batlló. From this a group of some 50 people constituted La Borda and began developing concrete plans for the project. There was a troubling point, however. Two people in extremely precarious situations squatted the derelict building that had to be demolished to make room for La Borda. 'It was like the original sin', a member admits, but adds that La Borda acted responsibly by struggling with the municipality to ensure that the two displaced people were rehoused in a satisfactorily way (Interview D).

While Can Battló in a La Borda member's words is 'a humus to start political projects', like the alternative housing initiative (Interview C), it should be noted that also the wider neighbourhoods of Sants and La Bordeta are nodes in Barcelona's social and solidarity economy, not least in the form of work cooperatives. Tellingly, in a recent charting of social and solidarity economy initiatives in Barcelona, the Sants and La Bordeta are termed the 'cooperative neighbourhood' (Fernàndez and Miró 2016). Several members of La Borda work in cooperatives in these neighbourhoods. This includes the architect cooperative LaCol, La Ciutat Invisible, a bookshop and publishing cooperative that also advices cooperative ventures, and the La Dinamo foundation for promotion of housing cooperatives, and people in these organisations are in turn inspired by or involved in La Borda as non-members.

Other alternative housing initiatives in the Barcelona area are also closely connected to their respective neighbourhoods – and neighbourhood activism (also Chapter 6). This is, for example, the case for the ongoing efforts to start a housing cooperative in the Vallcarca neighbourhood.[5] Cal Cases and La Borda are, in the words of two activists, models and friends of the Vallcarca initiative; but, 'Here is a more complex situation and we are fighting against big things.... It is going to be more difficult, but what we want to achieve is not just a place to live, it is also a kind of resistance against gentrification'. They are referring to the fact that Vallcarca through a messy planning process has experienced an 'urbanicide' that has left the neighbourhood with large tracts of vacant land (for maps, see Assemblea de Vallcarca 2016: 17). Many of these plots are owned by a large and rather notorious property company,

Núñez y Navarro, which, as the activists put it, 'like a vulture' waits for prices to rise. Gentrification researches would recognise this a classic 'rent gap' situation (Smith 1979). A housing cooperative is one of several initiatives by the Vallcarca neighbourhood assembly to resist gentrification. The group would have preferred to claim privately-owned land for the project, but it settled for a municipality-owned building plot for which the group negotiates permission to establish a housing cooperative along the lines of La Borda. This will not only ensure affordability, the activist emphasise; it will also help to block a future sell-off of municipality land. While still only at an initial stage, the visions for the project mixes individual housing units with substantial dimensions of common spaces and activities (Assemblea de Vallcarca 2016). Importantly, however, the visions also involve ambitions to open the project to the neighbourhood, and it is seen as intimately related to neighbourhood politics: 'We don't want to be a rose in a pile of shit', an activist says with reference to a future where the proposed housing cooperative could stand in a neighbourhood dominated by speculative Núñez y Navarro developments: 'we are fighting for our building but also for our neighbourhood where we are going to live.' Moreover, the activists recognise that their housing initiative necessarily must be part of a wider Barcelonan 'activism of the land', which says 'This piece of land will not be for private speculation.'

Although often linked to neighbourhood and urban activism, co-housing ideas are also getting traction in less overtly politicised contexts. One example is the organisation coHousing Barcelona, which is in the process of establishing right-of-use co-housing projects in the Poble Nou neighbourhood and the village of Arenys de Mar (Interview I; see also coHousing Barcelona 2019). Similarly, the consultancy cohousing_LAB provides assistance to groups that try to set up co-housing projects (Interview J; see also cohousing_LAB 2019). While drawing on some of the same elements as other initiatives discussed in this chapter, such actors are mainly political in the sense of promoting alternative forms of housing and living, including dimensions of sustainability. If still in embryo, this could indicate that some co-housing initiatives in the Barcelona area are moving closer to those found in countries like Denmark and Sweden (see also Chapters 1 and 2).

House and community

While alternative housing initiatives in the Barcelona area often are linked to neighbourhood activism and wider struggles, the immediate aim is a house. Designed by the LaCol architect cooperative, which includes La Borda members, the six-floor La Borda building amounts to 2900 m^2 of which approximately 300 m^2 are common areas. The latter includes a common kitchen, dining room, guest rooms and laundry. The building also includes a common patio and an adaptable multi-use space for children, meetings and other activities. Finally, La Borda has a 'care space', a sort of communal area where people can bath and relax. The building is divided into of 28 flats of varying size, labelled 'small' (40 m^2), 'medium' (50 m^2) and 'large' (76 m^2). Most flats are 'small' and 'medium', and all flats have a bathroom and a small kitchen. The relatively small flats are partly designed to encourage communal activities, but also, as a condition set by the municipality, to keep individual flats (including a share of common spaces) below the maximum size for social housing. Individual flats can be joined into larger units if more than two adults want to live together. At the street level, the building has space for a shop. In the spring of 2019, this space was rented by a small cooperative food shop.

La Borda is constructed to have a low environmental impact. This includes initiatives to save water and energy, for example by building with better insulation than required, and reflecting an aim of low car dependence, La Borda was – after struggles with the municipality – permitted to provide less parking space than usually required. But most eye-catching, and highly unusual in the Spanish context, the price-winning building is mainly constructed in wood (from the Basque Country). This and other initiatives aimed at ecological sustainability has added to the cost of the building, which again is reflected in the somewhat higher than initially expected price of shares in the housing cooperative. But in the words of a member, 'it is an investment in the future … we are going to pay less for water, heating, comfort … so, it seems expensive, but if you see the total, it is cheaper over a long period of time' (Interview C).

As with similar projects in and beyond Spain, funding has been the most complicated question for La Borda. As the community leases the land from the municipality, the primary expense is the construction of the building. This is budgeted to EUR 2.7 million, and the sources to cover this cost are manifold (for a detailed presentation, see La Borda 2018). Somewhat simplified, however, construction expenditures are covered by member contributions ('shares'), a loan through the credit cooperative Coop57 and a range of microloans organised through Coop57. The members have also sought to keep down construction costs by contributing their own work, particularly (but not exclusively) in the finishing of the raw building.

It remains to be seen how La Borda will unfold as a realised project. The process leading to the finished project has been highly collaborative and interlinked with related activities in the neighbourhood and in Barcelona more generally. Ecological sustainability is a prominent dimension, and although the right-of-use model with the requirement of purchasing a 'share' is prohibitive for some, the project emphasises social sustainability in the sense of providing relatively affordable housing. The La Borda community is also diverse when it comes to age and income. But in relation to nationality and politics, the community is more homogeneous. Almost all are Catalans and engaged in left-wing politics and activism.

The years to come will show to what extent this collaborative housing project will evolve into co-housing with significant dimensions of common activities aimed at everyday life. But as one member of La Borda put it during the planning stage, 'one of the goals of the cooperative is to break this privacy of families nowadays that really do not share much with the neighbours' (Interview D). Another member expanded on this issue:

> In a city like Barcelona there is a lot of individualism, and you can notice that in a building, because a lot of people [are] just passing by; there are no grassroots, links with you neighbours, and this makes the living more difficult, because you don't trust your neighbours, you don't feel confident with them, and you don't speak to them, and you cannot have relationships in which you can share, caring for babies and the children, for instance. And this means that your career is more difficult if you want to have children. … I think La Borda is a good way to think about that and to have such relationships in common.
>
> (Interview C)

Conclusions

Co-housing and related alternative housing forms arrived in Spain only recently and is still an emerging phenomenon in the Barcelona area. This development draws on experiences with co-housing in other countries, for example those covered in this book, and it could be said that co-housing activists in Barcelona are well-informed pioneers. Some projects have been realised, if in most cases only recently, and several initiatives are at some stage of implementation. While there are initiatives under way to form co-housing communities that take their point of departure in everyday life perspectives, many if not most alternative housing initiatives and projects in the Barcelona area are also framed as contributions to wider urban concerns and struggles, notably in relation to the seemingly permanent and mounting housing crisis and its roots in a housing system based on private property. Reflecting such political struggles (and prohibitive land costs), the favoured model is right-of-use housing cooperatives on land leased from the municipality, and 'co-housing' (*covivienda*/*cohabitatge*) has become somewhat synonymous with this model in Barcelona. Co-housing in this sense has been actively supported by the municipal government of Barcelona. But this has not been without challenges, and it remains to be seen whether the direct support from the municipality will be forthcoming in the future. There are, however, small but highly interesting moves towards right-of-use housing cooperatives that are independent of municipality owned land.

Why has co-housing, and alternative housing initiatives more widely, become so relatively successful in the Barcelona area? Part of an answer to this is undoubtedly rooted in intricate social-political histories and developments in and around Barcelona. But we can also point at some more immediate reasons. First, Barcelona has been strongly affected by the housing crisis, which has been augmented by the tourism industry and often predatory foreign direct investments in real estate. This is not merely confined to the recent housing-driven crisis, but has developed over at least two decades. There is, in other words, strong motivations to look for alternative housing models. Second, epitomised by the PAH, the city has become an epicentre of housing movements, which with Barcelona en Comú's 2015 rise to power in Barcelona Municipality gained some institutional support. Again, this is not confined to the recent years, but has evolved through longer histories of squatting and neighbourhood activism. Third, and more specifically, the regional government has recently introduced legislation that makes it easier (but not easy) to establish housing cooperatives, the favoured legal form of most co-housing and alternative housing initiatives and projects. Fourth, if not as housing cooperatives, Barcelona has a recent history of cooperativism in the production of housing – and, if halted by the Francoist regime, a longer history of cooperativism more generally. Finally, at least according to the Barcelona councillor for housing (Interview A), the city is currently blessed by a meeting between two generations that want to try something new – the older '1968' generation, which has the means, and the younger '15M' generation that has the practical-political experiences.

In terms of sustainable urban development, although as yet mainly represented by La Borda, co-housing projects in the Barcelona area are through technical and social initiatives clearly contributing to ecological sustainability in the local context. But it is in relation to social sustainability that co-housing and alternative housing initiatives are particularly interesting. Internally, there are hopes that co-housing can provide community and solidarity in everyday life, a counter to atomising tendencies in Barcelona and other metropolitan cities, which have been aggravated by increasing housing precarity. But if notions of equality and social justice are included in social sustainability, the greatest potential contribution of co-housing is arguably beyond individual projects and initiatives. As long as the right-of-use model of housing cooperatives are linked to socio-economic criteria, as currently required when the municipality leases out land for projects, there is little danger of co-housing becoming enclaves for the economically privileged. In this way, co-housing could help to provide affordable housing in an increasingly unaffordable city. But co-housing is unlikely to become anything but a tiny fraction of housing in Barcelona. Nonetheless, co-housing can in a wider social sustainability perspective help to advocate for alternative ways of providing housing, which can be applied beyond ideas about co-housing. Housing cooperatives is a case in point. But most profoundly, co-housing projects and initiatives could be (and to some degree are) nodes in broader political mobilisations for a more equal and just city. Two co-housing activists in the Vallcarca neighbourhood put this very vividly: 'They stole my city', one of them says with reference to the workings of real-estate interests, 'and finally I found a way of fighting not only in the political and ideological dimension, but for a piece of land. It makes a lot of sense' (Interview H). The other activist adds that although she has been political all her life, for the first time she 'can touch what we are fighting for'. The activists repeatedly emphasise, however, that their local struggle for a co-housing cooperative is embedded in social movements, the neighbourhood – and the city.

Referenced interviews

A. The Councillor for Housing, Barcelona City Council. Barcelona, 9 November 2018.
B. La Borda member. Barcelona, 22 March 2017.
C. La Borda member. Barcelona, 23 March 2017.
D. Five La Borda members. Barcelona, 18 November 2015.
E. Four Cal Cases members. Cal Cases, 19 November 2015.
F. Two La Borda members. Barcelona, 21 March 2017.
G. La Dinamo activist. Barcelona, 18 April 2018.
H. Two members of the Vallcarce neighbourhood assembly. Barcelona, 24 March 2017.
I. Architect with coHousing Barcelona, Barcelona. 8 November 2018.
J. Architect with cohousing_LAB. Barcelona, 8 November 2018.

Notes

1 In English as well as in Castilian and Catalan derivates (*covivienda* and *cohabitatge*), 'co-housing' is frequently used in Spain and Catalonia. But the housing form suggested is often different from what co-housing tend to mean in other countries. I will return to this issue.
2 The following is mainly based on material collected during a visit to the Cal Cases community 19–20 November 2015. Quotations are from a group interview during this visit (Interview E).
3 Cabré and Andrés (2018) translate the terms as 'cession of use', while Etxezarreta et al. (2018) suggest 'assignment of use' and 'right of use'. I here use the latter notion, which is most intuitive and points to the distinction between use value and exchange value (e.g. Harvey 2014: 15ff.) that is key to many alternative housing projects.
4 CUP originally argued that the few remaining plots of municipality-owned land should be prioritised for public housing (Rovira and Monge 2017). The party has subsequently adopted a more favourable position on leasing land for co-housing.
5 The following is mainly based on an interview with two activists from Vallcarce neighbourhood assembly (Interview H) and an outline of the context and ideas of the alternative housing initiative (Assemblea de Vallcarca 2016). The project is still in progress as 'Ruderal' (i.e. a 'plant' growing on waste ground or among rubbish!).

References

Adell, X. (2018) 'Colau "premia" con 209.000 euros a los radicales de Sants: Entidades vinculadas a los okupas, los comuns y la CUP reciben jugosas subvenciones', *Metrópoli Abierta*, Barcelona, 9 April 2018.

Aernouts, N. and Ryckewaert, M. (2018) 'Beyond housing: on the role of commoning in the establishment of a Community Land Trust project', *International Journal of Housing Policy*, vol. 18, no. 4, pp. 503–521.

Ajuntament de Barcelona (2016a) *Concurs públic per a la transmissió onerosa i constitució d'un dret de superfície sobre els béns patrimonials descrits per a destinar-los a la promoció construcció i gestió d'habitatges per part de les cooperatives d'habitatge en règim de cessió d'ús (cohabitatge)*. Barcelona: Ajuntament de Barcelona, Patronat Municipal de l'Habitatge.

Ajuntament de Barcelona (2016b) *The Impetus Plan for the Social and Solidarity Economy 2016–2019*. Barcelona: Ajuntament de Barcelona; Economia Cooperativa, Social i Solidária i Consum.

Ajuntament de Barcelona (2017) *L'Ajuntament resol el concurs per construir "cohabitatge" en cinc solars municipals.* http://ajuntament.barcelona.cat/premsa/ (25 February 2019).

Ajuntament de Barcelona (2019) *Segon concurs públic per a la transmissió onerosa i constitució d'un dret de superficie sobre els béns patrimonials descrits per a destinar-los a la promoció, construcció i gestió d'habitatges per part de les cooperatives d'habitatge en règim de cessió d'ús (cohabitatge), dividit en 3 lots.* Barcelona: Ajuntament de Barcelona, Institut Municipal de l'Habitatge i Rehabilitació de Barcelona.

Assemblea de Vallcarca (2016) *Cooperativa d'Habitatge Vallcarca.* Barcelona: Assemblea de Vallcarca.

Balmer, I. and Bernet, T. (2015) 'Housing as a common resource? Decommodofication and self-organisation in housing – examples from Germeny and Switzerland', in M. Dellenbaugh, M. Kip, M. Bieniok, A. Müller and M. Schwegmann (eds) *Urban Commons: Moving Beyond State and Market*, pp. 178–195. Basel: Birkhäuser.

Barcelona City Council (2018) *Barcelona Right to Housing Plan 2016–2025* (Qüestions d'Habitatge no. 21). Barcelona: Barcelona City Council, Municipal Housing and Renovation Institute.

Blanco, I., Salazar, Y. and Bianchi, I. (2019) 'Urban governance and political change under a radical left government: The case of Barcelona', *Journal of Urban Affairs,* doi: 10.1080/07352166.2018.1559648.

Blomley, N. (2004) *Unsettling the City: Urban Land and the Politics of Property.* London: Routledge.

Brysch, S. (2018) *Designing and building housing together: the Spanish case of La Borda.* Paper presented at the European Network for Housing Research (ENHR) conference, Uppsala, 26–29 June 2018.

Burón, J. (2016) 'The public policy challenges of Barcelona', in J. Palay and I. Santos (eds) *Qüestions d'Habitatge*, no. 20, pp. 5–9. Barcelona: Barcelona City Council, Municipal Housing Board.

Cabré, E. and Andrés, A. (2018) 'La Borda: a case study on the implementation of cooperative housing in Catalonia', *International Journal of Housing Policy*, vol. 18, no. 3, pp. 412–432.

coHousing Barcelona (2019) https://cohousingbarcelona.cat/en (14 June 2019).

cohousing_LAB (2019) www.cohousinglab.com (14 June 2019).

Colau, A. and Alemany, A. (2012) *Mortgaged Lives: From the Housing Bubble to the Right to Housing*. Los Angeles: Journal of Aesthetics & Protest Press.

COPHAB (2019) *COPHAB Map.* http://commoninghousing.net/cophab-map (24 June 2019).

Debelle, G., Cattaneo, C., González, R., Barranco, O. and Llobet, M. (2018) 'Squatting cycles in Barcelona: identities, repression and the controversy of institutionalisation', in M. A. Martínez López (ed.) *The Urban Politics of Squatters' Movements*, pp. 51–73. New York: Palgrave Macmillan.

Di Feliciantonio, C. (2017) 'Social movements and alternative housing models: practicing the "politics of possibilities" in Spain', *Housing, Theory and Society*, vol. 34, no. 1, pp. 38–56.

Di Feliciantonio, C. and Aalbers, M. B. (2018) 'The prehistories of neoliberal housing policies in Italy and Spain and their reification in times of crisis', *Housing Policy Debate*, vol. 28, no. 1, pp. 135–151.

Ealham, C. (2010) *Anarchism and the City: Revolution and Counter-Revolution in Barcelona, 1898–1937*. Oakland: AK Press.

Eizaguirre, S. and Parés, M. (2019) 'Communities making social change from below. Social innovation and democratic leadership in two disenfranchised neighbourhoods in Barcelona', *Urban Research & Practice*, vol. 12, no. 2, pp. 173–191.

Etxezarreta, A., Cano, G. and Merino, S. (2018) 'Las cooperativas de viviendas de cesión de uso: experiencias emergentes en España', *CIRIEC-España, Revista de Economía Pública, Social y Cooperativa*, no. 92, pp. 61–86.

Fernàndez, A. and Miró, I. (2016) *L'economia social i solidària a Barcelona*. Barcelona: La Ciutat Invisible and Barcelona Municipality.

Ferreri, M., Parés, M. and Cabré, E. (2019) *Emergent collaborative housing in Catalonia and the challenges of public-community 'co-production'*. Paper presented at the European Network for Housing Research (ENHR) conference, Athens, 27–30 August 2019.

Font, M. (2019) 'Què diuen els alcaldables de Barcelona sobre el cooperativisme d'habitatge en cessió d'ús?', *Crític*, www.elcritic.cat/mes/sostre-critic/que-diuen-els-alcaldables-de-barcelona-sobre-el-cooperativisme-dhabitatge-en-cessio-dus-26005

Garcia i Mateu, A. (2015) *Designing with Transitioning Communities: The Case of La Borda*. Barcelona: EINA.

García, M. (2010) 'The breakdown of the Spanish urban growth model: social and territorial effects of the global crisis', *International Journal of Urban and Regional Research*, vol. 34, no. 4, pp. 967–980.

García-Lamarca, M. (2017) 'From occupying plazas to recuperating housing: insurgent practices in Spain', *International Journal of Urban and Regional Research*, vol. 41, no. 1, pp. 37–53.

García-Lamarca, M. and Kaika, M. (2016) '"Mortgaged lives": the biopolitics of debt and housing financialisation', *Transactions of the Institute of British Geographers*, vol. 41, no. 3, pp. 313–327.

González, D. (2018) 'Colau subvenciona una tupida red de cooperativas de vivienda del entorno okupa', *El Nacional*, Barcelona, 10 April 2018.

Harvey, D. (2014) *Seventeen Contradictions and the End of Capitalism*. London: Profile Books.

La Borda (2018) 'Funding structure'. www.laborda.coop/en/project/funding-structure (22 April 2019).

La Borda (no date-a) 'About us'. www.laborda.coop (18 November 2015).

La Borda (no date-b) 'Grant of use'. www.laborda.coop/en/project/grant-of-use (21 February 2019).

La Dinamo (no date) 'Qué es la Dinamo'. http://ladinamofundacio.org (8 May 2019).

Lacol and La Ciutat Invisible (2018) *Habitar en comunidad: La vivienda cooperativa en cesión de uso*. Madrid: Fundación Arquia & Catarata.

Larsen, H. G. (2019) 'Three phases of Danish cohousing: tenure and the development of an alternative housing form', *Housing Studies*, vol. 34, no. 8, pp. 1349–1371.

Larsen, H. G. and Lund Hansen, A. (2015) 'Commodifying Danish housing commons', *Geografiska Annaler: Series B, Human Geography*, vol. 97, no. 3, pp. 263–274.

López, I. and Rodríguez, E. (2011) 'The Spanish model', *New Left Review*, no. 69, pp. 5–28.

Martínez, M. A. (2019) 'Bitter wins or a long-distance race? Social and political outcomes of the Spanish housing movement', *Housing Studies*, vol. 34, no. 10, pp. 1588–1611.

McCamant, K. and Durrett, C. (2011) *Creating Cohousing: Building Sustainable Communities*. Gabriola Island: New Society Publishers.

Palomera, J. (2014) 'How did finance capital infiltrate the world of the urban poor? Homeownership and social fragmentation in a Spanish neighborhood', *International Journal of Urban and Regional Research*, vol. 38, no. 1, pp. 218–235.

Pointelin, R. (2016) *L'habitat alternatif en Catalogne, un modèle émergent? La (re)naissance d'une «troisième voie», entre pragmatisme et utopie.* Girona: Universitat de Girona.

Rovira, M. and Monge, X. (2017) *L'habitatge a Barcelona: lloguer social i noves formes de tinença.* https://test.directa.cat/node/33154 (20 June 2019)

Singer, J. W. (2000) *Entitlement: The Paradoxes of Property.* New Haven: Yale University Press.

Smith, N. (1979) 'Towards a theory of gentrification', *Journal of the American Planning Association*, vol. 45, no. 4, pp. 538–548.

Sørvoll, J. and Bengtsson, B. (2018) 'The Pyrrhic victory of civil society housing? Co-operative housing in Sweden and Norway', *International Journal of Housing Policy*, vol. 18, no. 1, pp. 124–142.

Sostre Cívic (no date) 'Princesa49'. www.sostrecivic.coop/es/node/114 (20 June 2019)

Tummers, L. (2015) 'Understanding co-housing from a planning perspective: why and how?', *Urban Research & Practice*, vol. 8, no. 1, pp. 64–78.

Vidal, L. (2018) *El foment públic del cooperativisme d'habitatge en cessió d'ús a Dinamarca i Uruguai.* Barcelona: La Dinamo Fundació.

Vidal, L. (2019) 'Cooperatives islands in capitalist waters: limited-equity housing cooperatives, urban renewal and gentrification', *International Journal of Urban and Regional Research*, vol. 43, no. 1, pp. 157–178.

Wahlund, M. (2019) *Putting people back into the economy: urban restructuring and emerging alternatives in time of crisis.* MSc thesis in Human Geography, Lund University.

Part II

Co-housing as sustainable urban life?

5 Autonomy vs. government

Consequences for sustainability in co-housing

David Scheller and Håkan Thörn

Introduction

This chapter presents an analysis of six co-housing projects in Gothenburg and Hamburg, and how they are affected by support from, interaction with and regulation by, political institutions. Importantly, we will pay specific attention to questions concerning the consequences of different, legally instituted ownership and tenure forms for co-housing projects; whether, and how, tensions have emerged between municipal government and co-housing projects; and with what consequences for sustainability. More specifically, we examine how municipal governments support co-housing groups as part of their official sustainability agenda, and to what extent co-housing projects address or meet the different goals that are part of this agenda. How is 'sustainability' conceptualized in connection with co-housing policies and practices? To what extent is co-housing perceived as a solution to 'sustainability problems'? What are the similarities and differences between Hamburg and Gothenburg?

Gothenburg and Hamburg were selected as case cities because they are currently both involved in major urban restructuring, and have both launched programmes to support co-housing as part of their emphasis on promoting urban sustainable development through this process. In both cities, we will analyse support for co-housing groups that have a variety of tenure forms, and we argue that the extent to which co-housing provides alternatives to existing forms of housing is dependent both on the degree of autonomy in relation to municipal government, and on the extent to which different tenure forms enable more affordable housing. There are significant similarities between current processes of urban restructuring in Hamburg and Gothenburg (Scheller and Thörn 2018). Both are rapidly growing cities; the Hamburg region's population of 1.75 million is expected to grow by 100,000 (DUDE 2014: 9) in the next decade, while the Gothenburg region's population of 1 million is expected to grow by 175,000 over the same period (Västra Götalandsregionen 2014: 1). They are also facing housing crises: there is a lack of housing, and particularly affordable housing, with spiralling rents and growing gentrification. The political responses of government in each city are also similar, with heavy investment, subsidies and private-public partnerships, predominantly in former industrial areas and working-class neighbourhoods.

Ideologically, these strategies also place heavy emphasis on sustainability in policy documents and declarations, focusing on all three pillars of sustainability (ecological, economic and social), but rarely recognizing tensions or contradictions between them. Implicit or explicit definitions of economic and ecological dimensions are rather straightforward, as the goals of ongoing urban re-structuring are defined in terms of sustaining the cities' economic growth and increasing their climate adaptation, mitigation, ecosystem services and green spaces. In contrast, definitions of social sustainability are rather ambiguous, and vary depending on the context. For example, Hamburg city officials have argued that the changing demographic and social circumstances produce a demand for affordable housing as well as a need to create conditions for 'social mixing' (DUDE 2014: 70). In Gothenburg, the sustainability agenda has been tied to the preparations for the city's 400th anniversary in 2021. In connection with this, the municipality has formulated the Vision 2021 programme, to be implemented by local government institutions, business, civil society organizations and the university. The motto and goal of the 2021 official statement intends to combine all three dimensions of sustainability in a vision that, according to the municipality, is the result of broad participation (Göteborgs stad 2019a).

The following section will provide an analysis of the sustainability strategies of Gothenburg and Hamburg in relation to policies that address or affect co-housing projects. Against this background, we will present and analyse three co-housing projects in each city, selected mainly because they vary concerning tenure forms. However, we will also account for their history, profile, size, shared activities and to what extent their projects address or meet ecological, economic and social sustainability as defined in official discourses. Finally, our questions will be addressed through a concluding comparison of the cases and their relations to government strategies.[1]

Municipal support for self-build co-housing

Both Gothenburg and Hamburg are examples of how, in the context of the housing shortage that exists in many European cities, municipal support for co-housing often takes the form of support for self-build groups. In 2003, Hamburg launched one of the most ambitious municipal programmes to support self-build groups (*Baugemeinschaften*) and co-housing (*Gemeinschaftswohnprojekt*). The Department for Urban Development and the Environment established the Hamburg Agency (Agentur für Baugemeinschaften, see also Chapter 3) with a special programme to support housing communities. It should be emphasized that a self-build group in this context refers to people coming together to form an intentional community with the purpose of managing the building of their own homes. This means that the association does not actually build, but plans and commissions houses that have been constructed according to their needs and wishes. Not all self-build groups are co-housing projects, but in the two cities that we studied, an increasing number of co-housing projects are also self-build groups (two of which will be discussed below).

Inspired by Hamburg's model, Gothenburg has also begun to offer support for co-housing, partly linked to self-build co-housing groups. Explicitly referring to Germany, the Planning and Building Office has stated that the municipality had set a goal that 5% of new apartments should be produced by self-build groups; and that this should be regarded as an important measure to address social sustainability (Scheller and Thörn 2018).

To what 'sustainability problems' is self-build co-housing perceived as a solution by the cities? In a previous work, in which we analysed steering documents and interviews (Scheller and Thörn 2018), we mainly found similarities between Hamburg and Gothenburg in the following regards:

> *Economic sustainability*: In both Hamburg and Gothenburg, support for self-build co-housing is part of processes of de- and re-regulation of local planning and infrastructure to facilitate a market-based approach to the planning of land use and housing. This means that definitions of economic sustainability in this context are along the lines of the concept of 'smart growth'. The notion of smart growth in official discourses is to some extent ambivalent: on the one hand, since around 2000, it has been defined in purely economic terms as a new market-based strategy for land and housing development in local and regional planning; on the other hand, 'smart growth' has been defined as an over-arching planning strategy that is supposed to be able to integrate economic, social and ecological sustainability (Krueger and Gibbs 2008). From this perspective smart growth is seen as 'a way of organizing disparate elements of land use planning goals and approaches' (Krueger and Gibbs 2008: 1266), such as open-space preservation, regeneration, business improvement districts and the use of existing infrastructure. The latter perspective thus implies that ecological and social sustainability are subsumed within economic sustainability.
>
> *Ecological sustainability*: The meaning of ecological sustainability is quite coherent in this context, as definitions in both cities were shared by politicians, planners and architects: the buildings constructed should have low climate impact and facilitate resource-saving forms of living associated with co-housing, emphasizing urban sharing. For example, the Hamburg Agency's assessment criteria for accepting groups to its self-build programme include an ecology and energy vision.
>
> *Social sustainability:* We found four inter-linked definitions of social sustainability in this context: 1) *self-governance*; 2) *social cohesion*; 3) *social mixing*; and 4) *affordability*. The Hamburg programme's emphasis on *self-governance* was linked to the history of conflict between squatters and the municipality, as it was originally launched to meet what was

perceived as a justified demand for self-governance articulated by the squatter movement (Scheller and Thörn 2018, see also Chapter 3). In Gothenburg, the municipality's interest in supporting co-housing as a form of self-governance was partly a result of interaction with the co-housing association BoIhop (Live Together) (Gothenburg Planning and Building Committee interview 2015).

Support for co-housing is supposed to address the goal of *social cohesion* inasmuch as co-housing is believed to promote a sense of community within the house as well as social integration with the neighbourhood and the wider city. In the Hamburg case this approach was also directly related to the emphasis on *social mixing* in contemporary urban planning (Lees et al. 2008), by the inclusion of so called 'under-served' or 'under-represented' groups, i.e. disabled people, older people and migrants. The social mixing strategy also emphasizes the integration of housing with commercial enterprises and, more importantly, of groups with varying income levels. In Gothenburg, the municipality regards self-build co-housing groups as instruments of mixing in the sense that they can 'break up' socially homogenous areas, whether low- or high-income (Planning and Building Committee interview 2015). In areas with relatively low income, self-build co-housing (which in Gothenburg cannot be seen as affordable) can perform this function, while in areas with relatively high income, co-housing in the context of the affordable municipal housing stock (see below) could play a similar role.

Concerning the *affordability* goal, the strategies of the two municipalities in terms of support for co-housing differ. The Hamburg Agency's financial support for self-build co-housing is part of the Housing Development Programme (*Wohnraumförderungsprogramm*) that is provided by the city of Hamburg's public bank, Hamburgische Investitions- und Förderbank (IFB Hamburg). Depending on the individual income of households, members of housing cooperatives as well as private owners can apply for support from IFB Hamburg (IFB Hamburg 2019). In Gothenburg, the municipality has not introduced any subsidies, which means that self-build co-housing is not an affordable alternative (see further below). However, in order to counter this, the municipality has begun experimenting with applying conditions to the sale of land, reducing the price as a trade-off for affordable housing. It has also started to investigate the possibilities of introducing co-housing in the context of housing stock owned by the municipal housing companies, by letting blocks of flats to co-housing cooperatives. This would involve reducing rents in exchange for handing over maintenance responsibilities under a model of self-governance.

In the following sections, we will examine to what extent municipal strategies have affected co-housing projects in the two cities, and to what extent the co-housing projects address or meet the sustainability goals as defined by the municipalities.

Gothenburg co-housing projects

Stacken

Stacken (The Ant-Hill) co-housing project, founded in the 1980s, is located in a tower block house, completed in 1968 in the poor suburb of Bergsjön. Regarding *relations with government agencies*, Stacken, while clearly addressing ideas and demands regarding collective housing that were articulated in the alternative movement culture, was originally a project largely initiated 'from above', through a process involving a multiplicity of actors (including non-governmental actors) and policy levels (see Chapter 1). The municipal housing companies in Gothenburg participated in the process, and the state was represented in the seminar discussions through the National Board of Housing. Chalmers University of Technology, which initiated the process, did the planning for the remodelling of the house and also took on the task of finding tenants.

As soon as Stacken had been formed as a self-governing formal association, tensions arose around *the tenure form*, as several models were discussed between Stacken, the municipal housing company (Göteborgshem, today Poseidon) and the Tenants' Union. Stacken demanded a 'tenants' influence contract', which would give them full control over the administration of the building while each tenant still held a contract for an apartment with the housing company. The housing company, however, was not prepared to give up control of the house and instead proposed that Stacken should be sublet to its members in the form of a 'second-hand contract'. This was not accepted by the Tenants' Union, because such a contract would deprive individuals of the basic tenant rights that had been won through the struggles of the union in the early twentieth century. A compromise was eventually reached, which allowed for a subletting contract, but with the same tenant rights as a regular tenant's contract. In order to meet a demand from Stacken that its members should decide who could move in to the house, the agreement also meant that the municipal housing company had to make an exception from the rule that all its vacant apartments should be listed in its public queuing system. This changed in 2002, after the municipal housing company declared that they wanted to sell the house to a private developer. This move by the housing company has to be seen against the background of the de- and re-regulation of Swedish housing policy that had begun in the 1990s, favouring market principles (Thörn and Thörn 2018) and removing restrictions on selling municipal housing (see also Chapter 2). Stacken decided to buy the house, borrowed money from a government-owned bank and applied for a non-profit 'cooperative tenancy'.[2] This means that Stacken as an association owns the building and continues to sublet apartments to individual members, who in addition to rent pay a symbolic deposit (SEK 100/EUR 10). It also means that individual members cannot sell their apartments at the market price.

In its current organizational form as a self-governing, non-profit economic cooperative, Stacken is not dependent on changes in national and local housing policies, but autonomously decides the rent for its members. However, it did receive substantial public funding from both the national Swedish Energy Agency (Energimyndigheten) and Region Västra Götaland (the regional government) for its recent programme to renovate the house according to ecologically sustainable principles (see further below).

Regarding *social* and *economic* sustainability, Stacken is governed by democratic *self-governance*. The membership meeting, held once a month, is the governing body. All members can make proposals, and decisions need to be passed by a two-thirds majority vote. The elected board is responsible for implementing decisions made by the membership meeting and for running the day-to-day administration. The board is also responsible for the association's economy. The rent for individual members is highly *affordable* by Swedish standards,[3] and it is an important goal for Stacken to keep it that way. The average income at Stacken is considerably lower than the city's average, but higher than for the surrounding area in the poor suburb of Bergsjön.[4]

Social cohesion appears weaker today compared to the early period (see Chapter 2), at least if we consider the level of common social activities in terms of shared meals and other forms of everyday socializing in shared spaces. In the 2010s, the sense of collectivity was primarily linked with efforts to mobilize the members in a project to increase ecological sustainability, driven by a group particularly devoted to strategies for democratic self-governance and ecological and economic sustainability. Stacken does not have an elaborate *mixing* strategy when it recruits new members. Regarding *ecological sustainability*, Stacken recently launched a highly ambitious renovation programme that was completed in 2018. The whole exterior of the building was covered with solar panels, and today the building is close to fulfilling the criteria for a passive house. This reduces the need for additional energy for heating (according to estimates, Stacken will produce 90% of the electricity that it uses and its heating costs will be cut by 70%), and the house now even produces energy that can be sold to the grid. In line with its affordability approach, it was a high priority for the association that this renovation work came without a rent increase. One-third of the costs were covered by public funding and a grant from an environmental NGO (the Swedish Society for Nature Conservation). The rest was covered by a loan from an ecological bank (*Ekobanken*) at 1% interest, to be paid off over 16 years.

Trädet

Trädet (The Tree) is a co-housing project housed in a tower block house completed in 1958, which is owned by the municipal housing company Poseidon and located in the poor suburb of Kortedala (Trädet 2019). When Trädet was established as a co-housing association in 1983, it was modelled on Stacken (see also Chapter 2). In contrast to Stacken, the tower block house was not empty when Trädet's tenants moved in, in 1985, but the tenants already living in the house agreed to join the co-housing association. Trädet's form of organization is similar to that of Stacken.

Originally, Trädet adopted the same tenure form as Stacken. Trädet paid interest-bearing loans for the remodelling of the house and originally also paid for electricity, water and refuse collection, and was responsible for the maintenance of the house. In return for taking on these responsibilities, Trädet paid a lower rent for the house. Decisions on more long-term substantial maintenance (such as renovation) were taken through negotiations between Poseidon and Trädet. For this purpose, Poseidon established a fund to which Trädet paid an annual fee (AB Göteborgshem 1985).

Up to this point, relations between Trädet and the local government, represented by municipal housing company Poseidon, ran relatively smoothly. The agreement signed between the parties in 1985 was most favourable for Trädet. The fact that the general interest rate began to drop in the 1990s made it possible for Trädet to set the rents at highly affordable levels, even considerably lower than for other apartments in the area (which, according to Swedish standards, were affordable). For a number of years, the tenants even had one or two 'rent-free' months. Using money from the fund, they also initiated a self-organized, major renovation programme in the late 1990s (with tenants doing most of the actual work) (Trädet interview 2016). However, in 2010 Poseidon announced that they wanted to re-negotiate the agreement with Trädet. Again, this move by the housing company has to be seen in the context of a continued de- and re-regulation of housing policies at the national level in order to promote market mechanisms. Poseidon was aware that a new housing law would be passed in 2011, stipulating that municipal housing companies had to be managed according to 'business principles'. Initially, Poseidon offered Trädet the opportunity to buy the house in a similar manner as Stacken had done a decade earlier, but after an official estimation of the value of the house, Poseidon changed its mind (ibid.). Instead it presented a new contract with significant changes. Poseidon now takes care of and makes decisions on maintenance and renovation, and pays for electricity, water and refuse disposal. These changes came with a 40% rent increase.[5]

To soften the consequences of the rent increase for individual tenants, Poseidon agreed to introduce the new rent in steps over a 10-year period. During this process the members of Trädet experienced another downside of their tenure form: it was difficult if not impossible to get assistance from the Tenants Union. This is related to the fact that while individual members of Trädet can become members of the Tenants Union, Trädet, as an association, cannot. Moreover, if an individual tenant of Trädet asks the Tenants Union for assistance to oppose a rent increase, it would be Trädet, not Poseidon, that would be the counterparty. Consequently, members of Trädet would find themselves positioned on both sides in a conflict over a rent increase. In Sweden, if conflicts over rents cannot be solved through negotiation, the tenants are brought before the Tenancy Tribunal, supported by a lawyer from the Tenants' Union (the jury composed, in a corporativist fashion, of three members: one judge, one nominated by the Tenants' Union and one by the

Swedish Property Federation). In this case Trädet defended themselves against Poseidon, and lost, in the Tenancy Tribunal.

Trädet uses a democratic *self-governance model* similar to Stacken's, with a majority vote needed at the members' meeting for important decisions and an elected board running the day-to-day administration. In spite of the rent increase in 2010, the rent for individual members is highly affordable by Swedish standards and it is an important goal for Trädet to keep it that way.[6] The average income is considerably higher than in Stacken – and in the surrounding area of Kortedala – but lower than the average for Gothenburg and Sweden.[7] But the re-negotiation of the contract in 2010 deprived Trädet of the possibility to sustain its strategies for *economic sustainability* concerning the administration and maintenance of the house that had been developed in the early years. Regarding *social cohesion*, the regular shared meals are an indication that Trädet is a considerably more active association in everyday social activities than Stacken. Like Stacken, Trädet does not have a mixing strategy in its recruitment process, nor an elaborate strategy for *ecological sustainability.*

Under samma tak

Under samma tak (Under the Same Roof) was established in 2009 as a co-housing association. In 2015 it presented a programme for a self-build house, and in 2020 the members will move into a newly built four-storey house. The house is located in the district of Högsbo, a semi-central, partly industrial area south-west of Gothenburg's city centre that in 2014 was targeted as a 'prioritized development area' in the Planning and Building Committee's 'Development Strategy Gothenburg 2025' (Gothenburg Municipality 2014). Previously mainly inhabited by a low-income population living in rented flats, and owned primarily by municipal housing companies, the new plan's goal to create 'mixing functions' involves an 'upgrading' (ibid.: 15). Following protests against, and a public debate on, the possible gentrification effects in the district, the Planning and Building Committee announced that it would allocate land to affordable housing in Högsbo. In contrast to the Hamburg government (see below), Gothenburg municipality offered very little support for the project, and did not include the project in its support for affordable housing in the area (see further below). In order to achieve the goal of affordability, Under samma tak initially contacted the municipal housing company Familjebostäder, asking if it was interested in cooperating with the association on the project, including taking responsibility for building the house, acting as owner and letting the apartments to Under samma tak. However, after a period of discussion Under samma tak felt that the company did not have a sufficiently strong commitment to the project. Instead the members chose to reach an agreement with Trollängen, a private housing company specializing in sustainable housing. In its negotiations with the municipality on the price of the land, Trollängen referred to the municipality's decision to support affordable housing in the area, but eventually they had to buy at market price.[8]

Under samma tak's programme for its self-build co-housing project has a strong emphasis on sustainability: 'The association will work for a sense of community and foster economically and socially sustainable housing, and encourage residents to lead an ecologically sustainable way of life' (Under samma tak 2015). Trollängen, which eventually bought the land from the municipality at market price, builds and owns the property, and lets the individual apartments to members of the co-housing project. In essence, this is the same tenure arrangement as Trädet's, but with a private owner rather than the municipal housing company. Regarding *economic and social sustainability*, fulfilling the goal of affordability has been the biggest challenge, and disappointment, for the group. Initially the group set out a rent target that can be considered relatively affordable for newly built apartments in the Swedish context, but the price of land and construction costs made this impossible, and the co-housing group is now working with a rent level that cannot be considered affordable.[9] Further, the group has felt that their autonomy has been somewhat restricted during the construction process, as Trollängen has had a firm influence on some of the decisions regarding issues on which different opinions have been expressed within the group.

Under samma tak puts a strong emphasis on *social cohesion*. One of the strategies for achieving this is to organize a study circle for new members and to discuss a book titled 'Community and Cooperation in Collective Houses and Co-housing Associations' (Under Samma Tak 2018). Social mixing is also addressed internally in the sense that the association strives to create a mix of different generations, of families with children and singles, as well as disabled people. Under samma tak also puts a strong emphasis on ecological sustainability, and the Trollängen company was selected partly for this reason. With solar panels on the roof that will supply energy needs, the house will meet ecological standards comparable to a passive house (Ferrum Architects 2016). The authorities have accepted demands from the group to allow far fewer parking spaces for cars, and more for bicycles, per household than the norm stipulates. Trollängen organizes a car pool – tenants can join as an optional choice for a small rent increase.

Hamburg co-housing projects

Inter-Pares

The Inter-Pares (Between Equals) project was started in 2003 by a group of friends who came from the local squatting scene. Through monthly meetings over the course of a year, a group was formed around the idea of 'community-based, communicative, socially just and self-organized life and housing' (Inter-Pares 2019). In 2006, the group had the opportunity to buy a property in the former working-class district of Hamburg-Altona. A low-energy house

Table 5.1 Co-housing projects and relations with government

Name of co-housing association	*House/project moved in/ population*	*Ownership/Tenure form*	*Relations with government*
Stacken	Tower block, 8 floors, 35 apartments/ 1980/80	Cooperative ownership (non-speculative), sub-letting to members	Financial support from national and regional government for climate-friendly renovation
Trädet	Tower block, 10 floors, 39 apartments/1985/70	Rental contract between municipal housing company and Trädet, which sublets to members	Changing public housing policies affected the association's economic and social sustainability negatively
Under samma tak	Four story house, 59 apartments/ 2020/140	Rental contract between private housing company and Under samma tak, which sublets to members	Limited support from municipality for self-build project: allocation of land; exceptions from parking space regulation
Inter-Pares	Four storey house, 10 apartments/ 2010/26	Limited Liability Company (non-profit) with two collective shareholders	Limited support from municipality, counselling but no distribution of land
Heimspiel	Six storey house, 13 apartments/ 2014/39	Rental contract between large cooperative and Heimspiel, which sublets apartments to members	Support from municipal agencies and banks; distribution of land, special loan, counselling; funding guideline regulations
Möwe Altonah	Six storey house, 25 apartments/ 2019/90	Möwe Altonah as part of a small cooperative sublets apartments to members	Support from municipal agencies and banks; distribution of land, special loan, counselling; regulation of internal structure of residents

comprising ten flats was erected[10] and when the construction work was completed in 2010, 20 people moved in. The group consists mainly of white middle-class people between the ages of four and 68, often families with children. The majority of the residents are social workers, health workers and artisans. The rent can be considered highly affordable in comparison with the surrounding area.[11]

The group, which holds organisational meetings every second week, does not have strict rules concerning participation in communal work. Everyone contributes as much as they can and according to their individual competence. They also decided against having shared common spaces due to higher building costs. However, the garden and the rooftop are used collectively for events and parties. At the back of the site, behind a garden, is the alternative trailer park (Wagenplatz) Hospi, which has been there for over twenty years. Facing the threat of eviction, the trailer park group, together with the co-housing group, managed to find a way to save it.

Inter-Pares is a member of the Mietshäuser Syndikat (MHS, Apartment-house Syndicate) – a nationwide conglomeration of 141 collectively owned and self-organized houses and 17 project initiatives (MHS 2019). The Mietshäuser Syndikat defines itself as an alliance and solidarity network, and an association of established and upcoming projects. The co-housing projects are completely autonomous but limited by the syndicate's veto against re-privatization and commodification in order to block potential monetization. Its principles are built on the basic idea and slogan of the squatter movement: 'The houses belong to the people who live in them!' The aim is to avoid speculation and gentrification, and to create a space with stable rents for long-term self-organization.[12]

Surprisingly, given the Syndicate's origins in the squatter movement, a classical capitalist organizational form is used for the purpose of decommodification – a limited liability company (LLC). The residents of each cohousing project do not directly hold title to the property. Instead, the title belongs to a LLC that has been founded specifically for this purpose, comprised of two partners: the house association of tenants of a particular project and the overall Mietshäuser Syndikat association, of which all co-housing projects are members.[13] Through this form of organization, either shareholder can use its right to veto, if the other wants to sell or privatize the house. Twice a year a general assembly of the Mietshäuser Syndikat association is held in one of the bigger cities to discuss and approve new projects and organizational matters. Decisions are reached by consensus.

A critical factor for all projects is a lack of financial resources. The tenants do not need to contribute private savings; instead the equity is provided through microcredits called direct loans (*Direktkredite*) given by a larger network of friends and supporters (individuals, groups, collectives etc.) – people who want to support the project and who deposit their savings there and not in a bank account.[14] The project then refinances the loans through rents, over a period of up to 30 years, depending on the price of the house.

The mission of the Mietshäuser Syndikat includes an explicitly stated idea of ongoing solidarity on various levels: 1) through a financial transfer of a certain monthly amount per square metre from each house; 2) through open project spaces which are provided for meetings, workshops and solidarity events for neighbours and political initiatives; and 3) through knowledge transfer between settled groups and newcomers on questions such as how to deal with officials, banks, owners, architects, planners, etc. During the construction of their house, Inter-Pares cooperated with the Hamburg Agency, because it offered the possibility to work with a building facilitator (*Baubetreuer*), but they never became part of the agency, since this would have meant that the whole Mietshäuser Syndikat would have been a member.

Social sustainability is basically the focus of internal relations. Inter-Pares' intentional community is formed around the idea of the Mietshäuser Syndikat – of collectivization and decommodification of property. *Self-governance* is the basic principle for the collective maintenance of the building. Principles of affordability, self-organization, autonomy, solidarity and financial and knowledge transfer are integrated with each other. The group performs ongoing organizational and personal communication in order to maintain the building and the community, notably through a regular house plenum. There have not been many changes in the residential structure, meaning there is a consistency within the group. The residents also state that they have good relationships with the neighbourhood, especially with the other self-organized housing projects in the street. But there is not much exchange with the 'normal renters' in the area (Inter-Pares interview 2016). Inter-Pares has seen strong gentrification pressure in the surrounding area of Altona, which is a rental area. Some residents are very active in counselling other groups who want to realize a co-housing project. This knowledge exchange is not limited to Hamburg but also extends to Barcelona, with people from La Borda (see Chapter 4) coming to learn from the Mietshäuser Syndikat model.

Economic sustainability is strongly emphasized and interwoven with social sustainability. The Mietshäuser Syndikat's basic principle of taking houses off the speculative market provides the political foundation of the co-housing project. The legal form of an LLC is the foundation for collective property, autonomous self-organization, permanently low rents and secure housing for the residents in a long-term perspective. There is no internal financial transfer in Inter-Pares, but through the Mietshäuser Syndikat each house contributes to a fund with the aim of supporting new projects. With an expanding number of Mietshäuser Syndikat projects, the question of limits on growth has come to the fore.

Regarding *ecological sustainability*, residents argued that it has been trumped by economic considerations in the building process, in the sense that they decided to skip a number of ecologically sustainable elements in the construction process (such as building a timber-framed house), because they were too expensive. Accordingly, the group built an 'ordinary' low-energy house, but the energy standard is sufficiently high to be the last step before a passive house. Beyond that, particular attempts to save energy in daily life are individually driven and not part of the common agenda of the housing community.

Heimspiel

Heimspiel (Home Game) began in 2008 as a conglomerate of long-time neighbours and friends living in a house in Hamburg's Schanzenviertel district. Confronted with gentrification, rising rents, poor energy performance and extremely high heating costs, the idea of a multigenerational co-housing project grew as a way of building a stable and affordable home together (Heimspiel interview 2016). However, the members of the group do not consider themselves activists: 'We were not very political. Our main goal was to live together' (Heimspiel interview 2016). Instead of founding their own small cooperative, the group decided to collaborate with a large cooperative, Wohnungsbaugenossenschaft von 1904 e.G. (referred to from here on as W1904), that cooperated with the Hamburg Agency (see Chapter 3).[15] Together with W1904, the group was able to buy a piece of land and build a five-storey house with 13 flats for singles, couples and families. Heimspiel has become one of the first co-housing projects of the cooperative.

The residents in Heimspiel pointed out that in W1904 the financial barriers in terms of cooperative shares were 'ten times less' than in a small cooperative (ibid.). To become a member of the W1904 cooperative, the residents have to pay an initial EUR 30 access fee to the cooperative, and on top of that the obligatory cooperative shares: EUR 150 per square metre.[16] W1904 contributed the financial resources to buy the land, and for planning and constructing the building; and an architect was provided during the planning and construction phase.

This enabled the group to fulfil its co-housing aspirations through the Hamburg Agency's programme, which provided them with the land and advised them on loans, planning and construction. They have also worked with an intermediary, the Lawaetz Foundation (see also Chapter 3), which orchestrated the planning and construction phase together with the group.

Everybody in Heimspiel has a middle-class background and a job, except for one pensioner, and they mostly have middle-class jobs such as photographer, social worker, teacher. Decisions are made in a consensus-driven regular meeting procedure, while in difficult cases a three-quarter majority vote comes into play. Except for a shared garden, the group decided not to build shared spaces, because they had no specific plans for their use during the planning period and they were afraid of conflicts over the use of such spaces. The group would like to have permission to turn the street in front of the house into a playground without traffic. Their monthly meetings are only for socializing. They also state that they only have a few contacts with neighbours in the surrounding area, so far.

Heimspiel not only decided to work with W1904 to improve their chances of gaining support from the Hamburg Agency programme, but also to reduce the burden of self-administration. W1904 manages all the financial and maintenance obligations, and Heimspiel believes that this improves their resources and the quality of living together collectively – as well as making it more affordable (ibid.)

The group does complain about some restrictive practices of W1904, for example regulations on home decoration, shoes and toys in the stairways (fire protection). On the other hand, two board members of W1904 described the group as 'harmonic' and as 'a dream' in comparison with another project they are working with, where there are many internal conflicts. They also argued that it will be difficult for them to realize more projects due to rising building costs for relatively 'small numbers of flats' (W1904 interview 2016).

Regarding *relations with local government*, Heimspiel experienced some restrictions from the Hamburg Agency concerning the size of flats, which were needed to meet the proviso for subsidized housing. In this respect, the core group also had to find people with a certain income to ensure the right mix in order to get the subsidies.[17] Once Heimspiel was selected for the programme, there was hardly any further communication with the Hamburg Agency; the communication and organizational aspects were all covered by W1904.

Heimspiel puts considerable emphasis on *social sustainability* by prioritizing social relations and mutual support in the multigenerational context. In addition, W1904's definition of sustainability is first and foremost connected to social cohesion in the sense that right from the start it has emphasized ideas of community, solidarity and mutual support in everyday life as the foundations of their housing philosophy. This agenda is practised by offering community spaces in its houses for neighbourhood activities (but not in Heimspiel). W1904 also has an expanding European network of cooperatives sharing holiday flats and knowledge.

Besides the social emphasis, W1904 sees itself as at the forefront of *ecological sustainability* and experimentation with new technologies. *Ecologically*, the Heimspiel house fulfils the KfW-55 standard.[18] This means that a high level of cost reduction and energy savings has been achieved. Just like Inter-Pares, for Heimspiel the question of costs became a factor that made them give up ecological ambitions such as using natural materials in construction and to improve room climate. It was argued that affordability and stable rents are first and foremost the main goal.

Möwe Altonah

Möwe Altonah is a self-build co-housing group currently planning and constructing a six-storey apartment block with 100% social housing[19] in Central Altona (Neue Mitte Altona) – one of Hamburg's largest urban development areas. The motivation for starting the self-build co-housing group was mainly affordability and the sense of community that a self-organized project could offer in the light of a political intention to resist gentrification. They were accepted for the Hamburg Agency programme in 2011 as a member of an existing (small) cooperative, Wohnreform e.G., founded in 2002 (Wohnreform 2019). The project began when two circles of friends converged in Möwe Altonah. In 2015, there was a core group of about 35 people who were involved in the planning process. The age range extends from new-born to 60, but the group consists mainly of academics aged 30–50, families, some former squatters and political activists with 'relatively low income' (Möwe Altonah interview 2015). Most of them have a secondary school education or a university degree and are working – the majority in education. Nine people with disabilities (aged between 20 and 30) will join the development process at a later stage through collaboration with Living with Disabilities Hamburg (Leben mit Behinderungen Hamburg). Among the 90 future residents there will be 26 children, mostly of school age. People with a migrant background are underrepresented compared to the Hamburg average. The common goal is to live together 'long-term, in solidarity and friendship' (Möwe Altonah 2019). The targeted costs for rent are relatively affordable compared to rents in the area. *Democratic self-governance* is a key principle for the group and all decisions are made through the model of consensus. Work is organized in small working groups and they have realized that this work requires a significant amount of time and, moreover, social and cultural capital.

The building costs for the whole project are financed through a bank loan from IFB Hamburg, which will be paid off over 30 years. The private equity part of the bank loan is financed through crowdfunding and solidaristic signings of cooperative shares (Möwe Altonah 2019). The group tries to reduce the financial burden to pay the cooperative shares with crowdfunding campaigns that lower the financial barriers for low-income people (ibid.).[20] With the decision to become part of Wohnreform e.G., which compared to W1904 is a small cooperative with much less resources, the group not only had to get involved in the process of financial funding, but also in the organization of the planning and building process and, later, the maintenance of the house. In comparison with Heimspiel, this means more responsibility, but it also provides more autonomy from regulations and guidelines. Nonetheless, the building costs have increased by another EUR 900,000 due to technical construction delays, which made another loan from IFB Hamburg necessary (Möwe Altonah email interview 2019).[21]

Möwe Altonah describes its relation with local government, represented by the Hamburg Agency, in a more ambivalent and critical manner than Heimspiel. On the one hand, they profit from the Hamburg Agency's organization and its financial and capacity-building support for the project. On the other hand, they feel there are strong restrictions and regulations regarding the social composition and plans of the group. Because the house is dedicated to social housing, it has to follow strict legal obligations to qualify for subsidies from the city. This means that all residents need to report their financial situation to the Hamburg Agency and IFB Hamburg. Further, the group had to change their plans to include refugees and young adults with special needs, and instead give priority to accommodating people with disabilities, in line with the Hamburg Agency's demands. They also had to give up their plans to install a co-generation unit[22] (*Blockheizkraftwerk*) as a decentralized power source, due to a contract that the Hamburg Agency had signed with Vattenfall as energy distributor for the whole area (Möwe Altonah interview 2015). Due to financial problems, the size of the planned common spaces was reduced. The group has also been struggling with other financial obstacles, especially with the requirements by the Hamburg Agency and IFB Hamburg to include a low-income group in the programme, while at the same time financing the necessary shares in the cooperative. Further, while the group wanted to contribute to a car-free city, they needed to have a garage because their apartment block shares the same lot with four other buildings (but got permission for fewer parking places per household than the usual regulation stipulates). Moreover, a restaurant and business space were required in the building to serve the planned needs of the neighbourhood. The restaurant partner on the ground level faced some surprising requirements due to contract agreements already signed by the municipality, e.g. that the restaurant is only allowed to sell Carlsberg Beer[23] (Möwe Altonah interview 2015). In addition, the Agency had already chosen the construction company – an international corporation (ibid.). The group also found that the owner-occupied houses in the area got the more prestigious land next to a park, while the social housing units face the train track (S-Bahn).

Möwe Altonah explicitly emphasizes their political commitment to *social, ecological and economic sustainability.* As part of the small cooperative Wohnreform, and due to social housing benefits, they get long-term affordable rents and ongoing opportunities for a certain mix of social backgrounds. The bank checks whether household incomes still fulfill the funding requirements every five years. This can create a grotesque individual situation for people if their income rises. According to the social housing guidelines in the Hamburg Agency's programme they would need to move out. Nonetheless, their internal funding model provides some sort of a financial transfer within the framework of the official funding guidelines, meaning that those who can afford it can contribute more than others (Möwe Altonah interview 2015). *Ecological sustainability* is equally an important goal for the group, but it had to be adapted to the guidelines of the city, and in order to keep building costs affordable the targeted standard was not achieved. Further, the project creates economic dependencies, partly due to the process of lending money privately and partly due to the solidarity principle. This has created problematic responsibilities within the group, but it also stimulates the disciplining of personal plans for the coming years in order to deal with these dependencies.

Besides the 'community of solidarity' (Thomas et al. 2020) of the house, the group has explicitly planned to interact directly with the neighbourhood and the city by providing an open indoor common space and thus taking responsibility for the neighbourhood beyond the residential focus. At the same time, they encountered criticism from the broader left-wing Hamburg community, both for being gentrifiers and for 'selling out' their autonomy to the municipality. While they feel the accusation of being gentrifiers is unfair, they have realized that their closest neighbours have quite different ideas about housing, as they are surrounded by expensive ownership projects.

Conclusion

In this chapter we have analysed the role of co-housing in relation to the governing of 'sustainable urban development'. Focusing on Hamburg and

Table 5.2 Social and economic sustainability of co-housing cases

Name	*Self-governance*	*Social mixing*	*Cohesion*	*Affordability*	*Ecological strategies*
Stacken	Democratic self-governance – votes by members' meeting	No mixing strategy	Working groups, children's activities, working days. Shared spaces: café, free shop, kitchen and dining hall, children's playroom	Long-term high affordability	Passive House, solar panels
Trädet	Democratic self-governance – votes by members' meeting	No mixing strategy	Working groups, shared meals, children's activities, working days. Shared spaces: café, kitchen and dining hall, children's playroom	Affordable rent, but over time dependent on decisions of the municipal housing company	No significant ecological strategies
Under samma tak	Self-governance – board decides	Mixing strategy: intergenerational and apartments for people with disabilities	Working groups, shared meals. Shared spaces: kitchen and dining hall, children's playroom, orangery, roof terrace, three workshops, bicycle repair room	Not affordable	Solar panels, car pool
Inter-Pares	Democratic self-governance Consensus	No mixing strategy	No shared space except garden. House party once a year. Thematic working groups	Long-term high affordability	High efficiency standard; (KfW-55)
Heimspiel	Democratic self-governance but also house management by cooperative housing company	Mixing strategy: intergenerational	Internal community with mutual support	Long-term affordability	High efficiency standard (KfW-55)
Möwe Altonah	Democratic self-governance	Mixing strategy: intergenerational, different income groups, and apartments for people with disabilities	Internal financial transfer. Political aspirations of social, economic and ecological sustainability	Long-term affordability	High efficiency standard, low-energy house (KfW-40), no cars

Gothenburg, we examined how national, regional and particularly municipal government supports co-housing groups as part of their official sustainability agenda. We asked questions about relations between government and co-housing in this process and to what extent co-housing projects address or meet the different goals that are part of this agenda. To this end, we examined six co-housing groups' strategies to sustain their projects, and their relations with government. In particular, we were interested in the consequences of different legally instituted tenure forms.

The perspective in official discourses regarding how co-housing groups can contribute to solving 'sustainability problems' – and the definitions of sustainability that this involved – are rather similar in the two cities: economic sustainability is conceptualized in terms of 'smart growth'. In terms of social sustainability, the city governments put strong emphasis on the capabilities of co-housing to produce social cohesion, social mixing and self-governance; and to some extent also affordability. Regarding ecological sustainability, co-housing is believed to facilitate resource-saving forms of living, emphasizing urban sharing. In the cases where support for co-housing is linked to self-build projects, it is emphasized that the buildings constructed should have a low climate impact. We also found that in the official discourses, possible contradictions between the different dimensions were rarely recognized.

The extent to which a sustainability agenda is present varies greatly among our cases. The cases that most often referred to the official sustainability agenda were two of the self-build co-housing groups: Under samma tak and Möwe Altonah. This could be seen as a reflection of the fact that both groups were dependent on the municipality (most importantly for land allocation) and that both were established in the 2010s, when the sustainability agenda has become hegemonic in urban development (Scheller and Thörn 2018). For these two projects, this means that commitment to sustainability strategies is mandatory in order to be recognized as a legitimate actor. We also found that in all our cases, co-housing projects did have strategies that 'meet' key sustainability goals as defined in the municipal discourses, even though the co-housing communities may not always define them in the language of the official sustainability agenda.

While the definitions and practices varied in the cases we studied, they nevertheless shared some concerns that made their approach to 'sustainability' different from the municipalities, particularly regarding economic and social sustainability. Most importantly, economic sustainability was for the groups all about affordability. Generally, long-term rent stability and mutual support in an intentional housing community results in stable social security for the residents, who step out of the precarious conditions of a neoliberal housing market (Schröder and Scheller 2017). Further, while social cohesion in all cases was an important motivation to engage in a co-housing project, self-governance most often became the most important concern in the realization of the projects. 'Social mixing' in municipal discourses most often emphasizes 'mixing up' poor or working-class neighbourhoods by providing space for middle-class housing. However, in Hamburg, where public concern about gentrification is more strongly voiced than in Gothenburg, co-housing projects worry about the possible gentrification that the municipal mixing strategy may produce; and are eager to counteract tendencies that their own housing could become a middle-class enclave. Those co-housing projects that did see 'mixing' as a goal tended to see it as a question of the social composition of its members rather than in relation to the neighbourhood.

How then should we understand the relation between a co-housing group's autonomy and their ability to make co-housing sustainable? Möwe Altonah found their autonomy highly restricted by both formal and informal regulations and financial responsibilities stipulated by the Hamburg Agency. As a consequence, housing became less affordable than expected, the idea of a co-generation unit as a decentralized power source had to be abandoned, and plans to include refugees and young adults with special needs had to be changed. Further, in Gothenburg, Trädet's self-organized renovation project was interrupted when the municipal housing company, responding to a new national law that would make Swedish municipal housing companies more economically sustainable (by applying business principles), revised its agreement in a way that reduced affordability and self-governance (though it has to be emphasized that rents are still set at an affordable level by Swedish standards). At the other end, Stacken completed a highly ambitious climate-friendly renovation, with zero rent increases, thus sustaining their truly affordable rents. This was possible because Stacken has a high degree of autonomy as the owner of their house, with a non-profit cooperative ownership form. Equally autonomous in terms of ownership (as members of the Mietshäuser Syndikat), Inter-Pares has also been able to provide affordable and long-term secure housing for its residents. Just like Heimspiel they however down-prioritized ecological sustainability measures because they were too expensive. In the case of Heimspiel, it was not so much their own decision, as their autonomy was restricted by the some of regulations imposed on them by the large cooperative that they are part of. Under samma tak broke off their cooperation with a municipal housing company, instead cooperating with a private housing company that prioritizes ecological sustainability. While this cooperation facilitated the construction of a highly ecologically sustainable house, they felt that the company restricted some of their influence on the construction process, and even more importantly, they could not realize their initial goal of affordable rent for the residents.

These examples emphasize the significance of ownership forms for the potential to make co-housing sustainable. Non-profit self-ownership means autonomy and a strong capacity for affordability, because no third party can demand higher rents. While in three of our cases there seems to have been a tension between affordability and ecological sustainability, the case of Stacken demonstrates that there is not necessarily a conflict between the two. It should also be added that a significant difference between the groups that we studied concerned to what extent they defined their co-housing project as a *political* project, strongly emphasizing autonomy and non-market/non-profit housing. Those who did that came closest to realizing the kind of comprehensive sustainability agenda that the official discourses, at least rhetorically, celebrate.

With regard to the relation between autonomy and the capacity to realize sustainability goals we thus found an interesting paradox: the co-housing group among our cases that was most exposed to government strategies that strongly emphasize the sustainability agenda (Möwe-Altonah), also seemed to be least capable of fulfilling a comprehensive 'sustainability agenda', while the co-housing group with the highest degree of autonomy (Stacken) had the strongest capacity to realize both ecological and social sustainability goals.

With the reservation that it is risky to generalize from a few cases, we nevertheless would argue that this paradox may be seen as a function of the economic and political logics of contemporary urban development, in which one pillar of the sustainability agenda, economic sustainability, is defined and practised in terms of 'growth first' (Mayer 2016). This development, heavily conditioned by capitalist land and housing markets, and driven by public-private partnerships promoting de-regulation and re-regulation to further strengthen market-based approaches through 'smart growth', has led to rising property values and increased housing-related costs. This makes the goal of affordability in co-housing difficult to achieve, especially in cases of new-build housing. In this context, 'successful' co-housing can even contribute to processes of gentrification, with groups relatively strong in economic and cultural capital displacing weaker groups. Considering this situation, it may even be argued that local, regional or national governments' support for co-housing runs the risk of legitimising economically, socially and ecologically unsustainable large-scale urban restructuring. Thus, a key instrument for governmental support of affordable rents in co-housing projects is the provision of public land at moderate prices. As the example of Under samma tak shows, if public land is purchased at the market rate in an urban context, achieving affordability becomes impossible.

Interviews

Wohnungsbaugenossenschaft von 1904 e.G. interview, 30 June 2016, Hamburg.
Heimspiel interview, 14 May 2016, Hamburg.
Inter-Pares interview, 12 May 2016, Hamburg.
Möwe Altonah interview 19 October 2015, Hamburg.
Möwe Altonah email interview, 15 April 2019.
Gothenburg Planning and Building Committee interview, 8 October 2015, Gothenburg.
Trädet interview, 9 March 2016, Gothenburg.
Under samma tak, 22 November, 2018, Gothenburg.

Notes

1 This chapter is based on analysis of policy documents produced by the cities of Hamburg and Gothenburg, documents produced by co-housing associations and 26 interviews carried out in Hamburg and Gothenburg in 2015–2016, by the authors. We interviewed members of all six co-housing projects analyzed in the chapter, as well as planners, politicians, architects, public officials and representatives of housing companies (in Gothenburg) and large and small cooperatives (in Hamburg).

2 The price of the house was SEK 9 million. The state guaranteed security for a bank loan of 95% of this sum. For the remaining 5%, Stacken used money saved in a renovation fund.

3 In 2019 a 63-square-metre two-room apartment costs SEK 4,300 per month, electricity included.

4 In 2019: SEK 168,000 per year for Stacken, compared to 127,000 for the surrounding area in the poor suburb of Bergsjön; 285,000 for Gothenburg and 324,000 for Sweden (Hitta 2019; Göteborgs stad 2019b).

5 In 2019, the rent is 2.6 million SEK/year, which for the individual tenant means an increase from SEK 650 to 900 per square metre per year (Poseidon 2010; Trädet interview 2016).

6 In 2019, a 51-square-metre two-room apartment costs SEK 3,088 per month, electricity included.

7 In 2019 the average income was SEK 222,000 per year, thus considerably higher than the surrounding area in Kortedala (SEK 172,000) – but lower than the average for Gothenburg and Sweden (Hitta 2019; Göteborgs stad 2019b)

8 According to Trollängen, the municipality argued that the piece of land that Trollängen was interested in buying was not included in the plan to support affordable housing (while the neighbouring piece of land bought by another private housing company was included). Email conversation with Trollängen, 12 June 2019.

9 Initially the group set a target of SEK 1,400 per square metre per year, but in 2019 they were looking at a figure above SEK 2,000.

10 The project costs for the 591 square metres of land and the construction of the house with 808 square metres of living space and 211 square metres of commercial space reached EUR 2.85 million, which makes a rent of EUR 7.80 per square metre (including a EUR 0.16 per square metre solidarity transfer into the Syndicate fund).

11 In 2019, it was EUR 6.70 per square metre.

12 There are various forms and shapes of groups and houses, including a former army barracks with 285 residents in wagon communities, single-family houses for half a dozen people or medium-sized apartment buildings for 25 to 40 people (cf. MHS 2016: 80).

13 In Germany, the minimum core capital to form a LLC is EUR 25,000. The LLC's core capital is split between the house association (EUR 12,600) and the Syndicate association (EUR 12,400).

14 The supporter signs a contract directly with the house LLC, which provides low interest rates for the co-housing group and a transparent and non-speculative system of saving money for supporters.

15 In West Germany 28% of the 1,120 housing cooperatives, and in East Germany 39% of the 740 cooperatives are considered large with over 1,000 flats. W1904 has more than 3,800 flats with 4,500 members and is a member of the REX Group – a European network of housing associations with the aim of comparing working practices and sharing experiences between 11 members from five different European countries, which collectively manage some 450,000 dwellings in total.

16 Depending on the flat size, the cooperative shares range from EUR 6,000 for a 40-square-metre two-bed flat to EUR 16,500 for a 110-square-metre four-bed flat.

17 According to the founding guidelines set by IFB Hamburg for building communities, a single-person household would get funding for 30–50 square metres, a two-person household for 55–60 square metres and a three-person household for 65–75 square metres (IFB Hamburg 2019: 32).

18 A KfW-55 house only requires 55% of the standard set by the KfW Bank (100%) and is accordingly 45% more efficient in its annual primary energy demand and the transmission heat loss of the building.

19 Social housing in Hamburg is defined by a starting rent of not more than EUR 6.50 per square metre. To fulfill the goal of 3,000 rental flats in the social housing sector IFB Hamburg gives subsidies and funding (Hamburg 2019). For Möwe Altonah, this means that the majority of the future residents have to disclose their annual income. In fact, the majority declared their incomes as Level 1 or 2 on the IFB Hamburg index, which means that the annual income is below EUR 18,000 for a one-person household and below EUR 27,000 for a two-person household (IFB Hamburg 2016: 3). The income is checked every five years by IFB Hamburg and could also lead to a cancellation of funding if the requirements are not met anymore.

20 A family with two children has a maximum claim of 90 square metres of living space plus 2 square metres of communal space (IFB Hamburg funding regulation) and would have to pay EUR 38,800 for cooperative shares. A single parent who wants to move into a shared flat together with a child is accordingly entitled to 42.5 square metres plus 2 square metres of living space for themselves and their child – meaning EUR 17,800 for cooperative shares (Möwe Altonah 2019).

21 The Group has exerted political pressure and contacted the Hamburg Senator for Building, the Hamburg Agency and IFB Hamburg. Nonetheless, the new high loan will negatively affect the calculation of the rents. At the same time, the price for cooperative shares could be maintained through this effort.

22 A cogeneration unit is a system for the decentralized generation of heat and electricity, ideally situated in the house itself. Most use an internal combustion engine that burns fuels (diesel, gas, plant oil) or wood pellets. The surplus energy is fed into the local energy network and earns money for the house.

23 When Carlsberg – as the owner of Holsten – sold the brewery site to the city, a covenant was written into the contract stipulating that any hospitality establishment on the property could only serve Carlsberg beer.

References

AB Göteborgshem (1985) 'Hyresavtal 1985-02-13' [Rental contract, with date]. Gothenburg: Göteborgshem.

DUDE (Department of Urban Development and the Environment) (2014) 'Green, inclusive, growing city by the water. Perspectives on urban development in Hamburg'. www. hamburg.de/contentblob/4357518/9ac11792edd8de17e3119e1396474718/data/broschuere-perspektiven-englisch).pdf (17 October 2016).

Ferrum Architects (2016) *Bogemenskap på gång i Göteborg* [Co-housing on its way in Gothenburg]. Gothenburg: Ferrum.

Gothenburg Municipality (2014) *Development strategy Göteborg 2035*. Gothenburg: Gothenburg Municipality.

IFB Hamburg (Hamburgische Investitions- und Förderbank) (2016) *Einkomensvoraussetzungen bei einkommensabhängiger Förderung* [Income requirements for income-related funding]. Hamburg: IFB Hamburg. www.ifbhh.de/fileadmin/pdf/IFB_Download/IFB_Wohneigentum/IFB-Info_Einkommensvoraussetzungen.pdf (17 April 2019).

IFB Hamburg (Hamburgische Investitions- und Förderbank) (2019) *Baugemeinschaften – Förderrichtlinie für Baugemeinschaften mit genossenschaftlichem Eigentum* [Construction Communities – Funding Guidelines for Construction Cooperatives with Cooperative Property]. Hamburg: IFB Hamburg. www.ifbhh.de/fileadmin/pdf/IFB_Download/IFB_Foerderrichtlinien/FoeRi_Baugemeinschaften.pdf (17 April 2019).

Krueger, R. and Gibbs, D. (2008) '"Third wave" sustainability? Smart growth and regional development in the USA', *Regional Studies*, vol. 42, no. 9, pp. 1263–1274.

Lees, L., Slater, T. and Wyly, E. K. (2008) *Gentrification*. New York: Routledge.

Mayer, M. (2016) 'Neoliberal Urbanism and uprisings across Europe', in M. Mayer, C. Thörn and H. Thörn (eds) *Urban Uprisings: Challenging Neoliberal Urbanism in Europe*, pp. 57–92. Basingstoke: Palgrave Macmillan.

MHS (Das Mietshäuser Syndikat und die Hausprojekte) (2016) *Die Häuser denen, die drin wohnen. Selbstorganisiert wohnen, solidarisch wirtschaften* [The houses for those who live in it. Living self-organized, working in solidarity]. Freiburg: MHS. www.syndikat.org/wp-content/uploads/2017/02/broschuere_nr7.pdf (17 April 2019).

Poseidon (2010) 'Blockhyresavtal, Kollektivhuset Trädet, 1 July 2010' [Rental contract, with date]. Gothenburg: Poseidon.

Scheller, D. and Thörn, H. (2018) 'Governing "sustainable urban development" through self-build groups and co-housing: the cases of Hamburg and Gothenburg', *International Journal for Urban and Regional Research*, vol. 42, no. 5, pp. 914–932.

Schröder, S. and Scheller, D. (2017) 'Abgesicherte Fürsorge und fürsorgliche Absicherung in Gemeinschaft. Mehrgenerationenwohnprojekte als neue Formen der städtischen Reproduktion?', *sub\urban*. vol. 5, no. 3, pp. 23–42. www.zeitschrift-suburban.de/sys/index.php/suburban/article/view/313 (18 June 2019).

Thomas, S., Scheller, D. and T. Ehmann (2020) *Substanzielle Gemeinschaften: Selbstorganisation und Solidarität im Mehrgenerationenwohnen,* Wiesbaden: Springer VS.

Thörn, C. and H. Thörn, (2017) 'Swedish cities now belong to the most segregated in Europe', *Sociologisk forskning*, vol. 54, no. 4, pp. 293–296.

Under Samma Tak (2015) *Program för kollektivhus i Högsbo, Under Samma Tak*. Gothenburg: UST.

Västra Götalandsregionen (2014) Befolkningsprognos västra Götaland 2014–2030 [Population projection for Western Sweden 2014–2030]. www.vgregion.se/om-vgr/statistik-analys/analysportalen/2014/befolkningsprognos- vastra-gotaland-2014–2030/ (20 January 2017).

Webpages

Göteborgs stad (2019a) www.goteborg2021.com (15 April 2019).

Göteborgs stad (2019b) www.statistik.goteborg.se (15 April 2019).

Hamburg (2019) www.hamburg.de/pressearchiv-fhh/12137862/2019-02-05-bsw-wohnraumfoerderung-2019-2020/ (17 April 2019).

Hitta (2019) www.hitta.nu. (15 April 2019).

Inter-Pares (2019) www.syndikat.org/de/projekte/inter-pares/ (17 April 2019).

MHS (2019) www.syndikat.org/de/unternehmensverbund/ (17 April 2019).

Möwe Altonah (2019) www.moewe-altonah.de/de/informationen (17 April 2019).

Trädet (2019) http://nyatradet.wixsite.com/tradet/kollektiv (15 April 2019).

Wohnreform (2019) www.wohnreform-eg.de (17 April 2019).

6 Urban activism and co-housing

David Scheller and Henrik Gutzon Larsen

Introduction

In this chapter we look at the interrelations and dynamics between urban activism and the politics of co-housing. Drawing on our empirical investigations of Hamburg and Barcelona, the chapter explores the specific socio-political context of the politics of co-housing in the interplay of bottom-up organizing and top-down governance. Famously, in Hamburg, the houses in Hafenstraße were squatted in the early 1980s. After nearly a decade of violent battles between the police and the squatters, the city of Hamburg began to negotiate with the squatters, offering them recognition and financial support if squats were re-organized as legalized co-housing projects (see also Chapter 3). Over the years, Hafenstraße has hosted homeless, youth, political groups and refugees, and thus become a symbolic reference point in the struggle for self-organized and affordable housing for many urban activists. Squats with no housing, such as Rote Flora, legalized squats such as Hafenstraße and the more recently occupied Gängeviertel have become important nodal points and symbols on different scales, from the surrounding neighbourhoods up to the transnational scale. Barcelona also has a history of squatting, for example the Can Masdeu squat in the Collserola hills, Can Vies in Sants neighbourhood and Kasa de la Muntanya in the Gràcia district. But after the 2008 mortgage crisis hit Barcelona, with foreclosure and displacement affecting a large number of home owners, buildings all over the city have been squatted. Social centres have been established as spaces for mutual solidarity in specific neighbourhoods, such as El Banc Expropiat. Such spaces became hubs for political organizing by people hit by mortgage problems. At the same time, squatting relates both indirectly and directly to the development of the first co-housing projects in Barcelona (see also Chapter 4).

In our study of the politics of co-housing, we pay particular attention to squatting and related questions of urban activism. This investigation is structured according to three issues identified as particularly critical for squatting movements: relations to the state; whether to legalize or not; and intersections with broader movements. These three issues, which we use to structure our empirical investigations, are introduced in the first section. Following this, we discuss relations between co-housing, squatting and urban activism more generally in Hamburg and Barcelona. Finally, drawing on insights from the two cities, we discuss what we term the 'dialectics of the politics of co-housing'. This dynamic relation between grassroots organizing and top-down governance intersects in different political aspirations for co-housing – and eventually in what is understood as sustainable urban development. On the one hand, squatting and urban activism follow a political logic of empowerment, self-management, mutual self-help and solidarity. On the other hand, local city governments impose a political logic of urban governance, often with the aim of regulation, control, marketization and co-optation (Kuhn 2014). As we will see in our different cases in Hamburg and Barcelona, although they play out quite differently, the underlying contradictory political logics remain similar.

Urban activism in the crisis of neoliberal urbanism: an analytical perspective

Urban transformations have been shaped by neoliberalization processes during recent decades (Peck et al. 2009). At the same time, urban social movements have been described in their relation to the state as reactions to the several crises and the emergence of neoliberal urbanism (Mayer 2012b). As a result of this process, neoliberal urbanism – characterized by a growth-first approach, entrepreneurial forms of governance, privatization and polarization – has become the hegemonic modus operandi in many cities (Mayer 2016: 64–71). Nevertheless, the financial crashes of the 2000s have shaken this hegemony and neoliberal urbanism itself has fallen into crisis. This crisis has been challenged by a new convergence of counter- or alter-neoliberal and anti-austerity movements. As networks of urban social movements against the neoliberal city, different actors politicize and connect different protest fields, such as housing, climate change and refuge. Since the 2008 financial crisis these have included new actors and modes of organization in urban social movements that have evolved into deepening convergences of socio-political thematical backgrounds to address the crisis of neoliberalism (Mayer et al. 2016). These recent movements have been characterized as *post-autonomous* (Vollmer and Scheller 2018) to emphasize the relation between autonomous and institutional orientations to the state and to demands, and the involvement of different actors and actions. This can also be seen to imply democratizations of neoliberal post-democracy (Scheller 2019). In his conceptualization of *hybrid-autonomous* movements, Martínez emphasizes the collaboration of autonomous movements with new protesters who converge in opposition to the state:

> A hybrid autonomous initiative is one whose members do not accept the fate of remaining isolated alternatives to the dominant forces. Rather, they actively engage in creating strong or pragmatic bonds both with other autonomous islands, and, eventually, with state and even market

institutions, all the while facing the contradictions and unintended consequences that may likely occur.

(Martínez 2016: 259)

The novelty of what we will term post-autonomous urban social movements is a combination of autonomous strategies, such as direct action and civil disobedience, and more mainstream demands for grassroots-oriented institutional reforms and programmes tied to specific needs of citizens, for example sustainable social housing. In this chapter we will focus in particular on post-autonomous practices as constituted by three dimensions (Table 6.1). First, post-autonomous practices involve a shift in relations to the state. This is rooted in the autonomous criticism of political representation and refusal of institutionalized hierarchical organizational structures and leaders. But in post-autonomous practices, movements engage in strategic collaborations with state actors to foster institutional change. Second, post-autonomous practices involve an expansion of horizontal organizing beyond the traditional emphasis on direct democracy (Sitrin and Azzellini 2014; Graeber 2013). Historically rooted in the anarchist movement, but revived and popularized by the alter-globalization movement, the expansion of horizontalism involves elements of flat hierarchies (Sitrin 2006). This includes a post-identitarian mobilization of diverse actors (rather than a closed autonomous peer group), connection of different critical issues (e.g. in relation to racism, sexism and classism), self-reflection on the thematic boundaries of the movement (e.g. housing, precarization, refuge) and, related, the joining of forces in collaborative networks and actions that eventually may evolve from particularistic to generalized political demands (Marchart 2013; Scheller 2019). Third, traditional autonomous practices of direct action and non-violent civil disobedience remain political tools of post-autonomous movements, for example occupations, blockades, go-ins and take-overs of public events (Vollmer and Scheller 2018). But these tools are applied tactically by these new diverse actors, often to force political changes by the state. Moreover, a mixture of cultural and political action has been emphasized (Fraeser 2016; Mayer 2012a).

These dimensions provide our analytical lens for discussing movement activism in the politics of co-housing. To this end, we apply a historically and locally contextualized approach in the following analyses of movement activism in relation to co-housing in Hamburg and Barcelona. Many forces are at play in the politics of co-housing in these cities, of course. But we have found it particularly interesting to focus on squatting and – to various degrees – wider forms of urban activism that connect to grassroot struggles for sustainable communities, neighbourhoods and cities.

Hamburg: from autonomous squats to post-autonomous networks

Over the last three decades, Hamburg has been shaped by neoliberal urbanism and social urban movements alike, and urban policies have significantly followed the toolkit of growth first, entrepreneurial governance, privatization

Table 6.1 Characteristics of post-autonomous practice

Dimensions	*Post-autonomous practice*
Relation to the state	Critique of representation Not in sheer opposition to the state Strategic relation to institutions Aiming for institutional change
Horizontal organizing	Direct democratic decision making Inclusive post-identitarian politics Connection of diverse subject positions Self-reflection of thematic boundaries From particularities to generalization of claims
Direct actions	Civil disobedience Self-determination and appropriation Occupations, blockades, go-ins, take-overs Mixture of cultural and political action

and polarization (see also Chapter 3). The dialectics of these developments came to the fore with the 2008 crisis, which also hit Hamburg with rising housing insecurity and a public spending crisis. All over the globe significant cracks appeared in the global hegemony of neoliberal urbanism, and even hardcore neoliberal apologists had doubts whether growth could really be unlimited (Mason 2015). In opposition to policies of competitive city marketing and the capitalization of urban space and lifestyle, numerous and thematically diverse civil society initiatives have developed. Besides the autonomous movement, with a background in the occupations of the early 1980s, new actors have appeared: precarious and working poor, refugees, senior citizens, artists or small gardeners, all of which have started organizing in various neighbourhood initiatives and eventually through the city-wide Hamburg Recht auf Stadt-Netzwerk (Hamburg-Right-to-the-City-Network) (Birke 2016; Boeing 2011; Rinn 2016; Twickel 2011). Sustainable solutions to the housing crisis are a central link between the various movements within this network. Moreover, collaborative housing in general and co-housing in particular[1] appear as one of the pillars of grassroot demands for affordable and solidaristic urban policies.

The politics of co-housing in Hamburg is directly rooted in housing shortages and the lack of affordable housing. From this perspective, co-housing can be a political act of empowerment and mutual self-help, and co-housing can thus provide a possible solution for socially, economically and ecologically sustainable housing. Conversely, the federal state of Hamburg has in its relation to neighbourhood initiatives imposed a top-down urban governance by integrating co-housing in its political programme. However, this can be seen as a result of ongoing struggles by grassroots and as a political shift from zero tolerance towards the first co-housing projects established by squatting. As a result, we find co-housing projects with political self-awareness that are directly connected to the Hamburg Recht auf Stadt Netzwerk, such as Möwe Altonah, as well as co-housing projects such as Heimspiel that are aware of the squatting history and the current housing movement, but emphasize the lifestyle of internal mutual help and solidarity rather than the political contextualization (see also Chapter 5).

Relation to the state

For autonomous movements, such as the 'traditional' squatter's movement, relations to the state constitute a fundamental question that in the broadest sense is related to the movements' critique of representation on all scales (nation state, federal state, municipality, local borough). In order to approach our basic question regarding the dynamic relation between squatting, neighbourhood activism and the politics of co-housing in Hamburg, we differentiate between three generations of squatting (Amantine 2012). Probably the most famous example of the first generation of squats in Hamburg are the houses in Hafenstraße and Berhard-Nocht-Straße, located in the working-class neighbourhood near the harbour. Eleven houses were occupied in 1982 with the goal to preserve and renovate (*Instandbesetzt*) them in opposition to the city's plan to demolish them. The occupation was organized around the goal of anti-authoritarian and self-organized housing by a diverse group that was composed of long-time residents in the buildings – students, unemployed, homeless, housing activists and punks (see also Chapter 3). Importantly, this happened at a time when neoliberal policies were encroaching on the welfare state, particularly affecting young people, and causing unemployment and poverty (Mayer 2012b: 66).

Hafenstraße can be seen as a historic experimental space for early hybrid-autonomous associations, which Martínez (2016) exemplifies with the 15M movement in Spain (see further below). Support from the neighbourhood to stop evictions and demolitions was immensely diverse, including civil society actors, celebrities, churches and politicians, and intensified over nearly a decade of struggle. It could be seen as one of the first anti-gentrification movements in the city, which actively opposed the restructuring and marketization of a (former) working-class neighbourhood and introduced a new model of collaborative housing in Germany – collaboratively self-organized co-housing. These almost decade-long struggles for the preservation of houses in the Hamburg harbour area have become a symbol for counter-political movements in Hamburg and internationally. The projects were founded on a rigorous rejection of the destructive and repressive politics of the city council during the struggle. The squatting involved an explicit criticism of the political representation at the time and it has been continued ever since by new generations of squatters.

However, Hafenstraße was never occupied in direct opposition to the state. Rather, the occupation addressed local politics with the aim of stopping the demolition plans and establishing collective housing, and with legalization in 1995 came a shift in relations to state institutions. The precarious status and the poor condition of the houses have been described by the residents as stressful, further aggravated by the ongoing eviction threat and the prevention of renovation (Hafenstraße interview 2015). This changed when Hafenstraße was turned into a cooperative in 1995, and the houses have since been renovated with subsidies from the city. In 2007, the co-housing project planB for 40 people was erected in a vacant lot in-between the former squats. The legal form of a small housing cooperative provides a secure status for the houses, which are completely autonomously self-managed.

In the case of the occupation of Rote Flora in the Sternschanze, the squatters' goal was to preserve the former theatre from demolition and turn it into a social centre, a political and non-commercial subcultural hub for the neighbourhood (Rote Flora 2001). Rote Flora is an example of a 'traditional' autonomous initiative in direct opposition to the politics of representation, which acts on a very local level and includes an anti-systemic critique that challenges the privatization and commodification of housing. In the early years of the occupation, the city owned the building and even offered the squatters a contract, while at the same time threatening them with eviction. Eventually, no compromise was found, but at the same time no eviction was enforced. After another contract offer was rejected in 2001, the city sold the building to a private investor for EUR 185,000. The new owner promised that the status of the building would not change, but in 2012 made public that he considered selling it after having received an offer of over EUR 20 million for the building. As a result, the city first made use of its right to veto disposal plans for the building and later introduced a law that decrees that the building may not be sold (*Veränderungssperre*). The basic political tool of the squatters was in this case a threat of strong protests that would produce immense costs in case of an eviction attempted by the city. In October 2014, the building was eventually sold in an insolvency case for EUR 820,000 to the Lawaetz foundation – one of the general developers that were founded by the city in the aftermath of the 'Battle of Hafenstraße', acting as an intermediary between state and the (former) squats (see Chapter 3). But Rote Flora remains a non-legalized squat, and although not formally a co-housing project, Rote Flora is a key symbol of non-legalized autonomous squatting projects in the housing movement.

The latest wave of urban social movements can be seen in a similar way, as an anti-systemic criticism of the current state of political representation, described by Swyngedouw (2007) as the 'post-political city'. The protest articulations of these movements address specific deficiencies of current political policies, particularly the lack of affordable housing and non-commercial spaces and – connecting this with the precarization of artists and creative producers – the forced evictions or displacement of small gardeners and so forth. Most of the time, urban activists either refuse to work with state representatives and institutions, or construct a strategic relation with state actors, aiming for institutional change. Collaborations with politicians and municipal institutions (or their intermediaries) depend on the political issue and goal. Examples include negotiations to turn illegal projects into legalized co-housing projects, involving temporary collaborations with certain politicians and institutions. In the case of Hafenstraße, negotiations were conducted with Hamburg's First Mayor himself, whereas the Gängeviertel and Centro Sociale negotiated directly with the Municipal Council for City Development.

Driven by the political struggle, many urban activists have become highly professional and proficient in their work. As experts in their field, so to speak, they actively intervene in housing politics and establish a new active role in relation to the (traditional) state actors. They thus bring topics and alternative planning approaches to the formal political table. For example, elaborate plans and projects are worked out and proposed to the municipality. In the case of Esso Houses, a social housing complex that was torn down in St. Pauli, an initiative by residents with support from the Hamburg Recht auf Stadt-Netzwerk designed a plan for long-term sustainable affordable housing to be rebuilt at the same spot, instead of the proposed luxury condos. Mostly, such plans include strong notions of self-organization, self-management and collective ownership in both the relevant decision-making processes and physical structures.[2]

Horizontal organizing

Horizontal organizing and direct democratic decision making have always been at the foundation of the squatter movement. In the latest wave of urban social movements, the idea of horizontality also gives shape to internal organizational structures and modes of mobilizing. A flat and non-hierarchical mode of organizing and decision making is driving neighbourhood assemblies, working group meetings and/or user group meetings for self-organized spaces and the like. On the one hand, this reflects a refusal of traditional institutional modes of organization in hierarchical orders and, on the other hand, it appears as a convergence of different actors to communicate on the same level. Confronted with rising rents and gentrification, a basic question for many renters has become 'How can I arrange something that gives me the possibility to save my neighbourhood?' (RAS interview 2015). The collaboratively organized Centro Sociale can be seen as one example of these developments towards a politically self-organized neighbourhood. After it was opened as a non-commercial free space in August 2008, Centro Sociale became an important hub for the Hamburg Recht auf Stadt-Netzwerk. Moreover, right from the beginning it was set up as a political 'counter-sign' against gentrification in a highly commercial area in central Hamburg. It was designated as an urban common through a competition initiated by the city, which the collective won against other bidders. A cooperative was founded for the purpose of running Centro Sociale, which rents the property from the city. The collective demand for a reduction in the rather high monthly costs has yet to be accepted by the municipality. The cooperative currently has around 300 members, and about 26 initiatives, political groups and cultural producers use the space regularly. Money comes in through events, a bar and donations collected by an association (*Föderverein*). As an alternative collaborative space, Centro Sociale has now been an important symbol for the housing movement for over a decade. It became a central hub for alternative left counter-culture and the home for many political and cultural groups in the neighbourhood and beyond, based on volunteer and unsalaried work and horizontal self-organization. For example, Möwe Altonah and the Hamburg Recht auf Stadt-Netzwerk use the space for meetings.

In a similar manner, the Hamburg Recht auf Stadt-Netzwerk incorporates a horizontal and post-identitarian mode of organizing. The horizontality describes the internal structure, while the post-identitarian character focuses on the relationship between the inside and the outside (or the centre and the periphery) of different movements. In contrast to the autonomous movements, the boundaries of political identity are much more open and aim at convergence and collaboration between a highly diverse set of political concerns, subject positions and objectives. When the Hamburg Recht auf Stadt-Netzwerk emerged in 2009 (Birke 2016; Boeing 2011; Rinn 2016; Twickel 2011), it successfully managed to connect those diverse struggles all over the city. For example, autonomous projects such as Rote Flora are involved alongside the activities of ecological activists, artists, refugees, renters and gardeners.

The slogan 'right to the city' functions as a generalized nodal point for different struggles all over the city, with a capacity to connect various specific thematic claims. Claims to remain in the city centre, diversity, participation and self-organization constitute the foundation for a critique of the current crisis of neoliberal urbanism, particularly with regard to the core features of neoliberal urbanism: entrepreneurial city policies and the commodification and marketization of urban space (RAS 2017). Over 60 initiatives have participated in the network and its actions and events. 'Solidaristic' and 'social' housing city policies are a basic political claim that aligns with self-organized co-housing initiatives. This open logic of connectivity between different thematic struggles is implemented in the organization of events. For example, the parade 'We'll come united' illustrates how particular topics such as 'rents' and 'racism' have been discursively linked under the motto or slogan 'Let's get united! Housing and a solidaristic city for all. For a society without racism' (RAS Flyer 2018, our translation).

Whereas connections to other struggles in the city are made using the common signifier 'right to the city', boundaries between thematic political concerns and positions are also drawn. For example, the struggles of refugees are included, whereas right-wing populist groups are not. This illustrates the political logic of post-autonomous organizing, which integrates and excludes political positions according to their capability to connect to radical democratic and libertarian claims (Scheller 2019). Against this background, the politics of (co-)housing are articulated as an empowering right and a demand for affordable and collaboratively controlled housing for all that puts the affected actors in the centre.

Direct action

The emergence of horizontality in the organization of urban social movements in Hamburg, which we have described above, extrapolates another aspect that is rooted in the squatter movement. Horizontality constitutes the foundation for organizing direct actions of collaborative self-determination and appropriation – first of specific spaces and, second, with respect to having a say in political decision making. On the practical side, direct actions such as occupations, blockades of evictions, go-ins at institutions and take-overs of participatory events organized by city officials, define the political register of urban social movements. Traditionally, these practices and strategies have primarily been components in the political tool-set of autonomous groups, but they are now being used tactically by post-autonomous movements. One crucial difference between autonomous and post-autonomous approaches concerns the question of violence. While autonomous movements violently challenge the state's monopoly of violence, for the post-autonomous movements non-violent direct action is a driving factor, which follows the aim of a widened spectrum of mobilization.

In August 2009, more than 200 artists occupied Gängeviertel in a mixture of cultural festival and occupation. Somewhat surprisingly, they found that they were not evicted. The Gängeviertel is a former working-class neighbourhood in central Hamburg, which had been vacant for quite a while, and the complex of red brick buildings somewhat contradicts the surrounding high-rise modernist buildings of steel and concrete. Only four months after the occupation, the Gängeviertel was legalized and became a vibrant hub for a mixture of artists, cultural producers and small businesses as well as autonomous activists. This was the result of constant campaigns by the activists to gain support from the public. The city spent EUR 2.8 million to buy the whole building complex from the developer. Another EUR 20 million was invested in renovations and subsidies for social housing, artist studios, workshops and other cultural uses. Nina Fraeser (2016: 326) marks this as the emergence of a new squatting strategy in which the success of an occupation depends on its 'performative character' (Mayer 2012a) or, more critically, a 'marketing competence' (Eckhorst 2010). But this also became the starting point for a number of other protest actions and pamphlets.

The 'Not in our name manifesto' was presented to the public in Gängeviertel in 2009. As a collaborative work of numerous artists and cultural producers, it countered the marketization of subcultural production and producers for city branding purposes. Confronted with an uncertainty of status due to financial reasons and an immense influx of tourists in Gängeviertel,[3] the concept paper and campaign 'Komm in die Gänge' (Join the Gang) addressing the future of the project was launched by the activists in April 2010. The paper aimed at self-clarification of the autonomous status and the self-management of the building complex through the foundation of a cooperative to stabilize the collaborative project. The project was closely tied to the Hamburg Recht auf Stadt-Netzwerk and the struggles against privatization, luxury development, gentrification, displacement and the commodification of public spaces. This can be seen as an offensive to counter the transformation of the Gängeviertel into a tourist attraction and a city marketing tool (Fraeser 2016: 329). As pointed out by city developer Rolf Kellner, beyond being an experimental space for different kinds of collaborative housing and ways of working, the Gängeviertel has also become a meeting point for new co-housing initiatives elsewhere in the city (Gård 2013).

Besides rather traditional formats, other examples of non-violent direct actions make up the post-autonomous toolset of political actions around housing struggles in Hamburg. Other post-autonomous protest forms in Hamburg include various actions around the Esso Houses, for example a neighbourhood assembly, postcard action and a performance in front of the housing company in Munich.[4] Beyond this, a transdisciplinary planning office PlanBude was set up in 2014, right at the construction site in St. Pauli. It successfully integrated architecture, urbanism, social work, music and cultural studies, with the aim of co-designing a new grassroots-derived concept for affordable and self-managed housing for the Esso Houses. Such projects link the idea of self-organized and autonomous co-housing with the idea of social housing, as well as exploring new options for a long-lasting, political, large-scale collaborative housing movement. Such ambitious but feasible concepts put the needs of the residents at the centre. Long-term affordability, self-management and community building emphasize the use value (rather than the exchange value) and are conceptualized to balance social, economic and ecological sustainability.

Barcelona: an epicentre of hybrid autonomy

In Barcelona, as in other Spanish cities, neoliberal urbanism is virulent – and the effects as well as the responses highly noticeable. A manifest response is the occupation of housing. Such movements are heterogeneous, but as in the case of Hamburg, it is useful initially to distinguish some broad characteristics. Here, we can follow the tentative classification of three squatter identities in post-Francoist metropolitan Barcelona suggested by Debelle et al. (2018). While overlapping and blurring with broader urban and housing movements in contemporary Barcelona, these three identities represent a historical development.

First, and in a sense foundational in the history of squatting in Barcelona, is the *okupa* movement, which developed during the 1980s, taking inspiration from squatters' movements elsewhere in Europe (Cattaneo and Tudela 2014). Barcelona, like other Spanish cities, had during the rapid urbanization of the 1960s and 1970s experienced numerous cases in which migrants from the countryside occupied empty buildings. In contrast, as signalled by the deliberately unconventional spelling of *ocupa* (occupy), *okupa* emerged as a distinctly political and countercultural movement.[5] This movement was (and is) autonomous in the fundamentally anti-state sense, and its occupations often aimed at establishing social centres. Notably, and in advance of the broader urban mobilization over the past decade, squatters collaborated with neighbourhood movements concerned about real-estate speculation and gentrification. Although trying to avoid squatter stereotypes propagated by the media, the squatted social centre of Can Masdeu is a well-known outcrop of the *okupa* squatter movement in Barcelona, which is moving towards post-autonomous identity, while Can Vies in the Sants neighbourhood is an example of 'classic' *okupa*.

Second, occupation of housing has over the past decade experienced a significant revival in the form of broader housing movements in Spain. In Barcelona, this was represented by movements such as V de Vivienda (H for Housing) and, since February 2009, particularly by the Plataforma de Afectados por la Hipoteca (PAH, Platform for People Affected by Mortgages) (Colau and Alemany 2012). The PAH and its housing struggles are by now relatively well researched (e.g. Di Feliciantonio 2017; García-Lamarca 2017; Martínez 2019). For our purpose it is sufficient to note that for movements like the PAH and the neighbourhood assemblies that formed after the 15M, occupations are one of several tactics in the immediate defence of the housing-precarious and the longer-term struggles for a more just and affordable housing system. Like *okupa*, these movements occupy properties for the establishment of social centres. El Banc Expropiat (The Expropriated Bank), located in a vacant banking office in the Gràcia neighbourhood that was occupied in 2011, is in this respect a landmark. And to underline the crucial role of banks in the housing crisis (see Chapter 4), over a dozen banking offices have since been occupied (Debelle et al. 2018). But occupations have also come to include unsold or foreclosed housing units and buildings from banks. For the PAH, through its Obra Social (Social Work), this 'recuperation' of vacant properties from banks is a first step towards negotiating a social rent for the occupiers and as a means to pressure for legislative reforms. In mainstream media and public perception, these are often represented as (relatively) 'good' occupations as opposed to the 'bad' squats of a loosely specified *okupa* movement (Dee and Debelle 2015; Martínez 2019). Tactically, politically and personally, there are convergences between the occupations of the housing movements and the squatting of the *okupa*. But there are also some fundamental differences. For while housing movements like the PAH may engage in civil disobedience, the aim is legalization and legislative reforms. *Okupa*, on the other hand, was and is fundamentally opposed to any relations with the state, and this has sometimes led to frictions inside the movement, for example when Espai Social Magdalenes sought negotiation and legalisation. The PAH thus epitomizes post-autonomous initiatives, as it engages in reformist-institutional struggles rather than outright revolutionary-autonomous ones (Martínez 2016). This became very clear when the spokesperson of the PAH in 2015 became mayor of Barcelona for the governing minority of Barcelona en Comú (Barcelona in Common), a political platform (rather than 'party') that developed from the 15M and housing movements in Barcelona.

Third, Debelle et al. (2018) argue that a less clearly definable strand of activism has emerged, which uses occupations as an instrument to achieve more specific ends than the wider housing movements. Like the housing movements, however, these activists typically operate in the sphere of post-autonomous initiatives. When we next turn to the issue of alternative housing initiatives, we will see examples of this and other squatter identities or relations.

Relations to the state

As in the case of Hamburg, and already hinted at by the centrality of legality and illegality in the outline of squatter identities, relations with the state are crucial when it comes to the question of squatting, urban activism and alternative housing initiatives in the Barcelona area. Here, the state is in the first place the local state, the municipality, but issues often extend to the Catalan regional government (Generalitat de Catalunya) and the Spanish state. Unlike squatting and various forms of urban and housing activism, co-housing and kindred housing initiatives are an emerging phenomenon in the Barcelona area (see also Chapter 4). Nevertheless, there are by now initiatives at various stages of completion from which to draw examples.

In the first case – the ongoing attempt to establish a co-housing project in Barcelona's Vallcarca neighbourhood (Assemblea de Vallcarca 2016; see also Chapter 4) – the relations to squatting are mainly contextual. The project group from the neighbourhood assembly has from the outset opted for a legal course – to obtain a long-term lease on a plot of municipally owned land for a housing cooperative (for more on this model for alternative housing initiatives in Barcelona, see Chapter 4). In fact, the group has used its non-squatter identity instrumentally. As an activist ironically puts it: 'We are not squatters, we are nice people who can talk with the municipality' (Vallcarca interview 2017). Nevertheless, the activist hastens to add a telling 'but' to suggest that the municipality knows that relations easily can turn confrontational: 'we are going to negotiate with you, we are going to have a good relationship', the activist mimics a negotiation with the municipality: 'But remember that we are also fighting for all the neighbourhood.' In significant parts, this relates to the fact that neighbourhood assemblies, like that of Vallcarca, often have close links to squatters and potentially militant housing and neighbourhood activism. Although indirectly, the project also refers to squatting in other ways. Vallcarca is scarred by an abandoned road expansion project, which for a period left many houses vacant. Before they were demolished, some of these houses were squatted by people in need of housing. To mark this, one criterion in the group's selection of a plot for the project was that the plot had a history of squatting, and the neighbourhood assembly has more generally adopted support for housing-squatters as one of its three main initiatives on housing (the co-housing project being another) (Vallcarca interview 2017).

In the second case, the La Borda project in the La Bordeta neighbourhood, squatting – or, rather, the threat of squatting – plays a clearer if still indirect role in relations with the local state. The alternative housing project itself has from the outset been legal; in fact, the La Borda model of a non-speculative housing cooperative on leased municipally owned land is a key inspiration for Barcelona Municipality's current co-housing policy (see Chapter 4). But squatting in its post-autonomous form is lurking in the origins of the La Borda project. La Borda is located in Can Batlló, a former industrial estate the municipality planned to use for high-end housing and a park. This clashed with demands by activists in and beyond the La Bordeta neighbourhood, who wanted the vacant site for self-managed activities. As the municipality kept postponing its plans, neighbourhood activists and social organizations in the platform 'Recuperem Can Batlló: Can Batlló és per el barri' (Reclaiming Can Batlló: Can Batlló is for the neighbourhood) threatened to occupy the area. Eventually, the municipality and the campaign reached a compromise that allowed neighbourhood activists to take over and use part of the area (Eizaguirre and Parés 2019). One of the self-managed initiatives of the resulting Platform Can Batlló is what eventually became the La Borda project.

Finally, in the case of the 6 Claus (6 Keys) initiative, squatting comes to the fore. Located in the La Floresta neighbourhood of the Municipality of Sant Cugat, which effectively has become an affluent suburb of Barcelona, 6 Claus in 2015 seemed set to become an alternative housing project in a retrofitted former squat. But because of unclarities relating to the ownership of land, the project has (as we write) been on hold since June 2016 (6 Claus 2016). For our purpose, however, 6 Claus provides a good illustration of an attempt to form an alternative housing project based on squatting.[6]

La Floresta has a history of squatting, partly because a strong social network in the neighbourhood encourages young people to find ways to stay, and partly because the neighbourhood historically has had many vacant or even 'forgotten' houses, which were inviting targets for squatting. One of these buildings was a group of terraced houses that originally served as housing for teachers, Les Casetes dels Mestres (The Teachers' Houses). The building had been the object of squatting since 2005, but in June 2014, the group that became 6 Claus availed themselves of an opportunity the municipality – inadvertently – provided them with: the concept of *masoveria urbana*. This concept draws on the historically rural notion of *masoveria* (roughly translated as sharecropping), which transferred to the contemporary city entails that the owner of a property allows a tenant to use the property, for example in return for maintenance. This is 'a very good concept,' a key 6 Claus activist suggests, not least in a country that is currently 'a building cemetery' – that is, full of vacant buildings. But the activist also proposes that in the Catalan conservative bastion of Sant Cugat, the concept was mainly a 'gimmick' in the 2010 municipal election campaign. Nonetheless, for the activists, who for some years had repeatedly squatted and been evicted from Les Casetes dels Mestres, the notion was a gift. The 6 Claus activist relates their line of reasoning like this:

> The owner of the houses was the municipality; the municipality had this dead project [of *masoveria urbana*] for three years. It was like, what the hell, things just connect! Okay, let's openly say: 'Hey, municipality, if you have this project and you have this house, why don't you give an example?'

By re-squatting the building and at the same time applying to the municipality for *masoveria urbana*, in 2014 the 6 Claus activists started a long and difficult process of negotiations with the municipality. But with Sostre Cívic, an organization promoting cooperative projects in and around Barcelona, as an intermediary and eventually partner in the solution, the activists and the municipality in 2015 reached a deal in which the activists (through Sostre Cívic) would form what is in effect a housing cooperative with the right to use the property for 75 years (i.e. similar to the model applied in Barcelona Municipality, see Chapter 4).

The case of 6 Claus is thus a very clear example of a post-autonomous initiative, as the activists used squatting as an instrument to eventually reach a legal agreement with the local state for an alternative housing project. However, this strategy was not shared by all the activists. One group that had done much of the hard work in squatting Les Casetes dels Mestres could not accept legalization. Opposing this more traditional *okupa* position was another group, dominated by people from La Floresta, who wanted to negotiate and reach a compromise with the municipality. Eventually, after bitter internal conflicts, the 'hardliners' left for other squats.

Horizontal organizing

Although rarely directly related to squatting, but often to urban activism, the alternative housing initiatives and projects we have investigated in Barcelona are all committed to direct democracy and horizontal organizing. This is hardly surprising, as many of those engaged in these initiatives and projects are also active in the wider post-autonomous political landscape of Barcelona, which emphasizes horizontality and direct democracy through assemblies. 15M and the PAH are prominent if by no means singular examples of this (García-Lamarca 2017; Martínez 2016). But for the alternative housing initiatives and projects, this tends to feed into post-identitarian positions; that is, positions that go beyond an enclosed group and particularistic thematic. Emerging from the broader Platform Can Batlló and the neighbourhood assembly respectively, this could be said to be innate to both the La Borda and the Vallcarca projects. In addition, La Borda is integrated in the wider social and solidarity economy movement of Barcelona (Fernàndez and Miró 2016). But the 6 Claus project also seeks to go beyond its immediate identity. One of the key activists describes this as an inside and an outside 'circle of community': 'We want to connect this house with La Floresta, with this neighbourhood; we don't want to be an island' (6 Claus interview 2015).

It should be noted, however, that co-housing ideas are spreading beyond the environment of overtly political activists, for example through the organization coHousing Barcelona and the consultancy cohousing_LAB (see Chapter 4). While these actors are certainly activists in the sense of promoting alternative forms of housing and living, they are not in the same way linked to radical politics. In a sense, these actors are promoting forms of co-housing that are closer to those found in Denmark and Sweden, for example. Other merits untold, it remains to be seen if such projects will apply direct democracy and engage in horizontalism.

Direct action

Although the concrete examples are few, we have already seen that direct action plays a part in the establishment of some alternative housing initiatives in the Barcelona area. The threat of direct action was important in opening the Can Batlló area, and if only indirectly, this helped to put the La Borda co-housing project on track. In the case of 6 Claus and the squatting of Les Casetes dels Mestres, however, direct action was a key element.

As early as 2005, people who wanted to stay in the La Floresta neighbourhood had squatted flats in Les Casetes dels Mestres as they became vacant when teachers retired. This combination of legal residents as well as illegal occupants was difficult for the municipality and the police to handle. But eventually, around 2010, the last teachers retired and the whole building was squatted – and the squatters promptly evicted. This started a cycle of squatting and eviction. As narrated by one of the key activists, the squatters approached the municipality when it (notionally) adopted the concept of *masoveria urbana* (6 Claus interview 2015). But they did not get a reply. Therefore, as the activist put it, the squatters opted for the PAH strategy: 'we squat, then we negotiate.' More specifically, having ensured that their action would get favourable media coverage, in June 2014 the group re-squatted Les Casetes dels Mestres the day before the municipal council's monthly 'open door' meeting at which the squatters presented their demands. This, the activist points out, did not allow the municipality time to evict the squatters and gave them a platform to communicate that they were not 'rich kids' playing around, but people struggling for basic necessities. Moreover, the strategy made it possible for the squatters to communicate the non-violent nature of their direct action. In the summary of the activist, the message was:

> If somebody starts with violence, it will not be us, because we are not violent people; we prefer to go for the talking, not for violence. So, please, we trust that you as a responsible municipality will not send the police before talks.

In the assessment of the activist, this strategy forced the municipality into a process of negotiation that eventually resulted in a favourable agreement for 6

Claus – although not, as we have seen, for those demanding a hard line of continued illegality. As already noted, the project is currently (spring 2019) in a limbo, which the activists blame on Sant Cugat municipality (6 Claus 2016). And as the agreement between 6 Claus and the municipality is conditional on the project being started within five years, the municipality could eventually turn out to be the 'winner'.

Conclusions: the dialectics of the politics of co-housing

In this chapter we have examined the interrelations between urban activism and co-housing in Hamburg and Barcelona, where squatting often plays a direct or indirect role in the politics of co-housing. It has become clear to us that the politics of co-housing is shaped dialectically by two main forces.

On the one hand, and partly as a reaction to the crisis of neoliberal urbanism, we find grassroot movements of various sorts striving for co-housing and related alternative housing forms. Co-housing provides a collaborative alternative, which potentially and sometimes actively challenges the commodification, financialization and precarization of housing. It offers opportunities for appropriation, self-management and empowerment of the residents. The politics of co-housing aim for inclusive solidarity, self-help and mutual support. This contrasts with the deficiencies of neoliberal urbanism, expressed in soaring property prices and rising rents, commodification, displacement and gentrification, precarization of work and housing, and atomization and isolation of people as 'human capital' in constant competition. Although historically rooted in the autonomous squatting movement, current co-housing projects in Hamburg can be considered part of the post-autonomous wave of urban social movements. In Barcelona, most co-housing and alternative housing initiatives are similarly rooted in post-autonomous movements, but the autonomous heritage is much more alive and such housing initiatives are mostly close to radical urban activist movements. Besides the evident links between urban activism, squatting and co-housing in Hamburg and Barcelona – regarding relations to the state, the horizontality of organizing and the direct action approach – the idea of collaboration in co-housing can in its manifold ways be radical.

On the other hand, local governments have in several cities, including Hamburg and Barcelona, adopted, adapted or co-opted co-housing as political instruments. In terms of realizing a more just city, this can serve progressive ends. But co-housing policies are highly susceptible to being co-opted as a more or less deliberate way of governing radical and 'uncomfortable' activists, as a means to impose order on neighbourhoods and the city as a whole, or be instrumentalized in essentially neoliberal policies of entrepreneurialism and post-welfare state responsibilization. This shows the capacity of co-housing to be integrated in the logics of neoliberal urbanism following the lines of growth first, entrepreneurial forms of governance, privatizations and polarizations (see also Kuhn 2014).

In many emerging or existing co-housing communities in Hamburg and Barcelona, we see elements of post-autonomous political identities, which are historically rooted in radical urban social movements of the 1970s and 1980s, but do not necessarily identify with the autonomous political identity of these movements. Instead, these post-autonomous co-housing activists are hybrid collaborators in many processes and in the framing of their demands for a more socially just and long-term affordable city – in other words, a sustainable city for all. For most, this involves some form of compromise or cooperation with the (local) state. We suggest, however, that autonomous squatting movements remain crucial for the politics of co-housing in Hamburg and Barcelona. These movements keep open counter-state spaces and discourses, which can help to challenge co-optation and instrumentalization of the essentially reformist struggles that characterize most co-housing projects.

Referenced interviews

6 Claus interview, La Floresta, 22 November 2015.

6 Claus interview, Barcelona, 20 March 2017.

Hafenstraße interview, Hamburg, 20 October 2015.

Hamburg Recht auf Stadt-Netzwerk (RAS) interview, Hamburg, 20 October 2015.

Vallcarca interview, Barcelona, 24 March 2017.

Notes

1 See the introduction of this book for a distinction between collaborative housing and co-housing.

2 Affordable and sustainable community-led collaborative housing was one of the central anchor points for an international conference organized by the Hamburg Recht auf Stadt-Netzwerk and the Bundeskoordination Internationalismus (BUKO) in June 2011. Activists from different cities, countries and world regions discussed potentials and constraints of the slogan 'right to the city', analysed structural and political contexts, and exchanged practical experiences and strategies. A number of thematic papers have been published in the aftermath of the event (RAS 2011).

3 Within the first six months after the occupation more than 30,000 people visited the Gängeviertel (Komm in die Gänge 2010: 4).

4 It was in 2014 when parts of St. Pauli were declared a 'danger zone' (*Gefahrengebiet*) by the city – with reduced personal rights, people could be controlled and searched by the police without any specific reason. A person was filmed with a toilet brush in their belt during one of those checks. This picture went viral, and as a result, many residents carried toilet brushes with them in the streets – as a sign of resistance and solidarity.

5 Similar plays on conventional orthography were adopted by other squatter movements of the 1980s, e.g. the phonetic *BZ* – rather than *besæt* (occupy) – used by Danish squatters. Orthography can be a political marker. A subtle example is a pioneering study of housing occupations in Catalonia, which strikes a balance between the radical 'o*k*upación' and the conventional 'o*c*upación' by using 'o*ck*-upation' in the title (Obra Social Barcelona 2018).

6 The following is mainly based on interviews with 6 Claus activists (22 November 2015 and 20 March 2017). Covering the period June 2014 to January 2016, a rough timeline and various press material and information can be found on 6 Claus (no date).

References

6 Claus (2016) 'Clau Mestre'. https://projecte6claus.wordpress.com (8 March 2019).

6 Claus (no date) 'Recull de premsa'. https://projecte6claus.wordpress.com/recull-de-premsa (11 March 2019).

Amantine (2012) *Die Häuser denen, die drin wohnen!* Münster: Unrast Verlag.

Assemblea de Vallcarca (2016) *Cooperativa d'Habitatge Vallcarca*. Barcelona: Assemblea de Vallcarca.

Birke, P. (2016) 'Right to the City – and Beyond: The Topographies of Urban Social Movements in Hamburg', in M. Mayer, C. Thörn and H. Thörn (eds) *Urban Uprisings: Challenging Neoliberal Urbanism in Europe*, pp. 203–232. New York: Palgrave Macmillan.

Birke, P. and Henninger, M. (2012) 'Krisen und Proteste: Eine Annäherung an ihre jüngste Geschichte', in P. Birke and M. Henninger (eds) *Krisen Proteste. Beiträge aus Sozial. Geschichte online*, pp. 7–38. Berlin/Hamburg: Assoziation A.

Boeing, N. (2011) 'Recht auf Stadt – mehr als eine griffige Parole?', in *Transmitter 6/2011*. Hamburg: Freies Sender Kombinat.

Cattaneo, C. and Tudela, E. (2014) '¡El Carrer es Nostre! The autonomous movement in Barcelona, 1980–2012', in B. v. d. Steen, A. Katzeff and L. v. Hoogenhuijze (eds) *The City is Ours: Squatting and Autonomous Movements in Europe from the 1970s to the Present*, pp. 95–129. Oakland: PM Press.

Colau, A. and Alemany, A. (2012) *Mortgaged Lives: From the Housing Bubble to the Right to Housing*. Los Angeles: Journal of Aesthetics & Protest Press.

Debelle, G., Cattaneo, C., González, R., Barranco, O. and Llobet, M. (2018) 'Squatting cycles in Barcelona: identities, repression and the controversy of institutionalisation', in M. A. Martínez López (ed.) *The Urban Politics of Squatters' Movements*, pp. 51–73. New York: Palgrave Macmillan.

Dee, E. T. C. and Debelle, G. (2015) 'Examining mainstream media discourses on the squatters' movements in Barcelona and London', *Interface*, vol. 7, no. 1, pp. 117–143.

Di Feliciantonio, C. (2017) 'Social movements and alternative housing models: practicing the "politics of possibilities" in Spain', *Housing, Theory and Society*, vol. 34, no. 1, pp. 38–56.

Eckhorst, K. (2010) 'Besetzer mit Marketingkompetenz', *Jungle World*, 15. http://jungle-world.com/artikel/2010/15/40731.html (18 May 2019).

Eizaguirre, S. and Parés, M. (2019) 'Communities making social change from below. Social innovation and democratic leadership in two disenfranchised neighbourhoods in Barcelona', *Urban Research & Practice*, vol. 12, no. 2, pp. 173–191.

Europe Squatting Collective (2012) *Squatting in Europe*. Wivenhoe: Minor Compositions.

Fernàndez, A. and Miró, I. (2016) *L'economia social i solidària a Barcelona*. Barcelona: La Ciutat Invisible and Barcelona Municipality.

Fraeser, N. (2016) 'Fantasies of Antithesis – Assessing the Gängeviertel as a Tourist Attraction', in C. Colomb and J. Novy (eds) *Protest and Resistance in the Tourist City*, pp. 320–339. London: Routledge.

García-Lamarca, M. (2017) 'From occupying plazas to recuperating housing: insurgent practices in Spain', *International Journal of Urban and Regional Research*, vol. 41, no. 1, pp. 37–53.

Gård, L. (2013) 'Cohousing Hamburg – Rolf Kellner'. https://vimeo.com/55256736 (18 May 2019).

Graeber, D. (2013) *The Democracy Project: A History, a Crisis, a Movement*. New York: Spiegel & Grau.

RAS (Hamburg Recht auf die Stadt Netzwerk) (2017) 'Programmatic Basics'. www.rechtaufstadt.net/category/english/ (18 May 2019).

RAS (Hamburg Recht auf die Stadt Netzwerk) Flyer (2018) 'Aufruf zur antirassistischen' [Parade We'll come united]. www.rechtaufstadt.net/aufruf-zur-antirassistischen-parade-well-come-united/ (18 May 2019).

Komm in die Gänge (2010) 'Konzept für das Gängeviertel'. https://das-gaengeviertel.info/gaengeviertel/zukunftskonzept.html (18 May 2019).

Kuhn, A. (2014) *Vom Häuserkampf zur neoliberalen Stadt: Besetzungsbewegungen in Berlin und Barcelona*. Münster: Westfälisches Dampfboot.

Marchart, O. (2013) *Die Prekarisierungsgesellschaft: Prekäre Proteste. Politik Und Ökonomie im Zeichen der Prekarisierung*. Bielefeld: transcript.

Martínez, M. A. (2016) 'Between autonomy and hybridity: urban struggles within the 15M movement in Spain', in M. Mayer, C. Thörn and H. Thörn (eds) *Urban Uprisings: Challenging Neoliberal Urbanism in Europe*, pp. 253–281. London: Palgrave Macmillan.

Martínez, M. A. (2019) 'Bitter wins or a long-distance race? Social and political outcomes of the Spanish housing movement', *Housing Studies*, vol. 34, no. 10, pp. 1588–1611.

Martínez, M. A. (2019) 'Good and bad squatters? Challenging narratives and advancing anti-capitalist views of squatting in Western European cities', *Culture Unbound*, vol. 11, no. 1, pp. 165–189.

Mason, P. (2015) *PostCapitalism: A Guide to Our Future*. London: Allen Lane.

Mayer, M. (2012a) 'Beyond austerity urbanism and creative city politics', *City*, vol. 16, no. 5, pp. 558–559.

Mayer, M. (2012b) 'The right to the city in urban social movements', in N. Brenner, P. Marcuse and M. Mayer (eds) *Cities for People, not for Profit. Critical Urban Theory and the Right to the City*, pp. 63–85. London/New York: Routledge.

Mayer, M. (2016): 'Neoliberal Urbanism and Uprisings Across Europe', in Mayer, M., Thörn, C. and Thörn, H. (2016) *Urban Uprisings: Challenging Neoliberal Urbanism in Europe*, pp. 57–92. London: Palgrave Macmillan.

Mayer, M., Thörn, C. and Thörn, H. (2016) *Urban Uprisings: Challenging Neoliberal Urbanism in Europe*. London: Palgrave Macmillan.

Obra Social Barcelona (2018) *¡La vivienda para quien la habita! Informe sobre ockupación de vivienda vacía en Catalunya*. Barcelona: Obra Social Barcelona.

Peck, J. and Tickell, A. (2002) 'Neoliberalizing Space', *Antipode*, vol. 34, no. 3, pp. 380–404.

Peck, J., Theodore, N. and Brenner, N. (2009) 'Neoliberal Urbanism: Models, Moments, Mutations', *SAIS Review of International Affairs*, vol. 29, no. 1, 49–66.

RAS (Hamburg Recht auf die Stadt Netzwerk) (2011) 'Recht auf Stadt. Der Kongress'. http://kongress.rechtaufstadt.net (18 May 2019).

Rinn, M. (2016) *Konflikte um die Stadt für alle: Das Machtfeld der Stadtentwicklungspolitik in Hamburg*. Münster: Westfälisches Dampfboot.

Rote Flora (2001) *Positionspapier der Roten Flora zum Vertragsangebot*. http://m.roteflora.de/html/standpunkte_6.htm (29 April 2019)

Scheller, D. (2019) *Demokratisierung der Postdemokratie. Städtische soziale Bewegungen in Berlin und New York City*. Bielefeld: transcript.

Scheller, D. and Vollmer, L. (2018) 'Postautonome und postidentitäre Mieter_-innenproteste in Berlin und New York City', in R. Bürgin and A. Schoch (eds) *Urban Resistance / Städtische Widerstände*, pp. 139–158. Bern: Peter Lang.

Sitrin, M. (2006) *Everyday Revolutions. Horizontalism and Autonomy in Argentina*. London: Zed Press.

Sitrin, M. and Azzellini, D. (2014) *They Can't Represent Us! Reinventing Democracy from Greece to Occupy*. London/New York: Verso.

Swyngedouw, E. (2007) 'Impossible "sustainability" and the postpolitical condition', in R. Krueger and D. Gibbs (eds) *The Sustainable Development Paradox: Urban Political Economy in the United States and Europe*, pp. 13–40. New York: Guilford Press.

Twickel, C. (2011) *Gentrifidingsbums oder eine Stadt für alle*. 3. Aufl. Nautilus-Flugschrift. Hamburg: Ed. Nautilus.

7 Doing family in co-housing communities

Cathrin Wasshede

Introduction

In many co-housing communities, people have visions and dreams about 'another life', and alternative ways of organizing everyday life, family relationships and other close relationships that centre on sharing, collaboration and collectivity (see for example Sangregorio 2010; Jarvis 2011a; 2011b; 2019; Sargisson 2012; Grip et al. 2014; Sandstedt and Westin 2015; Lang et al. 2018). Co-housing in Sweden, and to some extent in Denmark, is almost always connected with the practice of shared meals and collaborative work (Vestbro 2010; Bendixen et al. 1997). Eating and working together are deemed an effective way of realizing social sustainability goals in the form of social cohesion and reducing loneliness in an individualized society, in which the traditional status of the family has declined to some extent (Sandstedt and Westin 2015; Schröder and Scheller 2017; see also Introduction). 'Children should have a hundred parents' (Graae 1967) was the caption of a newspaper article that inspired many Danish co-housing projects (see also Graae 1969). Further, when the association Bo i Gemenskap (Live in Community) was founded in Sweden in the 1970s, one of their main ambitions was similarly co-operation in the activities of everyday life, and to give children a better environment (Bo i Gemenskap n.d.). Co-housing is sometimes seen as being especially suited to low-income families and people living in single households with children (Lang et al. 2018; see also Jarvis 2011a). In their book about children and sustainable urban development, Christensen et al. (2018) call for more empirical research about children's everyday life and state that children have an ambivalent position in discourses on sustainable urban policy and planning:

> being at once superficially visible (in, for example, architects' drawings, vision documents, planning briefs and housing developers' brochures), yet still profoundly marginalized via the design and regulation of public and 'community' spaces.
>
> (Christensen et al. 2018: 4)

People in co-housing communities deal with at least two ideas of what a family is: one favouring the intimacy and privacy of the nuclear family and the other favouring the wider 'family', i.e. the community in the house – and sometimes even the neighbourhood and/or the city. Frictions between these two ideas often lead to ambivalences that are handled with the help of what is described here as emotional boundary work. The different ways of doing family that emerge among people living in co-housing communities shed light on the relationship between the individual and the collective, a recurring theme in research about co-housing (Lang et al. 2018).

The aim of this chapter is to analyse emotional boundary work relating to family in co-housing communities, with a special focus on shared meals, children's relationships and care, in order to discuss different aspects of the relationship between the individual and the collective. The chapter is based on empirical material from visits to six co-housing communities in Sweden and two in Denmark (further elaborated upon below). In almost all these communities, the kitchen and practices of cooking and eating together are said to be cornerstones for the sense of collectivity. Does cooking and eating together with a bigger group than the nuclear family in an everyday and mundane way affect definitions of and emotions surrounding family? If so, how? Further, the dream of a 'good childhood' is another cornerstone in many multi-generational co-housing communities, something which makes co-housing interesting to study in relation to definitions of family. Children in co-housing communities live with their own families, while at the same time they tend to have a sense of extended family through the social relationships in the house, and they often develop strong peer cultures with other children in the co-housing community. Meals in most co-housing communities take place in the family's own apartment and in the shared dining room, which means that children have (at least) two eating cultures, two groups to identify with and relate to – two 'hearts of the home' (Dorrer et al. 2010; Sandstedt and Westin 2015) to spend time in within the house.

Following this introduction, the theoretical perspectives used in this chapter are presented, providing a brief and selective view of earlier research on family, eating, and the boundaries between private and public in relation to co-housing communities. A short description of the method used, and the houses and interviewees, is given directly after that. This is followed by the main part of the chapter – the analysis of the empirical material, thematically structured around aspects of: eating; care and extended family relationships; children's relationships with adults in co-housing; and peer cultures and neighbourhoods. Finally, there is a discussion of the conclusions drawn from the analysis.

Theoretical perspectives and earlier research

Family and emotional boundary work

'Family' is created through a complex set of social relationships and mundane everyday practices (James et al. 2009a; Backett-Milburn et al. 2010; Morgan

2011; Ramos et al. 2017). There are many moral concepts, ideals and normative expectations of what constitutes a 'proper family' (Castrén 2017). The term moral is understood here as a way to discuss people's identities as moral beings, something that according to Andrea Doucet (2006) is a gendered process. Mothers and fathers often experience different moral responsibilities in relation to the family, which means that they feel differently about how they should act. In her research, Doucet found that mothers worry more about their children and their own role as mothers, and that they are more inclined to feel judged by others, than are fathers.

Many researchers claim that an analysis of networks of meaningful relationships is a better way to grasp 'family' than focusing only on the household (Mason and Tipper 2008; James et al. 2009; Morgan 2011; Castrén 2017). This is especially relevant when studying family practices in a co-housing context, since the family is potentially extended, and embraces more people than are included in the so-called nuclear family and the household itself. Extended family is a concept describing a chosen family, often used in studies about LGBTQ families, and may encompass biological family, household members, ex-partners, pets and friends (see for example Henriksson 1995). Even though family is so much more than (having) children, this chapter focuses especially on parenting and children in the doings of family. In their study of children and definitions of family, Mason and Tipper (2008) show how children put a lot of emphasis on care, love and support, and that shared biography and duration of the relationship matters when defining family and kinship. Bourdieu claims that fostering a 'family feeling' and a cultivation of an affective principle of cohesion are fundamental to family (Bourdieu 1996; see also Castrén 2017; Ramos et al. 2017). This emotional work is most often performed by women (Bourdieu 1996), as is the act of getting the family to eat together as a family (James et al. 2009b; Curtis et al. 2010; Morgan 2011).

In an effort to capture and understand people's emotional struggles around and at the edge of boundaries, the concept of emotional boundary work is introduced. It originates from Arlie Hochshild's (2003) concepts of emotional labour and emotion work, and the aspect added here is that of boundaries and the specific emotional work that is done in order to diminish, enlarge, overcome, create or reinstall a boundary, for example that between one's own (nuclear) family and the collectivity of the co-housing community, or between the co-housing community and the surrounding neighbourhood. Emotional boundary work is a way of navigating everyday life in a co-housing community, where people have to make a lot of micro-decisions, such as where to eat or who to invite to the dinner table. Hochshild says that the deeper the bond between people, the more emotion work it requires. Family is sometimes considered a zone free from emotional obligations and pressures, a place where one can rest, but according to Hochshild 'it quietly imposes emotional obligations of its own' (Hochshild 2003: 69). Since members of co-housing communities often cultivate strong social and emotional bonds with each other that are sometimes family-like, this concept appears particularly useful.

Family and eating together

Even if 'family' is mainly created and performed through networks of relationships, spending time under the same roof and eating together are still important aspects of doing family and creating family bonds. Some researchers argue that the idea of the 'proper meal' is essential to the idea of the 'proper family', and that individuals become connected when they eat together (James et al. 2009a; 2009b; Backett-Milburn et al. 2010; Curtis et al. 2010; Dorrer et al. 2010). In the view of Curtis et al. (2010) and James et al. (2009b), the shared family meal still retains its iconic status of what a 'proper family' does. Even if the food in itself may be important, it is subordinate to the social act of sitting around a table, eating together and actively cultivating a sense of family. As Lupton expresses it:

> It is not necessarily the food that is served at family meals that is considered important, but the ritual of sitting down to eat the meal. The 'family meal' and the 'dinner table' are potent symbols, even metonyms of the family itself.
>
> (Lupton 1996: 39, quoted in Curtis et al. 2010: 292).

Cooking and eating in co-housing communities are an important part of the organization of time in everyday life and may be seen as a kind of shared and/or distributed care.

The idea of the 'proper dinner' further involves a gendered division of labour, a heterosexual imperative, a generational hierarchy, and a class dimension. The food moralities are built on the idea of the mother cooking for her (heteronormative nuclear) family and the woman as the caregiver (Bourdieu 1996; James et al. 2009a; 2009b; Curtis 2010; Morgan 2011). From the establishment of collective houses in the 1930s onwards, co-housing has been a project that partly aims to liberate women from household work and enable them to be part of the work force. Sharing of household work, such as buying food, cooking and cleaning up after meals, has been a central aspect of the liberation of women (Caldenby 1992; Vestbro and Horelli 2012; see also Sandstedt and Westin 2015).

Further, to 'eat as a family' is often seen as a way to foster children; a 'moral crusade', in which children should learn the value of 'family' through the consumption of 'family food'. Adjusting to the family meal is seen as evidence of the child's commitment to and identification with the family (James et al. 2009b). It is a symbolic and, I would say, also material assertion of belonging to a particular culture (James et al. 2009a). It is material in the sense of food as a materia/matter that should be placed in the child's mouth, chewed, swallowed, and digested, and also in the form of other materialities, such as furniture, plates and cutlery, sound level, and the act of sitting together in a bodily disciplined way. The 'proper dinner' is also heavily connected to class distinctions. Research shows that there are differences between working-class and middle-class children's experiences of family, eating and autonomy or control (Corsaro 2005; Backett-Milburn et al. 2010; Curtis et al. 2010). In the middle-class families studied by Backett-Milburn et al. (2010), the shared family meal was seen as important and there was a high degree of parental control. This is in line with how Corsaro (2005) describes working-class children as being less controlled, having more autonomy and more free time to play informally, while middle-class children are more supervised and have more structured leisure time.

Since cooking, eating, and the dinner table in the dining room are central to the organisational structure of care and reproduction in the community, and ideas about the smaller nuclear family and the 'proper dinner' persist, a study of meals in co-housing communities can bring light to new and old conceptions of family.

Co-housing in between private and public space

Co-housing communities are interesting in yet another way, namely that they take place and are lived at the border between the private and the public (see for example Jarvis 2011b). This is especially tangible when it comes to the dinner table and the practice of eating together. Since co-housing is still a quite rare phenomenon, and since a lot of people are interested in this way that residency and family life are organized, there is a continual flow of visitors to the houses. In some co-housing communities that we have studied, there is a group specially designated to handle media, study visits and researchers. The visitors are often invited to join an everyday dinner, and if the visitors take photographs, they often picture members of the co-housing community cooking and/or eating together. This seems to be the ultimate image of life in a co-housing community. In their study of meals in the residential care of children and young people, Dorrer et al. (2010) found something similar; the dinner served as a display, a way to show the visitors the 'family-like' atmosphere that they have created in an institutionalized space.

Co-housing members in our study often claim their privacy, pointing to the fact that they have their own apartment with a fully equipped kitchen and their own door to close and lock. Still, collectivity and sharing are highly valued (cf. Jarvis 2011b; Sandstedt and Westin 2015). Helen Jarvis formulates this as 'mechanisms for greater sharing coincide with considerable protection of privacy' (Jarvis 2019: 268). This potential tension between privacy and sharing, or collectivity, is analysed in this chapter in terms of emotional boundary work. The home is taking place and being performed in different spaces; one's own small apartment and the shared spaces in the house, with a special emphasis on the kitchen and the dining room. Even if the home can never be seen as separated from larger society, and functions as a mediating link between society and the individual, it is often seen as a backstage space, a place in which people's individuality is guarded against external pressure (Hagbert 2016; see also Dorrer et al. 2010). The residents' emotional boundary work around family and home are thus interesting to study, since the co-housing community is both a private, semi-private and semi-public space (cf. Sargisson 2012).

Empirical material from Swedish and Danish co-housing communities

This chapter builds on interviews with 18 co-housing residents, where the doings of family in co-housing communities are analysed through the lenses of meals, children and care. Interviews were carried out during 2015–2018 with people living in six different co-housing communities in Sweden; two in Gothenburg, two in Stockholm, one in Malmö and one in Lund; and in two communities in Denmark; one in a suburb of Copenhagen and one small collective in Christiania, Copenhagen. The co-housing communities vary in sizes, between 35 and 63 apartments, as well as in tenure forms; associations subletting from municipal housing companies, cooperative rentals and private ownership. All but one cook and serve several shared meals a week. Two of the communities invite people from the neighbourhood to take part in cooking and eating together on a regular basis. The interviewees are listed below, using pseudonyms for surnames and the specific co-housing community they belong to in order to preserve anonymity:

IP1: Fredrik, The Boat, Lund, single father with two children.
IP2: Louise, The Boat, Lund, single mother with two children.
IP3: Jessica, The Flower, Gothenburg, single mother with one child.
IP4: Rut, The Arch, Stockholm, woman with grown-up children.
IP5: Karen, The Garden, suburb of Copenhagen, woman with two children.
IP6: Lis, The Garden, suburb of Copenhagen, woman with two children.
IP7: Anna, The Square, Stockholm, woman with two children.
IP8: Ida, The Window, Malmö, single mother with one child.
IP9: Per, The Flower, Gothenburg, single man with no children.
IP10: Liselotte, The Flower, Gothenburg, single woman with two grown-up children.
IP11: Martin, The Plant, Gothenburg, single father with two children.
IP12: Hugo, The Flower, Gothenburg, single man with grown-up children.
IP13: Moa, The Flower, Gothenburg, 12-year-old girl.
IP14: Kerstin, The Plant, Gothenburg, single woman with grown-up children.
IP15: Sigrid, The Flower, Gothenburg, 18-year-old girl.
IP16: Bente, The Utopia, Copenhagen, woman with two children.
IP17: Axel, The Plant, Gothenburg, single man part-time parenting two children.

IP18: Sara, The Square, Stockholm, single mother with one child not living in the co-housing community but participating in cooking and eating there.

Challenging the nuclear family?

Eating as a family

The kitchen is often talked about as 'the heart of the house'. Almost all co-housing communities we have visited have a big shared kitchen and a big dining room, which is in line with earlier research (Vestbro 2010; Sargisson 2012; Sandstedt and Westin 2015; Lang et al. 2018). The dining room is often used for other activities as well, such as playing games, chatting with each other, meetings etc. The residents cook together on a rolling schedule and they eat together two to six days a week. Following previous research, this can be seen as a benefit especially for women and single parents (Caldenby 1992; Jarvis 2011b). One single father, Fredrik, in The Boat in Lund, says:

> It is very positive to live like this, when you are single with children and work, it is a hell of a service to get cooked meals every second day. And the social closeness as well. When you work nine to five it is nice to just come home and sit at a set table and leave the dishes to someone else.
>
> (Fredrik, The Boat, Lund)

One single mother in the same house however complains about her children not wanting to eat in the shared dining room:

> Finally, I am freed from cooking and then I have to cook something else for them anyway, because they don't like the food! I was pissed off.
>
> (Louise, The Boat, Lund)

Another single parent, Jessica, living in The Flower in Gothenburg, says that it is easier to get her child to eat when they join the larger group:

> It is a social benefit to sit there and eat with all the others, not sitting at home by ourselves and nagging about finishing the food … it is a group […] it is no fun to interrupt the playing and go home to eat.
>
> (Jessica, The Flower, Gothenburg)

The emotional boundary work in these three quotes deals with the two different dinner tables; the table in the private home and the shared table in the community's dining room. For Fredrik it is a nice solution to the time pressure he experiences in his everyday life, and he seems to move easily between the two different dinner tables. Louise, on the other hand, is struggling with her anger, stemming from being forced back to her private kitchen by her children. Even though it is not explicitly stated in the interview, it is easy to imagine how she tries to convince her children to accept the meals served in the shared dining room. In the last quote, the shared meals are described as a solution to avoid bad feelings, i.e. *nagging*, around the private dinner table. In all three quotes, the shared dinner is mostly talked about as a benefit, a service, or a mutual exchange, while the social bonds and social cohesion it might bring are only mentioned by Fredrik. However, in other quotes, the emotional and social aspects are in focus.

The cooking duty and the social bonds that practical work may result in are mentioned in earlier research (cf. Sargisson 2012; Sandstedt and Westin 2015; Jarvis 2019), as well as in the interviews in this study. One interviewee with grown-up children explains this with the help of a metaphor, a choir:

> Cooking together is like having a choir. It is a really important activity and there are lots of resources in every person that really can strengthen each other, in the cooking teams. […] One could say that every tune is very important. […] To cook can be very creative and we inspire each other a bit, with different dishes. […] In a choir you have to focus on cooperation, otherwise it doesn't sound good at all. And it is the same in a cooking team.
>
> (Rut, The Arch, Stockholm)

Further, the practice of cooking and eating together seems to force the residents in the house to handle irritations and resolve conflicts. Several interviewees talk about the 'impossibility' of cooking and eating together when there are unresolved conflicts. One example of this:

> We just can't walk around being mad at each other or talk bullshit about each other, because we are supposed to sit down together and cook and eat together and socialize.
>
> (Louise, The Boat, Lund)

Another interviewee, Bente in Copenhagen, says that the kitchen is the heart of the house, and the space that holds the house together socially, since they have to be able to eat and have a nice time while doing so. Jarvis (2019) emphasizes that it takes considerable effort to work together and that the intentionality that characterizes co-housing communities carries high demands for cooperation and dialogic conversations, especially when conflicts arise. Further, Jarvis argues that intentional sharing and collaboration are more about ethical social relationships and micro-social interactions than about individual mutual exchange. This corresponds with some of the findings in this study regarding family practices in co-housing communities, where relationships and emotions are central.

Since people in co-housing communities do 'family activities' together with more than just the few people that normally make up the nuclear family, they find themselves dealing with 'family emotions' even outside the nuclear family. They are involved in emotional boundary work that aims to create a kind of extended family feeling and a strong sense of social cohesion (cf. Bourdieu 1996; Fonseca et al. 2018). Having 'a nice time' at the dinner table could also be seen as an important part of creating the 'proper dinner'. One way to handle irritations and potential conflicts is to conceptualize and treat the neighbours as relatives:

> It is like an extended family, but … you know how it is with relatives, some of them you barely know, and some of them you meet once a year and some never, and some of them you don't like, but you are still relatives. It is a bit like that here. There are some [people] that you feel like: 'oh, my god, here they come with their stupid opinions again' at a meeting. But afterwards you eat together and talk about something. Just like with family; you have to spend time together. You have to get along with each other. […] You live together a bit more than as neighbours and a bit less than as nuclear family.
>
> (Louise, The Boat, Lund)

Solving conflicts and having a nice meal together may be seen as a way to create not only a 'proper dinner', but also 'proper feelings' towards the community and the individuals living there, in the ongoing work of organizing everyday family life. Axel, who lives in The Plant in Gothenburg, expresses this in a similar way to Louise above, and adds that it also has to do with having a shared history with the other people in the house, and with the house as such, just like you have with your relatives (cf. Mason and Tipper 2008). It is not only the individuals who live in the house or the family that you identify with and create a history with, you also identify with the bigger entity – the community/house as such. Axel even talks about how thinking about moving to another co-housing community makes him feel like he would be cheating on the house. Here, the house is talked about in terms usually used in discourses about committed loving relationships. Solidarity, loyalty and identification are thus ingredients of the emotional boundary work done by Axel, as is potential guilt.

In The Garden, a co-housing community, situated in a suburb of Copenhagen, the two mothers Lis and Karen talk about the importance of the act of cooking and eating together and how people that leave the community often stop participating in this some time before they leave:

> I think there is a pattern for many of the persons that have left; first they withdraw from eating together … [and when] they [even] stop bringing food home it is a sign that they are on their way out. For us, the collective cooking is vital.
>
> (Karen, The Garden, suburb of Copenhagen)

Withdrawing from the cooking and eating is understood here as a step towards withdrawing oneself from the community, something which again positions shared meals as being at the very heart of the emotional boundary work of the community – of belonging together (cf. Dorrer et al. 2010). Withdrawal from the collective meals implies new boundaries around the 'we', and potentially a return to, or a strengthening of, the smaller (nuclear) family. Further, it is described as a signal of changing boundaries and relationships with the other members of the community.

Although most interviewees are positive about the act of cooking and eating together, there are also problems connected with it. For some of the interviewees, the sound level in the shared dining room is too high. This has sometimes led them to take food to eat in their own apartments. For others, often parents with small children, the shared dining room is deemed 'too social', and is said to distract the children's attention from the food:

> The children didn't eat anything. Exciting things were happening all the time and we tried … we found a corner where we could sit so that our children could not see all the others. We were ruthless; no one else was allowed to sit with us, it was a case of: 'now we are eating and *afterwards* you can play'.
>
> (Anna, The Square, Stockholm)

The emotional boundary work here implies an interesting way of combining collectivity and privacy. The family insists on eating in the shared dining room, but makes efforts to create a boundary between their own family and the community. Anna says that the collective meal is sometimes a tempting 'trap' for her, since she needs the chat with other adults and enjoys not having to cook for her own family. However, she talks about it in an ambivalent way and says that her mother sometimes accuses her of spending too little time with 'her own family'. She says that maybe her mother is right, maybe she should spend more time with her own children:

> Over the last year we have been talking about having a special day every week when we *always* eat at home, to get a little more of that … just us. That thing people have at the dinner table, that's the time when you can sit and talk, *everyone* together.
>
> (Anna, The Square, Stockholm)

Here, it is the interviewee's mother who imposes emotional boundary work on the interviewee. In this quote *everyone* means everyone in the nuclear family, not in the co-housing community. When she eats in the collective dining room, Anna sometimes ends up sitting together with another family, talking to their children – about everyday things:

> For the last two days I have been sitting and eating together with another family, since my children have been away on activities. […] I know them

> very well. So, I sit there with the father, the children and their aunt. […] And it is exactly the same [a family conversation about mundane things].
>
> (Anna, The Square, Stockholm)

In her emotional boundary work, she struggles with an urge to protect her own small nuclear family from the bigger 'family', i.e. the collective, and we see the two parallel ideas about family: the first is about the privacy, intimacy and exclusivity of the nuclear family; the other about sharing with and belonging to the larger 'family', the collective (cf. Castrén 2017). Interestingly, Anna finds herself ending up with another 'nuclear family' when she eats in the collective dining room, which makes her think about her own family and arouses feelings of ambivalence: is she spending enough time with her own children, her own family? The same theme is covered in an interview with a single mother, Ida, living in The Window in Malmö, who says that she would rather have three days of eating collectively, than four, so that she can spend more time with her son:

> I want three [meals a week], because we don't have time to see each other. We come directly from kindergarten and we go to the dining room … and afterwards he wants to stay and play and we don't get to our apartment until seven, maybe half past seven. […] And then it's time to go to bed. So, we have no time *at all* to spend with each other.
>
> (Ida, The Window, Malmö)

In this quote, which is a simple but good example of emotional boundary work, it is implicitly said that it would not be easy for her to just stay at home and eat with her son when a collective dinner is served in the communal dining room. She is navigating in relation to, or on the boundary between, the small family and the bigger community, reflecting upon her 'duties' and wishes as a parent and member of the community, as well as on her son's needs.

One mother, Jessica, who lives in The Flower in Gothenburg, talks about how her own family space can be disturbed by the openness of the co-housing community. She says that there was a time when there was almost always 'another child' eating at their private kitchen table or when her own child ate at other people's homes. This annoyed her a little. She thought that the eating situation was too disruptive and that her child did not eat enough or too late. So she put an end to it and declared that she and her child should eat alone – sometimes even on shared meal days. Instead, they went down and fetched the food and took it back to the apartment. Jessica reinstated a version of the 'nuclear family', in that, while being a single mother, she indeed protected the small private family. In the empirical material collected in this study, it is the mothers in particular who talk about the need to strengthen and/or protect the smaller family unit – none of the fathers interviewed discuss this. The mothers describe in quite a detailed way the emotions and thoughts that arise when boundaries between the nuclear family and the co-housing community become visible. They are doing emotional boundary work and are trying to navigate between two different ideas of family and/or community.

Care for each other and extending family relationships

Many interviewees talk about how they help each other with daily activities such as fetching the children from school or kindergarten. This is helpful, especially if you are a single parent. As Per, a single man with no children who lives in The Flower in Gothenburg, says in an interview: 'In a co-housing community it is really easy for a single parent to live and still have a normal life.' Another example of this is when a parent cannot get home on time due to job obligations or other things and can quite easily ask a neighbour to go downstairs to check that the child is fine, or to help the child get something to eat. The close relationships and the fact that the children usually know the other adults in the house very well, makes it easier to ask for help. In the following example, this is even extended to children who have lived in the co-housing community before and are only visiting the house:

> The children were guests in the house [visiting a particular family], and they stayed in an apartment by themselves. So, their mum called from Halmstad the other night: 'well, NN says he has got a headache, can you go and check in on him?' So, I walked over with an aspirin.
>
> (Louise, The Boat, Lund)

Care is, in this quote, described as being distributed in a way that implies that at least some of the people living in the house actually see each other as people they can count on, to involve in the more intimate family sphere.

This way of organising the everyday care of children is not, however, just a question of getting and giving help. It is also a way of giving your children something different, something you can't give them yourself. Ida, in The Window in Malmö, says that she really wanted her child to have an extended family, a bigger family than just the two of them. Close relationships with other children of the same age are desirable for her, as well as relationships with other adults:

> I want him to connect with other adults who can be his guides in the same way as I am. Of course, I am the one who has the main responsibility and should be most important to him, but I want him to experience other norms and values than mine. And other boundaries as well.
>
> (Ida, The Window, Malmö)

This is an example of how a person, with the help of the co-housing community, strives to expand the networks of meaningful relationships for her child and herself, and how this is a way to create a new form of family.

Several of the interviewees talk about how the children experience new and different things due to the fact that they spend time with other families. They take turns taking each other's children to the forest, the public swimming pool or the garden, for example. In some families the children are allowed to play computer games a lot and in others not at all. They learn to cope with different family cultures and rules. The interviewees' stories about what they want and (often) get for their children are examples of how intentional sharing and collaboration are ways to create ethical social relationships that demand a lot of emotional work (Jarvis 2019). For one interviewee, Jessica, in The Flower in Gothenburg, it took some time to adjust to the culture in the community. At first she felt reluctant to let her daughter move freely around the house and eat at another family's dinner table:

> In a family it becomes very self-contained, when you live with just your own child, or with a child and father and so on … you spend almost all the time with each other after work and you eat and go to bed. But here … she is at somebody else's place, suddenly she is at a friend's apartment, and I just feel: OK, what am I supposed to do now? […] [the daughter asks]: 'Can I eat at their place? Can I go with them to their place?' Wait, is it OK, how are you supposed [to know], is she allowed?
>
> (Jessica, The Flower, Gothenburg).

Besides emotional boundary work, this is a learning process. Shifting perspective from the nuclear family to the community requires new ways of handling everyday activities, thoughts and emotions. The reluctance towards new eating activities can also be seen as a sign of the strong position of the 'proper dinner' in relation to the 'proper family' and what is seen as the new 'proper community'. Where, when and how is a dinner supposed to take place to be 'proper'? It is a question of identification with and commitment to the (right) family (cf. James et al. 2009b).

There are however other stories, in which care is not shared and/or distributed. Some parents talk about how disappointed they were when their neighbours in the house would not help out at all with the children. Kerstin and Axel, both living in The Plant in Gothenburg, had high expectations about a helpful, sharing environment and realized that it was sometimes hard to ask for help, that people were not interested in helping each other and that everyone, more or less, had to care for themselves and their own children. A mother of two children, Anna, in The Square in Stockholm, says that she thinks all parents ought to take part in caring for the children in the house when they are in shared spaces such as the play room. She says that she often sits there helping the children to resolve conflicts, for example, and she complains about parents who do not sit in the play room, and is morally quite upset about this:

> […] while others just remain sitting happily at the dinner table and kind of notice that there is chaos going on out there, and they see their

> own child. And they think it is really good that another adult is taking care of it.
>
> (Anna, The Square, Stockholm)

Sharing everyday life activities, such as cooking, eating, cleaning and repairing things, sometimes seems to nurture a feeling of 'family'. There are several stories about long-term relationships that have started in the co-housing community (cf. Mason and Tipper 2008). Liselotte, who lives in The Flower in Gothenburg, talks about her relationships and those of her son, who is now an adult:

> They were the same age, we had like four guys in the house who were the same age. And at least three of them still stick together, and it is really wonderful, as I am like an aunt to his childhood friends, and I'm not close to my birth family; I have no contact with my parents any longer. It is almost as if you start a family here in the house. The mothers of these children are still my best friends. [...] We have become a social family so to speak. [...] They are like my sisters, they mean a lot to me. [...] In a way, it is like an extended family; the things a family does, we did together.
>
> (Liselotte, The Flower, Gothenburg)

She also incorporates her neighbours' relatives in her and her children's lives:

> Well, people have big families that come here every now and then [...] that I have met over the years. And they indirectly become part of the collective. [...] In a strange way, we become like one huge family since we know more about each other.
>
> (Liselotte, The Flower, Gothenburg)

This quote illustrates a family-centred worldview, but, importantly, combined with an extension of the traditional nuclear family, and it emphasizes strong social bonds in doing 'family activities' together. It also shows that the duration of the relationship is a central aspect (cf. Mason and Tipper 2008). Liselotte and her friends in the house have consciously cultivated a sense of cohesion and intense, lasting, emotional family bonds (cf. Bourdieu 1996; Jarvis 2019), for example through spending holidays and celebrating birthdays together, even involving each other in their own network of relatives. Another person, Martin, a single father living in The Plant in Gothenburg, says that living in a co-housing community entails an evening out of the differences between biological family and other forms of family kinship. He values the fact that other adults can tell him when he is doing something wrong as a parent, since it makes him feel less alone in his parenthood. However, other people talk about the emotional tensions that this closeness and interfering in each other's parenting may cause:

> That's one of the biggest taboos we have. […] At the same time, one has to struggle with that … other adults telling your children what to do … I want them to.
>
> (Ida, The Window, Malmö)

The idea behind this is to create an environment in which parents can take care of and foster each other's children in a mundane way, i.e. a redistribution of care and the creation of an extended family. Louise, in The Boat in Lund, describes how this can lead to teenagers revolting against the whole house:

> The teens can be a quite tough period because they perceive the *whole* house as a mother that they have to defy. […] One of them had a sign on the apartment door saying 'I hate co-housing' or 'I hate all of you'.
>
> (Louise, The Boat, Lund)

The house has become the parent/family and the teenager is doing emotional boundary work in relation to the whole community. The small nuclear family has been opened up and extended. From the adult perspective, this opening up towards greater collectivity is a help; Louise mentions how the whole house knows about and is engaged when a teenager in the house has problems, for example with drugs.

Children's own relationships with adults in the house

In some interviews, children are described as relationship builders:

> Sometimes, having children is a little like having a dog … [laughs] a small ice-breaker that helps the adults. […] Once when I was in the shower, he [the three-year-old son] had walked to a neighbour because he wanted her help letting a cat out [from our apartment]. […] He has no problem using other people here.
>
> (Ida, The Window, Malmö)

Martin, in The Plant in Gothenburg, describes a similar situation:

> Recently, when my parents were here visiting me, they told me that a child had come to my apartment asking for something. It was a three-year-old child so they didn't understand what he/she said.
>
> (Martin, The Plant, Gothenburg)

Here, children are described as active agents in creating caring relationships and it is also possible to see them as creators of emotional boundary work; it is easy to imagine that the parents have to deal with emotional work when faced with situations like this where children cross borders. However, this is mostly described in positive terms in the interviews, as a safety net for the children. Some of the interviewees, both adults and children, say that the children can knock on any door in the house and be sure to meet someone who will help them or socialize with them; others however say that it is mostly other parents who help out. Maybe we can talk about the co-housing community as not only semi-public (cf. Sargisson 2012), but also semi-private (cf. Jarvis 2011b). The private homes seem to be quite open, at least when it comes to letting children in – and out.

Another example of children creating meaningful relationships beyond the nuclear family is described by a man, Hugo, in The Flower in Gothenburg. He is 77 years old and has lived in the house for many years, at first with his two children and now by himself. He has an 'open door' and many of the children in the house visit him on a regular basis. They know that they can come to him for a chat, candy or just hang around. One of the children, who visits him quite often, lives with his mother, a single parent, and Hugo speculates on whether he is a 'father figure' to the boy. Further, Hugo says that he is an unofficial caretaker in the house, and that people often come to him if a drain is blocked, and 'sometimes they come if their soul is blocked too' (Hugo, The Flower, Gothenburg). Fredrik, in The Boat in Lund, says something similar when describing his son's relationships with other adults in the house:

> Now he is very happy about it [living here], he has established contacts here with adults that could be seen as extra grandparents. [...] And it's good, because he doesn't have so much contact with his real grandmother and grandfather.
>
> (Fredrik, The Boat, Lund)

Here, again, we see how interviewees use 'family words' to explain the relationships in the house and how this is part of the emotional boundary work. The word *as* in '*as* extra grandparents' is interesting since it indicates that they are not 'real' grandparents – who later in the quote are explicitly mentioned as *real* – a fact that underlines the distinction between the biological family and the chosen extended family that is made possible in the co-housing community.

Peer cultures and neighbourhoods

As discussed above, children are seen as a group that has a lot to gain from the social networks in co-housing communities. This is especially emphasized in relation to children's relationships with each other and the peer cultures they cultivate (see for example Corsaro 2005). Several of the interviewees talk about the children's relationships with each other in terms of siblings: 'They run around and feel at home with everyone and they feel almost like extra siblings,' as one mother says (Louise, The Boat, Lund). Eighteen-year-old Sigrid, living in The Flower in Gothenburg, talks about how two younger children in the house have adopted her as their big sister and that they come to her almost every day. Even though the interviewees use 'family words' when describing children's relationships with other children in the house, they qualify them with words such as '*like* siblings', '*almost like* a sibling relationship', and '*some kind of extra* siblings'. Some interviewees even reject the word sibling and instead describe the relationships children have with each other in terms of cousins:

> It's not like siblings, absolutely not. Even if they see each other every day and have slept over at each other's places and stuff like that … but it is not … I think it's like the way they know their cousins anyway; you have played together and you know each other. […] It is some sort of cousin-thing.
>
> (Anna, The Square, Stockholm)

Even though Anna is using 'family/relative words', she adds distance to the nature of the relationship by using cousins instead of siblings. Implicit in this quote is that the children in the co-housing community are not to be seen as part of the same (nuclear) family. The distinction between one's own (nuclear) family and the collectivity in the community is reinforced, and the smaller nuclear family is seen as something different. A 12-year-old girl, Moa, in The Flower in Gothenburg, describes her relationship to a boy in the house in the following way:

> The guy I told you about, he lives upstairs.… It is like my second home, because … we grew up together. Totally. We spent time with each other every day when we were younger, and every day now. We have daily contact and so on.
>
> (Moa, The Flower, Gothenburg)

Here, it is the shared biography and the length of their relationship that is emphasized when defining their relationship and the way his home acts as a second home for her (Mason and Tipper 2008).

In both The Flower and The Plant in Gothenburg, some of the interviewees describe the children as a big flock that spends a lot of time together. They play outside, and inside in special play rooms and on the stairs; they hang around at each other's homes and sometimes they eat at each other's place on days when there is no shared meal. It is talked about as a 'unique' 'child context' and as something the children create on their own: 'They have created it by themselves' (Kerstin, The Plant, Gothenburg); 'they choose each other freely everyday' (Jessica, The Flower, Gothenburg). According to Jessica it also works as a kind of safety net for the parents:

> When she [the daughter] was four years old, I didn't dare to let her go outside, but eventually I saw that they stuck together.
>
> (Jessica, The Flower, Gothenburg)

The 12-year-old girl Moa talks about how she and the other children in her co-housing community have a kind of 'club'; they often play together outside and they take care of each other. She says that because she is one of the oldest, she never leaves the yard before the small children are gathered up and go inside. Moa could not see herself leaving them alone outside:

> If everyone wants to go home and a small child stays outside, then someone has to stay and make that child go home. Because you don't leave someone there. It is very important to us.
>
> (Moa, The Flower, Gothenburg)

The care, love, and support that Mason and Tipper (2008) argue is important for children when defining family is accomplished here by the children themselves. They care for each other. Age is relevant here, in the sense that the older children take responsibility for looking after the younger ones. Moa's care for the children in her house can also be understood in terms of emotional boundary work. She navigates emotionally between different boundaries; that between her own family and the bigger community of the house, and that between the children in the co-housing community and the neighbourhood.

Moa also describes the ease with which the children in the co-housing community find each other:

> You get home from school and you see kids playing: 'well, I will join in, I just have to drop off my school bag first.' So, you see kids outside, you meet in the café, 'yes, after dinner we will play outside'. It's easy to make friends here. It's sort of best friends forever. And when we are bored, we go down there [to the play room] and find something to do. And when you have finished playing and are breathless, you lay down and check your smartphones and just talk. We have our funny moments. You burst into laughter down there. Because you have a lot of fun and stuff. That's a good part; that you laugh a lot in this house.
>
> (Moa, The Flower, Gothenburg)

The play room is an extra home space for the children in the house, where they meet, play, talk and have fun together. This extra room is also a potential place to be without too much adult supervision (cf. Corsaro 2005). Of course, the location and architecture of play rooms have a big influence on the potential for privacy. If the room is located close to other shared spaces in the house, and if the room has walls made of glass, there is less privacy for the children. But in the quote above Moa describes it as a free zone where the children meet each other and have lots of fun. Her description is very vivid and emotional, and it makes the experiences of play, physical activity and emotions essential for their relationships and commitment to one another.

Having such a tight group of peers, as described above, means there is a risk of creating strong boundaries with the surroundings, with people who do not belong to the group. In the interviews, people talk about the neighbourhoods in very varied ways. There seems to be an ambition to be inclusive and welcome children from the neighbourhood, expressed by both adults and children in the co-housing communities, which is in line with the idea of sharing (cf. Sargisson 2012; Sandstedt and Westin 2015). Moa says:

> We often play hide-and-seek. If they ask if they can join, we absolutely say yes. We welcome everybody.
>
> (Moa, The Flower, Gothenburg)

Still, there is a distinction here between 'we' and 'them'. 'The others' are sometimes described as 'not nice' and Moa talks about a situation when 'the others' had caused trouble by teasing the younger children and how she and some other children from the co-housing community had scared them off.[1] Further, 'the others' are seen as living isolated lives. One example of this is: 'In other houses they don't talk with each other. They barely know who is living in their house' (Moa, The Flower, Gothenburg). In this quote we can see how the girl is committed to and identifies with her co-housing community and that the sense of collectivity that she feels there is experienced as something good – and unique. She explores the boundary emotionally, with her effort to embrace 'the others' and include them in the 'we', but there is no doubt that they are distinctly different from each other, at least when it comes to social life inside the houses. The emotional boundary work that she is doing is thus (re)creating the boundaries between the co-housing community and the surroundings. This is similar to the phenomenon in nuclear families, where clear boundaries are drawn with other families, and a feeling of something unique and self-providing is nourished. Children in co-housing communities have (at least) two 'families' to commit to and identify with; their own family and the collective in the co-housing community, and hence two boundaries that demand emotional work.

Discussion and conclusion

People in co-housing communities tend to relate to a large number of people when creating/doing family. They often have strong and extensive social networks with the other people in the house, and several of our interviewees use 'family words' like aunt, sister, siblings, extra grandparents etcetera when describing their own and their children's relationships with the other people living in the house. The meals – planning, buying, cooking, eating and cleaning up after dinner – in co-housing communities have at least three functions: 1) the ease in everyday life you experience when the dinner is already bought, prepared and cooked by other people; 2) the social bonds that may be created through working together on chores such as cooking and cleaning up; and 3) the opportunity to socialize while eating together with other people. This sharing of everyday activities seems to cultivate family-like relationships. The residents have to do a form of emotional work that is often connected with the larger family beyond the nuclear family – one example is how they say that they have to resolve conflicts, since they eat together and want to have a nice time with each other while doing so. Care may be a significant aspect here. Who cares for whom? Is there such a thing as collective care, and if so, what is it and where are the boundaries between it and private care? There are ambivalences around how open and involved in the community the interviewees are, want to be or feel that they should be. Some interviewees reject collective activities and family words and instead try to protect the smaller nuclear family, for example by eating in their own apartment, 'as a family'. In some cases, the choice to eat in one's own apartment is just a way to solve practical problems, such as a high sound level or other distractions in the shared dining room.

Co-housing communities are discussed as semi-public (see for example Sargisson 2012), but they are also semi-private (see Jarvis 2011b). The most private space, one's own apartment and family, is opened up, socially and emotionally, and often visually. They have to deal with other parents' ways of raising children and they often know a lot about each other. To sum up, many of the interviewed people living in co-housing communities definitely open up the nuclear family and extend networks that are 'family-like'. At the same time, some interviewees also talk about a need to strengthen the smaller nuclear family in relation to the community. It is here that they do a lot of emotional boundary work. They struggle with where to draw the line between the privacy of the small family and the collectivity of the community in the house. Sometimes these efforts come from external pressure, most visible in the example of the woman whose mother thought she spent too little time with her own family. However, pressure also arises in more subtle and invisible ways, such as in the form of norms, ideals and discourses about the 'proper family', which consists of heterosexual parents and their children eating a healthy and enjoyable dinner together. The meal in co-housing communities is interesting to study in relation to this. It could be seen as a symbol of the very boundary between two different ideals about how to live your everyday life in a socially sustainable way. It is a question of belonging or not; to which group do I belong? Which group do I cook for and eat with? Which group can I rely on? And what happens to other groups when I identify with one group? Opening up to shared meals, and collectivity in general, also means losing a little of the control you might have over your child(ren), and over the actual food you and your children eat. You let other people in. You let other people decide what meals to serve. You let your children learn about other ways of living, other norms, other 'family cultures'. Further, there is a high degree of social control in co-housing communities, which is described by most interviewees as a very positive thing, but by some as a negative and painful thing, especially if you are involved in a conflict in the house. Further research is needed about the conflicts, and conflict management, in co-housing.

In the interviews, children are talked about as social agents creating their own social relationships, often going beyond their own families' networks. In a co-housing community this may be more intense, more expected, than in 'ordinary housing', since the children's space is extended and they are part of bigger social networks than their nuclear family. They actually live together with more people. They share *home spaces* with other people – children and adults of different ages. Home spaces are spaces in a building that are usually seen as belonging to the home, such as living room, kitchen, dining room, play room. The children's sense of home is probably extended, when compared with children living in a traditional apartment with their own family. Even though there may be clear boundaries between one's own apartment and the shared spaces, there is a possibility that the children do not experience those boundaries as strongly as the adults do and have less preconceived ideas of what a family is and what a home is – or should be. If so, children in co-housing communities have an 'extended sense of home'. It is not just about extended family. It is also about the extended home.

Interesting questions arise regarding what a 'proper family' and a 'proper meal' is to people living in co-housing communities. They relate to and (re) construct at least two contradictory discourses around both family and meals. The first is about an alternative life; a family that opens up, shares and extends beyond the limits of the traditional nuclear family, among other things through collective cooking and eating. The other is about keeping the smaller family intact, protecting it against too many impressions and potential disorder, for example in relation to the collective eating situation. Some interviewees find themselves spending less time with their own children than they want to. So, even if they spend time with a child in the house, it is not the same as spending time with their own child. Of course, this is not surprising. It is just a good example of the emotional boundary work that people living in co-housing communities possibly have to do often. Further, it is related to ideas about the 'proper house'. What does a 'proper co-housing community' look like? And; what is a 'proper home'? For many, but not all members of co-housing communities it is a political and ethical question, about creating new forms of everyday life that contribute to a more sustainable and inclusive society, now and in the future. The tensions between privacy and collectivity that take place in co-housing communities mirror the same tensions in society in a more general sense; and a question that has kept sociologists and other researchers occupied for many years: How are societies possible?

Note

1 The particular context of the co-housing community can be noted as contributing to a sense of 'we' and 'them'. The house is located in a quite poor and racialized area on the outskirts of Gothenburg, whereas the co-housing residents are relatively 'white' and with a higher average income than in the surrounding neighbourhood.

References

Backett-Milburn, K., Wills, W., Roberts, M. and Lawton, J. (2010) 'Food and family practices: teenagers, eating and domestic life in differing socio-economic circumstances', *Children's Geographies*, vol. 8 no. 3, pp. 303–314.

Bendixen, E. L., Dilling, L., Holten, C., Illeris, S., Illeris, G., Bjerre, B. and Rasmussen, B. (1997) *Sættedammen i 25 år.* Hillerød: Sættedammen.

Bo i Gemenskap (n.d.) www.boigemenskap.se/boigemenskap.se/Forskargruppen_Bo_i_Gemenskap.html (18 April 2019).

Bourdieu, P. (1996) 'On the family as a realized category', *Theory, Culture & Society*, vol. 13 no. 3, pp. 19–26.

Caldenby, C. (1992) *Vad är ett kollektivhus?* Gothenburg: Chalmers University of Technology.

Castrén, A-M. (2017) 'Rebuilding the family: Continuity and change in family membership and relationship closeness in post-separation situations', in V. Cesnuitytė, D. Lück and E. D. Widmer (eds) *Family Continuity and Change: Contemporary European Perspectives*, pp. 165–186. London: Palgrave Macmillan.

Christensen, P., Hadfield-Hill, S., Horton, J. and Kratfl, P. (2018) *Children Living in Sustainable Built Environments: New Urbanism, New Citizens.* London, New York: Routledge.

Corsaro, W. A. (2005) *The Sociology of Childhood* (2nd edn). London, California, New Delhi: Sage Publications.

Curtis, P., James, A. and Ellis, K. (2010) 'Children's snacking, children's food, food moralities and family life', *Children's Geographies*, vol. 8 no. 3, pp. 291–302.

Dorrer, N., McIntosh I., Punch, S. and Emond, R. (2010) 'Children and food practices in residential care: ambivalence in the "institutional" home', *Children's Geographies*, vol. 8 no. 3, pp. 247–259.

Doucet, A. (2006) *Do Men Mother? Fathering, Care, and Domestic Responsibility.* Toronto: University of Toronto Press.

Fonseca, X., Lukosch, S. and Brazier, F. (2018) 'Social cohesion revisited: A new definition and how to characterize it', *Innovation: The European Journal of Social Science Research*. doi:10.1080/13511610.2018.1497480

Graae, B. (1967) 'Børn skal have hundrede forældre', *Politiken*, Copenhagen, 9 April 1967, pp. 49–50.

Graae, B. (1969) 'Den store familje', *Politiken*, Copenhagen, 16 March 1969, pp. 49–50.

Grip, E., Kärnekull, K. and Sillén, I. (2014) *Gemenskap och samarbete i kollektivhus och bogemenskap.* Stockholm: Migra förlag.

Hagbert, P. (2016) *A Sustainable Home? Reconceptualizing Home in a Low-Impact Society.* Gothenburg: Department of Architecture, Chalmers University of Technology.

Henriksson, B. (1995) *Risk Factor Love. Homosexuality, Sexual Interaction and HIV Prevention*. Gothenburg: University of Gothenburg, Department for Social Work.

Hochshild, A. (2003) *The Managed Heart. Commercialization of Human Feeling.* Berkeley, Los Angeles, London: University of California Press.

James, A., Kjørholt, A. T. and Tingstad, V. (2009a) 'Introduction: Children, food and identity in everyday life', in A. James, A. T. Kjørholt and V. Tingstad (eds) *Children, Food and Identity in Everyday Life*, pp. 1–12. London: Palgrave Macmillan.

James, A., Kjørholt, A. T. and Tingstad, V. (2009b) 'Negotiating family, negotiating food: Children as family participants?', in A. James, A.T. Kjørholt and V. Tingstad (eds) *Children, Food and Identity in Everyday Life*, pp. 35–51. London: Palgrave Macmillan.

Jarvis, H. (2011a) 'Alternative visions of home and family life in Christiania: Lessons for the mainstream', in H. Thörn, C. Wasshede and T. Nilson (eds) *Space for Urban Alternatives? Christiania 1971–2011*, pp. 156–180. Stockholm: Gidlunds förlag.

Jarvis, H. (2011b) 'Saving space, sharing time: Integrated infrastructures of daily life in cohousing', *Environment and Planning A*, vol. 43 no. 3, pp. 560–577.

Jarvis, H. (2019) 'Sharing, togetherness and intentional degrowth', *Progress in Human Geography*, vol. 43 no. 2, pp. 256–275.

Lang, R., Carriou, C. and Czischke, D. (2018) 'Collaborative housing research (1990–2017): A Systematic review and thematic analysis of the field', *Housing, Theory and Society*, doi:10.1080/14036096.2018.1536077

Mason, J. and Tipper, B. (2008) 'Being related: How children define and create kinship', *Childhood*, vol. 15 no. 4, pp. 441–460.

Morgan, D. H. G. (2011) 'Locating "family practices"', *Sociological Research Online*, vol. 16 no. 4, p. 14.

Norton, A. and de Haan, A. (2013) *Social Cohesion: Theoretical Debates and Practical Applications with Respect to Jobs*, World Development Report. www.researchgate.net/publication/313040601_Social_Cohesion_Theoretical_Debates_and_Practical_Applications_with_Respect_to_Jobs (8 April 2019).

Ramos, V., Gouveia, R. and Wall, K. (2017) 'Coresidence as a mechanism of relational proximity: The Impact of household trajectories on the diversification of personal networks', in V. Cesnuitytė, D. Lück and E. D. Widmer (eds) *Family Continuity and Change: Contemporary European Perspectives*, pp. 187–210. London: Palgrave Macmillan.

Sandstedt, E. and Westin, S. (2015) 'Beyond Gemeinschaft and Gesellschaft. Cohousing life in contemporary Sweden', *Housing, Theory and Society*, vol. 32, no. 2, pp. 131–150.

Sangregorio, I-L. (2010) 'Collaborative housing from a woman's perspective', in D. U. Vestbro (ed.) *Living Together: Cohousing Ideas and Realities Around the World*, pp. 114–123. Stockholm: Report Division of Urban and Regional Studies in collaboration with Kollektivhus NU.

Sargisson, L. (2012) 'Second-wave cohousing: a modern Utopia?', *Utopian Studies*, vol. 23, pp. 28–56.

Schröder, S. and Scheller, D. (2017) 'Abgesicherte Fürsorge und fürsorgliche Absicherung in Gemeinschaft', *sub\urban, Zeitschrift für Kritische Stadtforschung*, vol. 5 no 3, pp. 23–42.

Vestbro, D. U. (2010) (ed.) *Living Together: Cohousing Ideas and Realities Around the World: Proceedings from the International Collaborative Housing Conference in Stockholm 5–9 May 2010*. Stockholm: Report Division of Urban and Regional Studies in collaboration with Kollektivhus NU.

Vestbro, D. U. and Horelli, L. (2012) 'Design for gender equality: the history of cohousing ideas and realities', *Built Environment*, vol. 38 no 3, pp. 315–335.

8 The social logic of space

Community and detachment

Claes Caldenby, Pernilla Hagbert and Cathrin Wasshede

Introduction

A history of co-housing visions and practices that spans over more than a century shows that this phenomenon has offered an answer to various problems over time: from a shortage of domestic staff, which made it difficult for middle-class women to work in the 1930s, to the loss of a sense of community, felt by many as a widespread social problem in the 1960s and 1970s, and the rise of ecological concerns over recent decades (see also Introduction). The problems described are thus ideological, economic, social, as well as ecological.

In addition to understanding the political, organizational and everyday life aspects of co-housing, as outlined in previous chapters, this chapter explores the materialization of co-housing practices into built form. In her research on co-housing Sargisson (2014) found that its utopian dimension is a product of the architects just as much as of the co-housing residents themselves. We argue here that co-housing as an answer is also a spatial organization that has shown some important characteristics over a long period of time, and that there is what could be called a 'social logic of space' in co-housing. The spatiality of social sustainability is, according to Shirazi and Keivani (2019), an under-researched field, and in this chapter we add to this research by discussing the spatiality of co-housing and its relation to questions of urban social sustainability, with particular respect to the dialectic of community and detachment.

Moss Kanter, in a study of American housing collectives, emphasized two processes in the creation of 'commitment' to a collective: on the one hand, 'detaching' from the surrounding context and, on the other hand, 'attaching' to the collective (Moss Kanter 1972, quoted by Goodwin and Taylor 1982). This dual process of internal attachment or community and external detachment could also be interpreted spatially. The early predecessors of co-housing, from Owen's 'parallelograms' and Fourier's 'phalanstères' to the modernist Soviet and Swedish 'collective houses' of the 1930s (see also Chapter 2), were all complex internal spatial organizations detached from the urban context and placed as 'buildings in the park' (*hus i park*). Co-housing projects from the 1970s onwards have in turn been described as falling into two 'models': the 'Danish' 'dense-low' (*tæt-lav*) style of a cluster of low-rise houses and the 'Swedish' more concentrated, often high-rise multi-family building (Gresleri 2015; see also Sargisson 2014; Chapters 1 and 2). The Danish model is quite widespread in the Anglo-Saxon world and it has similarities to eco-villages (Marckmann et al. 2012). While there tends to be an assumption that certain types of structures better promote social cohesion than others, it will be asked here whether these two seemingly different models of co-housing are really spatially different as far as 'internal' community and 'external' detachment are concerned.

An extreme version of how inward-oriented community and society-related detachment can manifest itself is the gated community, which seeks to physically as well as socially exclude those who are perceived as not belonging. Most co-housing projects would disavow these types of exclusionary practices, although the risk of self-segregation and the tendency for social and ethnic homogeneity in co-housing communities has been pointed out (Jakobsen and Larsen 2018; see also Chapter 2). Critical examinations of co-housing as a form of private residential community highlight the need for a more cautious interpretation, for example by problematizing an 'introverted' spatial organization (Chiodelli and Baglione 2014) and the risk that co-housing projects could function as segregated 'islands of community' (Droste 2015; Sørvoll and Bengtsson 2019).

The questions discussed in this chapter are what implications the spatial logic of co-housing may have for its social logic, and the challenges or tensions that might emerge. The chapter focuses mainly on Sweden, yet makes some historical references and comparisons to studies carried out in other countries, which, we argue, also makes it relevant to discuss the socio-spatial implications and models of co-housing addressed beyond the Swedish context.

The chapter first provides a broader theoretical base, departing from what Hillier and Hanson (1984) called 'space syntax'. Space syntax is used here not as a precise measuring technique, but rather as a heuristic tool to discuss fundamental concepts of spatial relations. The questions concerning co-housing that are raised, such as the detachment from or openness to the local context, or the logic of the internal community, circle around terms such as *transpatial* or *spatial solidarity* and *distributed* (*ringy*) or *non-distributed* (*tree-like*) structures of space. After this theoretical section, a historical perspective is presented, exploring ideals as well as built examples, where a rational social and spatial logic, rather than notions of community, can be seen to have dominated collective housing ideas of the early 1900s, mainly focusing on predecessors to co-housing in Sweden and the Soviet Union in the 1930s, known in Swedish as '*kollektivhus*'. We then look at how different waves of co-housing, from the 1970s onwards, can be understood in the analytical framework of space syntax, and in relation to the two 'models' of co-housing mentioned above. More specifically, we then also relate this to empirical insights from Swedish co-housing projects, based on interviews with residents in five co-housing communities located in Stockholm, Gothenburg, Malmö and Lund respectively. The chapter ends with a discussion of how co-housing can deal dialectically with the potentially vicious circle between 'internal' community and 'external' detachment.

An analytical framework of space syntax

In their book *The Social Logic of Space* (1984), Hillier and Hanson develop what they call a 'space syntax' – as a way of analysing spatial configurations, helping architects and planners to explore the possible social effects of their spatial designs. A key notion developed is that buildings are different from other artefacts: 'Insofar as they are purposeful, buildings are not just objects, but transformations of space through objects' (Hillier and Hanson 1984: 1). Hillier and Hanson talk in particular about the relevance of *spatial continuity* and different aspects of *solidarity*, with respect to the internal as well as external spatial organization of building complexes. Space syntax is presented not as a theory of the principles of solidarity – they leave that to anthropologists and sociologists – but as a 'more modest', spatial theory of 'encounter systems' (ibid.: 224). According to this view, building interiors can have a *transpatial solidarity*, meaning that the internal spatial relations are structurally similar, but this also relies on upholding an external boundary, which can have a 'segregating effect', to protect the interior structure. Hillier and Hanson claim that:

> The duality of inside and outside adds a new dimension to the relation between *social solidarity* and space. A solidarity will be transpatial to the extent that it develops a stronger and more homogeneous interior structuring of space and, in parallel, emphasizes the discreteness of the interior by strong control of the boundary.
>
> (Ibid.: 145)

This can be contrasted with the *spatial solidarity* of a whole settlement (e.g. an urban district or city) at a larger scale, which is based on 'contiguity' (immediate adjacency of spaces) and encounters, and thus also on less elaborate interiors and weaker boundaries (ibid.: 145). We emphasize here the similarity of the concepts of *transpatial* and *spatial solidarity* to the dialectic of internal community and external detachment of co-housing, as well as the implications for the wider solidarity that co-housing can or cannot be seen to contribute to.

Hillier and Hanson moreover argue that space has to do with ordering, control and power (ibid.: 147). This is analysed through the concepts of symmetry/asymmetry and distributedness/non-distributedness. Being friends is a symmetric relation; if I am your friend you are also my friend. Being a boss and an employee is an asymmetric relation; if I am your boss you are not my boss. The same goes for spaces. A symmetric relation, a distributed space, means that two spaces have the same relation to the exterior. An asymmetric relation, a non-distributed space, is where one space is accessed only through the other space, which means it is controlled by the other space. An interior with a high share of distributed space has a *ringiness*, you can access rooms in more ways than one, while an interior with a high share of non-distributed space has a tree-like structure (ibid.: 148).

This is further developed in terms of an *elementary building*, i.e. a building with an interior that opens directly on to the spatial continuity outside. This is typical of the tent or hut, but also the small parish church and the traditional shop as a hole-in-the-wall. In the deeper, non-distributed interior, there is an interface between the *inhabitant* and the *visitor* from outside, who enters the shallower, distributed part of the interior space. But all buildings are not elementary. Typically, public institutions such as hospitals, prisons and schools, are what Hillier and Hanson call *reversed buildings.* Buildings of this kind 'have evolved and diversified substantially in the past two centuries' (ibid.: 184).

Reflecting upon the 'industrial bureaucracies' of contemporary social systems, Hillier and Hanson argue that space today has a certain social logic that underlines the reproduction of asymmetric and non-distributed relations as inherent principles of a class society. One aspect of this is that the system wants to avoid solidarity, such as the forming of close communities, among groups at the lowest levels of society, in order to avoid revolutions against the system. The spatial solution to this is what Hillier and Hanson call 'a new urban genotype'. It comes in two principal forms: 'hard' and 'soft' (ibid.: 266). The hard form has an asymmetric and non-distributed syntax, with a strict separation of inhabitants that lowers the risk of excessive solidarity. This form corresponds to the anonymous large-scale housing units ('*unité d'habitation*') of Le Corbusier, and, maybe paradoxically, the typical Swedish co-housing unit. The soft form consists of small, fragmented units with few, non-random and highly controlled encounters. The garden cities of Ebenezer Howard can according to Hillier and Hanson be seen as a key ideological statement of the soft form, and eco-villages as well as Danish and Anglo-Saxon co-housing projects can be seen as following this syntax. Co-housing – as building complexes detached from their context – will be explained here as *reversed buildings,* or a *new urban genotype,* and the Danish and Swedish models will, following Hillier and Hanson (1984), be referred to as the *soft* and *hard* versions of this genotype.

In contrast to this, Hillier and Hanson's vision of a society 'democratically deployed in space' is based on large communities, dense local encounter spaces, and mixed social labels. It is above all 'locally and globally open, distributed, and un-hierarchical' (ibid.: 262). Co-housing is not specifically mentioned by Hillier and Hanson, but they do mention Robert Owen's factory communities and Fourier's Phalanstère (usually included as early predecessors in histories of co-housing) as forerunners of the 'new urban genotype' that they criticize. By emphasizing the too-often-neglected spatial organization of society, Hillier and Hanson may seem to be close to becoming spatial determinists, giving a simplistic negative description of the 'new urban genotype' and a correspondingly over-idyllic vision of an un-hierarchical democratic city. The point of this chapter is to critically explore this, underlining that space can have unexpected *social logics*, and discuss what implications this might have for notions of community and detachment in co-housing.

Modernist collective housing

As mentioned above, Owen's factory communities and Fourier's Phalanstère are often described as early forerunners of co-housing (Vestbro 1982; see also Introduction). They are large housing units, sometimes also working units, with a complex inner organization, set in landscapes of different kinds. A 'parallelogram', as described in Owen's vision of the ideal society in the 1820s, is typically a large building, raised on a platform, detached from the surrounding landscape. It can be understood as a *reversed building* with a *transpatial solidarity*. The parallelograms are figures of order against a more or less chaotic, or at least unimportant background. They are literally 'utopian' in the sense of belonging to 'no place' specifically.

Many of the collective housing projects of the 1920s and 1930s, built or unbuilt, that were designed by architects in the Soviet Union and Sweden, have a similar spatial structure. They are free-standing units, isolated from their surroundings, similar to what are known in Swedish as 'buildings in the park'. This is usually understood as typical of the urban planning models of modernism, but can also be found in more classical collective housing projects in the early 1900s. Furthermore, free-standing buildings in a park are also typical of nineteenth-century institutions. They are what Hillier and Hanson (1984) call the 'new urban genotype', usually of the 'hard' form.

The inner spatial structure of the modernist collective housing projects is a large, coherent and widespread unit. It often consists of a tree-like structure of long corridors from which the individual rooms or apartments are reached. In the centre, close to the entrance, is a more ring-like structure of common spaces with dining rooms and other facilities. The complex inner organization, as well as the isolated urban situation, are both typical of the 'new urban genotype'.

Just to underline that there are other, slightly different possibilities, the 'central buildings' or 'one-kitchen houses' built in several European cities in the early 1900s must be mentioned. In the co-housing tradition, they are often called 'the first collective houses' (Vestbro 1982: 50–61). The very first could be Fick's central building in Copenhagen, dating from 1905. It is an ordinary upper-middle-class house with apartments of three to five rooms. But the kitchen is replaced by a small kitchenette in the apartments, and 'food lifts' from a central kitchen to the apartments. Tenants bought food from the central kitchen, but they had no common spaces. Seven employees served the 26 apartments, a considerable reduction in the need for servants, compared to each family having their own housemaid. Actually the 'one-kitchen houses' can be seen as a solution to the growing middle-class 'servant trouble' – the difficulty of finding and affording housemaids (Caldenby and Walldén 1979: 153). In this sense they are reversed buildings with residents occupying the deeper cells – the apartments – and the employees as 'inhabitants' controlling the knowledge of household work. However, they did not search for community in their internal spatial organization, and they did not mark the boundaries to their surroundings, but rather anonymously merged into the ubiquitous late-1800s grid of perimeter blocks. Further, they did not seem to form any transpatial solidarity.

The first collective houses in the Soviet Union emerged in the mid-1920s, after the civil war and with the relative stabilization of the economy (Caldenby and Walldén 1979: 42). In 1925–1926 there was a competition in Moscow organized by Mossoviet, the Moscow city council. There was an obvious belief in the economic advantages of large-scale solutions, which also led to complex spatial organizations. The project comprised a house for some 750–800 inhabitants with apartments of different sizes for single persons and families, providing six square metres per person. There were to be no kitchens, showers or toilets in the apartments, but such facilities were shared on each floor. There should be a central dining room, also used for meetings, as well as a central laundry, library and day nursery. The winning entry, and the first co-housing project to be built, in 1929, has a palace-like structure around a large courtyard, with all the characteristics of the institution-like 'new urban genotype': a complex tree-like structure relatively isolated from its context. At the same time, it shows a transpatial solidarity similar to 'houses of transition type' (Caldenby and Walldén 1979: 63) from the same time.

The most iconic of the little more than a handful of modernist co-housing projects built in the Soviet Union is Dom Narkomfin in Moscow. It was finished in 1930 as one of a small series of experimental buildings. The client was the People's Commissariat of Finances of the Russian Soviet Republic. It is a six-storey building with galleries on every second or third floor leading to double-height maisonette apartments. At the same time, it leads to a tree-like structure with apartments arranged like twigs on the branches of the two galleries. The apartments were large for the time (60–90m^2), including a kitchenette. Beside the apartment building, connected by a covered bridge, is a glazed, cubic building with day nursery and kitchen for food to take home. There are few common social spaces. On the flat roof there is a villa for the People's commissar himself, like a bridge deck, completing the image of Dom Narkomfin as a ship. The 'mobile home' concept, with minimal sleeping cabins, similar to those on an ocean liner or overnight train, was a much-cherished model for modernist housing. Dom Narkomfin stands on pillars, pilotis, in a park, as if independent of its context, ready to sail away into the future.

A project for a 'collective house' (*kollektivhus*) in Stockholm was presented in late 1932 by a group of 'socially interested' people (Caldenby and Walldén 1979: 176; see also Chapter 2). The main argument behind it was the need to reform the 'traditional family life', basically making it possible for middle-class women to work by providing help with organizing cooking and child care. The plan was to start by building at least one of a group of three 10-storey houses in Alvik in the western outskirts of Stockholm. The open site would make it possible to add new houses to the first one. Each house should have small flats (23–35 m^2) along corridors. On the entrance side, they planned for one attached building with a day nursery and another with a restaurant and common facilities. Again, we see the institution-like building in a park, the 'new urban genotype'. Another important part of the project was to make it possible to start a 'free school' based on modern educational ideas. Economic calculations showed that at least 100 households, but preferably 200, were needed to make the day nursery and restaurant work. The calculations also showed that to afford to live in the house, a family with two children would need a yearly income almost twice that of a working family with two breadwinners. The Alvik project was never built. The site was owned by the municipality and they seemed sceptical of the whole idea.

Instead, the group was given a much smaller plot on John Ericsson street in a rather central location in an ordinary perimeter block (see also Chapter 2). The eight-storey house had 57 apartments, most of them with one or two rooms. Apartment windows looked towards the south and the sea, and away from the neighbours on the opposite side of the street, thus showing a certain degree of detachment. The ground floor had a day nursery and a restaurant, which was open to the public and also served the inhabitants, with food delivered through 'food lifts' directly into the apartments. The building was finished in 1935. In an exhibition the year before, it was presented as 'individual culture through collective technology' (Caldenby and Walldén 1979: 199). Community between the inhabitants was not an issue. Gradually the services became too expensive for the inhabitants. The day nursery was taken over by the municipality and the restaurant became an ordinary public restaurant.

From the late 1930s to the mid-1970s, almost 20 collective houses were built in Sweden (Vestbro 1982). They were all of the 'hard' form described above – multi-family houses with services on the ground floor and often in a relatively free, suburban location. The problem to be solved by the collective houses in the 1920s in the Soviet Union, and from the 1930s to the 1970s in Sweden, was rationalization of household work, enabling women to work. Neither community nor solidarity were an issue. Living in a collective house was a practical solution, for those who could afford it, but not very much of an ideological statement. At the same time, the spatial logic of the 'new urban genotype' was the potential community created within the collective house, and the potential detachment offered from the surroundings.

The first wave of co-housing: living in community

The new generation of collective houses initiated in Sweden in the 1980s, which can be said to constitute part of the first post-war wave of co-housing, had a different understanding of the problem to be solved. Community now became much more important, in a society understood in many ways to cause alienation. As a product of the alternative social movements of the 1970s, choosing to live in co-housing also became more of an ideological statement than it had been for earlier generations. Whether this also had spatial implications for the type of co-housing communities established in Sweden in the 1980s is another question, particularly considering that several of the co-housing projects were retrofits of buildings constructed decades before.

Palm-Lindén (1992) discusses a selection of Swedish 1980s co-housing communities from the point of view that interests us here, 'spatial structure and social life'. From an estimated total of some 40 Swedish co-housing projects from the 1980s, Palm-Lindén has selected nine remodelled as well as newly built houses for analysis. They are all of what she calls the BIG type, based on the programmatic ideas of the group 'Live In Community' ('Bo I Gemenskap', see Chapter 2). Palm-Lindén uses space syntax for a more formal analysis than we do here. Her focus is on the 'transition zone' or the 'interface' (*mellanzonen*) between the private apartment and the urban context, which usually means staircases and corridors leading from outside the house to the apartment.

The BIG group's model for organizing housing communities stressed the socio-spatial benefits of reducing private space by 10% in order to maximize shared space and facilities (Vestbro and Horelli 2012; Sargisson 2014). In most of the 1980s Swedish co-housing projects, common spaces are seen as an extension of the apartment, which is slightly smaller than normal, but still has a normal-sized kitchen. Common spaces include above all a dining room and a large kitchen, but also a variety of other spaces such as carpentry workshops, play rooms, rooms for sewing and weaving, and photo labs. Many projects also included a day nursery, run as a cooperative or by the municipality (Palm-Lindén 1992: 53).

The two early Gothenburg examples, Stacken (The Ant-Hill) and Trädet (The Tree) (see Chapters 2 and 5), both in remodelled ordinary high-rise multi-family buildings from the 1950s and 1960s, can be described as very 'deep', tree-like structures with few 'rings' – understood as one room having more than one connection to other rooms, in space syntax associated with a non-hierarchical social logic. Except for the two parallel communication systems of stairs and elevators, Stacken was found to have two rings, both added during the remodelling: the hobby room, which could be reached from a separate entrance, and a complex of kitchen, dining room and day nursery (nowadays turned into a play room) on the fifth floor. In Trädet, there is only one ring: a complex of kitchen, dining room and café.

Summarizing her study, Palm-Lindén describes what she calls a 'paradox' in the spatial organization of the Swedish 1980s co-housing projects (Palm-Lindén 1992: 194). Most of them have what she calls a 'deep' system of spaces where the transition zone, the corridor, is a cul-de-sac. Lower buildings with an interconnected, 'ringy' transition zone are unusual, and the 'controlling' transition zone, as in a central hall, is rare in the co-housing examples studied by Palm-Lindén. This means, somewhat paradoxically, that the most common co-housing building type in Sweden is that which differs least from ordinary houses. This was the case in both remodelled and newly built co-housing projects, which showed no great difference in spatial structure. When trying to explain this, Palm-Lindén emphasizes the strong individualism of the Swedish co-housing inhabitants, who did not want to feel overly 'controlled'. With a few exceptions (see Chapter 2), the projects were bottom-up initiatives, not centrally planned utopian projects – even if the owner of the house is usually a municipal housing company.

Palm-Lindén combines her space syntax analysis with interviews in three of the houses to find what she calls the 'social meaning of spatial characteristics' (Palm-Lindén 1992: 149). Her conclusions are fairly cautious. Transition zones that are 'ringy' connect different parts of the building, but they also give inhabitants different options to move around. They may thus act as both connecting and separating. You can choose different paths through the building, depending on how keen you are on meeting people. The degree of 'privatization' of the spaces, like adding furniture or decorating the transition zone, depends on how 'segregated' the spaces are. Cul-de-sacs are more privatized than the most 'integrated' parts of the building, which many people pass through. Common spaces located together encourage use, and well-integrated common spaces near the entrance allow for more spontaneous meetings and use, compared to common spaces located deep in the building.

The focus of Palm-Lindén's study is the internal organization. She does not discuss co-housing projects in space syntax terms as 'reversed buildings' of the 'new urban genotype', even if her description of the 1980s projects as deep, tree-like structures points in this direction. Thus, the point could be made here that the 1980s Swedish co-housing projects had a spatial organization that was quite similar to the first generation of modernist collective houses. But it could also be argued that the different agenda, working together on tasks such as cooking, cleaning, gardening etcetera, instead of having employees do the work, meant that residents had taken control over the knowledge of household work and that they tried to create community. Together with a general ideological sympathy for 'solidarity', this meant that the co-housing projects of the first wave were modified examples of reversed buildings, sharing the tendency towards a combination of attachment and detachment.

The second wave of co-housing: further distinction between the two models

A second wave of co-housing spread across the world in the 1990s, including countries such as the UK and USA, where we had not seen many co-housing projects previously. In a survey carried out by the Italian architect Gresleri (2015), around 20 selected co-housing projects are categorized as belonging to the second wave. Gresleri agrees with what he calls the 'common opinion' that, if the Soviet examples of the 1920s are excluded (along with the Swedish examples of the 1930s), co-housing began in Denmark in the 1970s and then spread to Sweden and later on to other countries all over the world (Gresleri 2015: 24).

With his focus on spatial aspects, Gresleri identifies the two main 'models' of co-housing as discussed above, the Danish and the Swedish, and adds a third middle way, the Dutch model (Gresleri 2015: 42, based on Fromm 1991). He is careful to emphasize that these models were not planned but grew 'spontaneously' in different ways in different countries. The Danish model consists of a relatively small number of apartments in low buildings, often spread out in an open landscape. The Swedish model is a more compact and vertical structure, often with more apartments than the Danish. The Dutch model (*centraal wonen*) is similar to the Danish in the construction of low buildings with a separate 'common house', but apartments are in smaller 'clusters' of four to eight apartments with common space for dinners. The similarity to the Swedish model is, according to Gresleri, that the Dutch tenure form is rented flats. It is worth emphasizing that all his Danish examples, except one, are owner-occupied units, while all the Swedish ones are rental arrangements. The Anglo-Saxon examples (two each from Canada, UK and USA) are all owner-occupied. This is an important difference, even if somewhat exaggerated and simplified in Gresleri's selection (see the Chapters in Part 1 of this book, and the Conclusion, for a more nuanced discussion of different forms of tenure and their different impacts on the social dimensions of co-housing).

The Danish and Swedish models could easily be seen as examples of Hillier and Hanson's 'soft' and 'hard' forms respectively: the garden city and the large housing unit, the two principal forms of general housing developments in the twentieth century. But this also means that, according to the theory of Hillier and Hanson, the two forms have something in common spatially – as examples of reversed buildings with non-distributed and hierarchical spatial relations. The ideological basis for this is what they call 'the correspondence theory of social and spatial groups' (Hillier and Hanson 1984: 268); meaning that similar social categories of people are living spatially together and separate from others, whether in a garden city or a large housing unit. Another term for this, which Hillier and Hanson don't use, is segregation. As a consequence, they claim, the more a society grows, the more you will have of the institution-like reversed form of buildings, with a transpatial solidarity rather than a relation to its immediate surroundings. The question of interest for us here, in relation to questions of urban social sustainability, is the need for a more open, local urban solidarity. If co-housing of both the Danish and Swedish models runs a risk of creating socially and spatially closed and detached communities for members only, what would it take to open them up to their surroundings?

In the following section we address this question by examining how residents in five co-housing communities in Sweden, located in the urban areas of Stockholm, Gothenburg, Malmö and Lund respectively, negotiate social and spatial relations at the intersection between strong transpatial solidarity, upholding a sense of community *within* the co-housing, and accessibility to the neighbourhood and a more externally oriented spatial solidarity. The section is based on interviews that offer thematic insights that are analysed with respect to the social and spatial logics implied, outlining key issues and potential spaces of conflict, as well as the negotiation of these.

The negotiation of community and detachment in co-housing

The spatiality of social encounters

Fiolen is a co-housing community situated on the outskirts of Lund, in the south of Sweden, built in 1993 by the local public housing company and designed in collaboration with future residents. It consists of 24 sub-let apartments, built in the form of two-storey houses in a perimeter shape around an almost enclosed common yard. The shared spaces in the house – kitchen, dining room, play room, guest room, gym, laundry and hobby room – are placed in a cluster in the middle. The neighbourhood is suburban and the co-housing project is adapted to its context in scale and design, but at the same time somewhat detached from the neighbouring houses in its typology, as Fiolen is a larger and more introverted building. You can only enter through the front door, which is locked, or through the garden. In scale it has some similarities to the Danish model, with its 'dense-low' characteristics, but as a coherent unit with interior communications to apartments, and in its tenure form, it clearly belongs to the Swedish model.

The residents are nonetheless keen to invite neighbours in and to include so-called vulnerable groups in society. Examples of this are arrangements such as pub evenings, salsa courses and activities involving refugees who have permanent residence but are in need of housing. One man in Fiolen says:

> For example, we celebrated the national day with them [the refugees] and we had Afghani kite flying and other things. So, yes, I think that we try to be open to the neighbourhood so to speak.

The clustering of the shared spaces inside the house, and the fact that the residents have to walk through them to get to their own apartments, seem to make it easy for the residents to spend time there and to meet one another:

> The apartments are in the flanks. But everyone has to pass through down there, everyone has to go in to the laundry room, the kitchen. You meet everyone.

Further, the shared spaces have no apartments on top, so having a party there does not bother people in the apartments. The accessibility of the shared spaces is emphasized in the interviews. One person talks about how she can go to the dining room and just join a party or a cosy evening around the fireplace if she feels like it. Another person, a single father with a small child, says:

> If you don't manage to go out, if it's pouring with rain, there is still a big space to be in. One can run around and play and … even if I have a big two-room apartment, and [NN] has a lot of toys, it is still valuable. […] Personally I can also feel a bit locked in sometimes so it is nice, you can come down here and light a fire.

Further, the residents cook and eat together several days a week, something which is talked about very positively, also in relation to space:

> It is still the core, that we eat together, we use these [spaces] … every second day it is very empty down there, when no one is there. I think that is really sad. It is empty and no lights and no one … and then every second day.

This quote is interesting since it contradicts the stories about how they always meet one another in the shared spaces, on their way to their apartments. Maybe it is a question of intensity in the social encounters, where the cooking and eating together is a more focused and intense sociality than just meeting each other occasionally, on their way to their apartments (for further discussions about cooking and eating, see Chapter 7).

The importance of the location of common spaces

The importance of where common spaces are located within the internal spatial organization of co-housing and how that relates to its use is further highlighted in several of the examples studied. The fact that the kitchen, dining room and café in the co-housing project Trädet in Gothenburg are placed together on the first floor in a ringy form, partly as an addition to the existing building, makes the space fluent and lively. The members of the community spend a lot of time in these spaces, mostly related to cooking and eating, but they also sit in the café reading a newspaper, watching football games on the TV together, celebrate special occasions, etcetera. The play room is not part of the ringy structure, which makes it a potential free zone for the older children in the house (see Chapter 7), since it is not as visible and accessible as the other rooms. Another important space in Trädet is the outdoor terrace, which is reached from the dining room and from the outside. Trädet arranges an 'open house' for the public every now and then with festivities and information about living in a co-housing community, with the underlying goal of communicating and socializing with the immediate neighbourhood as well.

The spatial organization of the common spaces in Trädet can be contrasted with Stacken, where most of the shared spaces in the house are located on the fifth floor, including a dining room and a kitchen that are only used during collaborative work days, meetings or certain social activities – and that can be booked by residents for private events. On the same floor there is also a play room, which according to some interviewees has to be locked, since the children are not taking enough responsibility for keeping the room tidy.

The reason for placing the common spaces on the fifth floor was technical: the structure of the building was originally so tightly designed that it was not possible during the remodelling to make the necessary openings in load-bearing walls on lower floors. Whether this played any part in the later disuse of the dining room is open to discussion (cf. Chapter 2). On the ground floor there is a space that can be used as a café, as well as a carpentry workshop and a sauna. The fact that the common spaces are placed on different floors in the house and that the building is tree-like in its structure, as well as the fact that the residents don't cook and eat together on a regular basis, makes the spatiality challenging in relation to creating potential internal solidarity and enabling more spontaneous social encounters.

Both Trädet and Stacken are clear examples of the Swedish model of co-housing as reversed buildings, spatially detached from the local context, as is also typical of the modernist urban plan. Trädet, with its terrace, is a bit more open to the surroundings, while Stacken, which was recently upgraded to passive house standard and clad with solar panels, symbolically stands out even more clearly than it did originally, sending the message of being an alternative.

'Us' and 'them': co-housing in an urban context

Some co-housing projects particularly emphasize the social function they seek to serve in the neighbourhood, by providing space for activities that are becoming scarcer with the continued privatization of urban spaces and dismantling of the Swedish welfare society, such as community youth centres. Södra Station (South Station) is a co-housing project in an attractive part of central Stockholm. It was built in 1987 by a public housing company and has 63 apartments. From the start, the tenure form was rented apartments, but in 2010 they were remodelled for tenant ownership. The co-housing is part of a 1980s urban renewal project made up of perimeter blocks that were intended to be part of a mixed urban area. The co-housing building – like most other buildings in the area – has locked doors at the front, while the courtyard is shared with other houses. However, considering the openness and transparency at the back, Södra Station may be called a spatial hybrid. Most of the common spaces (kitchen, dining room, play room, TV room, etcetera) are situated on the entry floor and are only accessible by the residents, contributing to the detachment of the co-housing from its surroundings. The open and ring-like structure of the common spaces enhances the transpatial solidarity and contributes to the social cohesion and sense of community in the house. Yet on the entry floor, at the back of the house, Södra Station has a double-height room with an entresol that has café-like seating and a ping-pong table, accessible from both the shared spaces inside the house and directly from the outside. There is a door leading to the pedestrian and bicycle path outside, and the room has big windows facing this path, which makes it even more exposed and accessible from the outside. Here, the teenagers living in the house often spend time together with their friends. The co-housing community also arranges pub evenings, concerts and parties in this room, to which they invite people from the neighbourhood, as well as friends and their friends.

One woman talks about this semi-public space in positive terms, but says that the room is sometimes 'occupied' almost entirely by 'outsiders', i.e. teenagers from the neighbourhood, and not from the house. They know how to get in and they have a place to go. The problem, according to this interviewee, is that this may keep the younger children who live in the house from going there. They are a little afraid to claim their right to the ping-pong table when the room is full of older teenagers. On some occasions the residents have also had problems with youth smoking cigarettes in the room. At some point, the adults of the house decided that it was totally okay for the teenagers to have friends and friends' friends there, but when the teenagers of the house go home to their respective apartments, they can't leave their friends there, they have to make them go home too.

This is also a question of 'generations' of children: when the house's own teenagers are too old to spend time in the ping-pong room it still attracts teenagers from the neighbourhood, since it has become an established place to meet. This means that there is a potential 'risk' that the room will be used more by outsiders than by young people in the house, something which makes explicit the tension between internal needs of the residents and ideals of accessibility for the neighbourhood. The ping-pong room has become a semi-public space (cf. Sargisson 2012) and this raises some questions: who is responsible for talking to the teenagers in the room – if a 'talk' is needed? And furthermore, who has access to the house? In a sense, the spatial organization can be said to shape the social relations in the co-housing community, where the openness at the back of the house contrasts with the otherwise detached character of the house – mirrored also in the aspirations to connect with the neighbourhood.

A similar case is brought up in another interview. The Stacken co-housing (described above), had bought a big trampoline and placed it outside the house, that is, extending the spatial connection between the inside and outside. It attracted a lot of children from the neighbourhood. On some occasions there were conflicts, and one interviewee (a single man with part-time parenting responsibilities on and off) describes the ambivalences this caused:

> It brought a lot of responsibilities, you have to take responsibility and tell off other children who do not live in our house, and this led to a lot of conflicts [about] how the co-housing community operates in society, and there were discussions about putting up big fences so that no one else could [come], and it became rather emotional in relation to … who can afford a trampoline? Who has the right to a trampoline? These are the kind of political, philosophical issues that came up in relation to this.

The trampoline, like the ping-pong room in the example above, became a semi-public place, and the residents in the co-housing project had to deal with questions concerning spatial solidarity versus detachment from the surroundings, with the risk of reproducing a sense of 'we' and 'them', in opening up the space for external use. Both cases can be seen as illustrative examples of dual spatial intentions. The trampoline activated space outside of the otherwise tree-like structure of Stacken, and the ping-pong room become an easily accessible and less hierarchical space, both offering social functions that blur the socio-spatial boundaries of the internal co-housing community and the wider neighbourhood.

Co-housing as urban acupuncture?

Another example of the dual spatial intentions of co-housing is SoKo, Sofielunds kollektivhus. It was built in 2014 by the municipal housing company in Malmö, in the south of Sweden, in between the traditional perimeter block plan of central Malmö and the more open modernist areas to the south. The block consists of a mix of co-housing, ordinary apartments and lower terraced houses ranging from two to six storeys high. All the apartments are rented. The SoKo co-housing has 45 of the 170 apartments in the block.

This project was conceived as a sort of 'urban acupuncture', a strategy officially adopted by the public housing company and other builders in Malmö to make areas more attractive through small strategic interventions. The larger context of redevelopment here is an 'urban corridor' stretching from the city centre, through the neighbourhood of Sofielund and onwards to a stigmatized modernist housing area, Rosengård. SoKo was built by a private builder on the commission of the municipal housing company, but initiated by and designed together with a local co-housing group. The co-housing project was specifically seen as providing an 'innovative' alternative housing form and contributing to making the area more attractive, with an emphasis on the role of diversity and creating a dense 'urban character', providing common spaces on the ground floor. SoKo's 45 apartments range from small studios to six-room units for 'apartment collectives' within the larger co-housing. The ground floor has several common facilities that are visually open to the surroundings as well as to the courtyard, including an entry hall, laundry, kitchen and dining room, living room, play room, etc. The house is L-shaped, with one internal staircase in the corner, and most apartments are accessed through open galleries and staircases that also function as balconies with personal furnishings, and as social meeting places. The house is also connected to a large terrace on the roof of the terraced houses. Together with the rest of the block, SoKo forms a semi-closed courtyard. The spatial organization tries to open up the co-housing to its immediate neighbours, through the open galleries and roof terrace, as well as the ground floor activities. As a form of urban acupuncture, it also has the ambition to influence the wider urban context.

A young female resident, who was part of the group involved in the architectural design of the house, describes how she imagines that the shared spaces located on the first floor, with its large windows and a door that opens on to the street, can go beyond simply serving the co-housing community. She hopes that SoKo will provide a platform for various social and cultural activities that are open to the neighbourhood. Being more broadly active in urban and housing rights issues herself, the interviewee also sees the space as a resource for mobilizing activism and knowledge dissemination through open lectures or meetings. The spatial relation of this common space is in a sense a distributed space, with the potential for a wider use than for the co-housing community alone. But at the same time, it relies on the inhabitants of the house to actively welcome visitors. Potential tensions regarding the use of the common spaces and the house demand negotiations.

SoKo is thus an interesting example of how weak spatial boundaries, and the tension between designing for transpatial versus spatial solidarity, can be perceived as problematic. In the urban context of Sofielund, where the co-housing project is conceived as part of a socially sustainable urban development – including an opportunity for residents to self-organize and more or less autonomously manage their building – there is also a conflict between being open to the neighbourhood and preserving a sense of security. The layout of the building and the semi-open block structure mean that the inner courtyard is accessible to outsiders, something which was identified by an interviewee as a topic of debate within the co-housing community. After several bike thefts and incidents of people not living in the house walking up to the roof terraces, there were discussions about putting up gates to enclose the courtyard, or restrict access to the staircases. As one interviewee, a young man, expresses it:

> We did not understand the problem. You can enter the house from the ground level.... The staircases are open. So, you can go up, anyone can go up and enter our exterior corridors. And we have our apartment doors locked but ... well ... it feels ... some people feel unsafe then ... because we had some thefts in the beginning ... The solution could be to put up 'cages' to the staircases ... so that no one could enter without a key. And that would feel somehow sad, but we will see what we ... It is exactly that conflict between sort of ... having a closed yard or an open yard?

When planning the house, the residents-to-be were also keen to create a spatially open atmosphere internally, but all the openness and the many glass walls and windows are not without problems. A woman in the house talks about how she feels uncomfortable in parts of the shared living room, because she can be seen all the time – through the glass walls and windows:

> I think it's really unpleasant ... the transparency when you sit there.... It's a sort of openness.... You sort of want to see and meet, have eye contact.

> But it is as if you are sitting and hanging around and you don't have contact with anyone else. It is as if you are in a little cage … people can see you, but there is no contact. You are in a cage of glass.

It sounds as if she is describing the typical panopticon, where you are (potentially) watched all the time. Another example of the relation between architecture and social life in Sofielund is the question of visibility and privacy materialized by the windows in the apartment doors. Every apartment door has long, narrow windows. One interviewee told us that they wanted those windows to enhance the openness towards the surroundings, and to give an opportunity for children and animals to look out. Interestingly enough, many of the people living there had put up curtains to prevent transparency. They protected their private space, as they did not want their neighbours and/or visitors to be able to see into their kitchen and/or living room. The ideal of openness and visibility turned out to be problematic in practice.

The Swedish co-housing model in context: summing up our cases

All our empirical examples here are of the 'Swedish model' or the 'hard form' discussed above, with one coherent building with common spaces, usually (but not exclusively) near the entrance, and apartments reached by stairs and lifts. The tenure form is mostly rented apartments owned by municipal housing companies, except for Stacken, which is organized as a rental cooperative, and Södra Station, which is tenant-owned. The spatial solutions tend to foster internal attachment and community, and an external detachment, or put in other words: transpatial solidarity rather than spatial solidarity with the wider neighbourhood. As we have seen in the examples, the context varies from suburban, with the co-housing project as a more or less clearly distinguishable built form, or 'buildings in the park' (Fiolen, Trädet and Stacken), to a denser and more urban context, with the co-housing buildings constituting part of an urban block (Södra Station and SoKo). The denser urban context also seems to include an expectation of openness to the immediate surroundings, both from residents and planners. But such openness also has its problems.

Dialectic utopias? Concluding discussion

Since the beginning of modernity there has been a utopian aspect to collective housing ideas, in their position as an alternative to 'ordinary' housing (see, for example, Sargisson 2014). At the same time, co-housing is shaped by its contemporary society, its problems and its economic and legal framework. Co-housing is thus a recurring (spatial) answer to changing (social) questions.

Drawing on David Harvey (2000), the Dutch architect Guillermo Delgado questions 'the fundamental division between the notion of utopia of social processes and utopia of built form' (Delgado 2012: 430). Instead, he proposes what he calls 'dialectic utopias' that:

> contain the process-driven component and open-end tendencies of utopias of social processes as well as the aim for materialization that characterizes utopias of built form.
>
> (Delgado 2012: 430)

Even though spatial layout and physical environment do not cause interaction and socialization, but rather provide or preclude them (Shirazi and Keivani 2019: 117–118; Sargisson 2014), in this chapter we have shown examples of how spatiality and sociality are engaged in a dialectic negotiation, with specific consequences for co-housing communities and their relations to the surroundings.

Hillier and Hanson (1984) can also be said to deal with utopias. The built form of co-housing can be seen as related to what they call the 'new urban genotype', the 'reversed building', appearing with the modernization of society over the last two centuries. In relation to co-housing, this comes in two main models, the Danish low-rise, garden-city-like project and the Swedish high-rise, large housing unit, corresponding to the 'soft' and 'hard' forms of Hillier and Hanson. As illustrated in our empirical examples, both are mainly based on creating internal, 'transpatial solidarity', and correspondingly, again following the argument of Hillier and Hanson, face problems when it comes to spatial solidarity with their surroundings.

The empirical insights provided above underline that the socio-spatial relations of co-housing are often conflicting. On the one hand, there is a need for privacy among the individual households and to uphold a sense of security in and around the home. On the other hand, the underlying idea of many co-housing projects is social and spatial solidarity, both internally (strengthening the social cohesion of the co-housing community itself) and externally (providing a social function to the neighbourhood or the wider urban context). This paradox also emerges when co-housing is used in urban planning as a form of 'urban acupuncture', i.e. to open up an area in order to contribute to social sustainability on a larger urban scale. The SoKo co-housing community in Malmö is a good example of this. At the same time as the community is expected to, and wants to, be open to the surrounding neighbourhood, there is a need to uphold clear boundaries in order for the co-housing community to function internally.

Another utopian built form, proposed by Hillier and Hanson, is an alternative to the new urban genotype, consisting of 'large, non-corresponding, encounter-rich' urban communities. This, in their view, would offer a democratic, and non-hierarchical distribution of space – which in turn would correspond to less hierarchical social relations, and a more democratic social system. It is quite likely that co-housing as we know it, as reversed buildings, does not fit into this utopia outlined by Hillier and Hanson. There is a risk of reaching an impasse here between co-housing as a built form that generates conflicts between internal community and external detachment, and a utopia of a more or less non-corresponding – that is, a non-segregated, all-encompassing – urban community. As we have seen, co-housing residents have to deal with these conflicts on a day-to-day basis through negotiations between internal community and spatial solidarity with the surroundings. There are no easy ways out of this, but Delgado's dialectic utopia might offer a strategy, emphasizing the potential of co-housing to actually become an alternative that is open to wider engagements in urban struggles, and to develop ways to provide access to housing for those not currently accommodated by the housing market, and who are usually not part of the existing, often homogenous co-housing communities. This goes beyond pure spatial organization, but as Delgado stresses, co-housing communities 'as built form have some capacity to generate urban transformations'. Yet, the challenge for moving forward is how to learn from empirical insights in co-housing practice to create new housing that 'will have not only some capacity, but socially necessary capacities to re-join separated urban tissues and social groups' (Delgado 2012: 441).

It is particularly relevant here to consider that if we are to understand co-housing as a form of collaborative civil-society-driven housing alternative, as argued by Sørvoll and Bengtsson (2019), it needs to more actively deal with the challenges of how to contribute to external (spatial) solidarity and the potential for realizing political, utopian, goals beyond the direct interests of the co-housing residents themselves. Although co-housing offers a type of housing that can mobilize internal, transpatial solidarity, fostering community between residents – more or less strengthened by the internal spatial organization – it could also be part of attempts to provide space (both more symbolically and literally in the form of actual meeting places in the city) for political action, urban activism and solidarity with under-served groups in society, as also attempted in some of the cases of the Swedish co-housing studied.

Interviews

Stacken, Gothenburg: Male, single, part-time parenting responsibilities, April 25 2016.
Sofielund, Malmö: Female, single, April 10 2015.
Sofielund, Malmö: Female, single, children, April 10 2015.
Sofielund, Malmö: Male, single, April 10 2015.
Södra station, Stockholm: Female, married/cohabitant, children, April 17 2015.
Fiolen, Lund: Male, single, with children, April 4 2018.
Fiolen, Lund: Female, single, children, April 4 2018.

References

Caldenby, C. (1992) *Vad är ett kollektivhus?*. Göteborg: Chalmers Tekniska Högskola.
Caldenby, C. and Walldén, Å. (1979) *Kollektivhus: Sovjet och Sverige omkring 1930*. Stockholm: Byggforskningsrådet.

Caldenby, C. and Walldén, Å. (1984) *Kollektivhuset Stacken*. Göteborg: Bokförlaget Korpen.

Chiodelli, F. and Baglione, V. (2014) 'Living together privately: for a cautious reading of cohousing', *Urban Research & Practice*, vol. 7, no. 1, pp. 20–34.

Delgado, G. (2012) 'Towards Dialectic Utopias: Links and Disjunctions between Collaborative Housing and Squatting in the Netherlands', *Built Environment*, vol. 38, no. 3, pp. 430–442.

Droste, C. (2015) 'German co-housing: an opportunity for municipalities to foster socially inclusive urban development?' *Urban Research & Practice*, vol. 8, no. 1, pp. 79–92.

Goodwin, B. and Taylor, K. (1982) *The Politics of Utopia: A Study in Theory and Practice*. New York: St. Martin's Press.

Gresleri, J. (2015) *Cohousing: Esperienze internazionali di abitare condiviso* [Cohousing: International experiences of living together]. Busalla: plug_in.

Harvey, D. (2000) *Spaces of Hope*. Berkeley: University of California Press.

Hillier, B. and Hanson, J. (1984) *The Social Logic of Space*. Cambridge: Cambridge University Press.

Jakobsen, P. and Larsen, H. G. (2018) 'An alternative for whom? The evolution and socio-economy of Danish cohousing', *Urban Research & Practice*, doi: 10.1080/17535069.2018.1465582

Lang, R., Carriou, C. and Czischke, D. (2018) 'Collaborative housing research (1990–2017): A Systematic review and thematic analysis of the field', *Housing, Theory and Society*, doi: 10.1080/14036096.2018.1536077

Marckmann, B., Gram-Hanssen, K. and Christensen, T. H. (2012) 'Sustainable living and co-housing: evidence from a case study of eco-villages', *Built Environment*, vol. 38, no. 3, pp. 413–429.

Palm-Lindén, K. (1992) *Kollektivhuset och mellanzonen: Om rumslig struktur och socialt liv*. Lund: Lunds universitet.

Sandstedt, E. and Westin, S. (2015) 'Beyond Gemeinschaft and Gesellschaft: Cohousing Life in Contemporary Sweden', *Housing, Theory and Society*, vol. 32, pp. 131–150.

Sargisson, L. (2012) 'Second-wave cohousing: A modern utopia?', *Utopian Studies*, vol. 23, no. 1, pp. 28–56.

Sargisson, L. (2014) 'Utopianism in the Architecture of New Urbanism and Cohousing', in K. Bradley and J. Hedrén (eds) *Green Utopianism: Perspectives, Politics and Micro-Practices*. New York, London: Routledge.

Shirazi, R. and Keivani, R. (2019) 'Spatiality of social sustainability: Social activity and neighbourhood space', in R. Shirazi and R. Keivani (eds) *Urban Social Sustainability: Theory, Policy and Practice*. New York, London: Routledge.

Sørvoll, J. and Bengtsson, B. (2019) 'Autonomy, democracy and solidarity. The defining principles of collaborative civil society housing and some mechanisms that may challenge them', *Urban Research & Practice*, doi: 10.1080/17535069.2019.1573267

Vestbro, D. U. (1982) *Kollektivhus från enkökshus till bogemenskap* [Collective houses from one-kitchen houses to co-housing]. Stockholm: Byggforskningsrådet.

Vestbro, D. U. and Horelli, L. (2012) 'Design for Gender Equality: The History of Co-Housing Ideas and Realities', *Built Environment*, vol. 38, no. 3, pp. 315–335.

9 Co-housing as a socio-ecologically sustainable alternative?

Pernilla Hagbert

Introduction

The development of sustainable living environments is increasingly recognised as an imperative task in mitigating climate change and reducing the ecological impact of modern society, in the strive for a safe and just operating space for humanity within planetary boundaries (Raworth 2012). Efforts within the construction industry, coupled with strengthened legislative measures both in the EU and in national building codes, have driven the emergence of for example low-energy buildings, improved building processes and materials, and an integration of eco-efficient technology in new sustainable urban development projects throughout Europe. At the same time, critical calls for sustainability transition underline the need for larger shifts in societal systems, including the overhaul from a fossil based to a fossil free energy mix, and the reconfiguration of for example transport and housing infrastructure (Markard et al. 2012). This is understood not only as a technical challenge, but requires significant societal, cultural and economic changes (van den Bergh et al. 2011). Empirical insights further underline the barriers for, but also limitations of an eco-efficient, techno-centred interpretation of sustainable housing development (Hagbert and Bradley 2017; Hagbert and Femenías 2016; Storbjörk et al. 2018).

Meanwhile, growing environmental concerns and calls for climate action have increased the wider interest in developing forms of living that might enable a lower ecological footprint. The latest wave of co-housing, as explored in previous chapters of this book, can be framed in this discourse as developing at a rather paradoxical junction between socio-ecological concerns and urban governance strategies. On one hand, co-housing can be said to tap into a growing group of socially and environmentally conscious residents pursuing alternative housing that is expected to offer affordable, low-impact solutions. On the other hand, co-housing claims of sustainability must also be understood in relation to a prevalent 'ecological modernisation' logic in contemporary urban governance. Building upon a modernist worldview that sustainability challenges can be met with the use of science and technology, an 'eco-modernist' framework highlights the possibility to combine improved environmental performance with social and economic development (Lidskog and Elander 2012), particularly under the guise of concepts such as 'green growth'. This further ties into notions of sustainable consumption and building, where a key ecological modernisation idea supposes using market mechanisms to steer towards less environmentally harmful production and consumption (Spaargaren 2000). This framing in turn relies on an understanding of residents as customers that might be influenced to make better purchasing choices, rather than as co-actors in creating alternative solutions in their own right (Hagbert and Femenías 2016, Hagbert 2016).

As Scheller and Thörn (2018) note, the concept of sustainability expressed in relation to urban development programs in which new co-housing projects are situated, often functions as an empty signifier. As such, sustainable urban development encompasses various dimensions of socio-ecological concern within a rather vague formulation of what needs to be done. A key aspect in relation to sustainability in co-housing, whether understood as a social or economic dimension, is the question of affordability (see the Introduction, as well as the Conclusion of this book). In addition, social sustainability in discourses on sustainable urban development often relate to for example social cohesion (or mixing) and self-governance (Chapter 5) – linking to notions of community and integration – rather than more overarching social justice aspects, including challenging prevailing socio-metabolic systems in housing production and provision. When it comes to ecological sustainability, the meanings found across the national and urban contexts studied in this book, spanning from Sweden to Germany (see Chapter 5), but also in discourses in Denmark and Spain (see Chapter 1 and 4), include a focus on low climate impact from construction and the facilitation of resource-saving forms of living – associated with co-housing as a type of housing that emphasises sharing.

The claims made by co-housing proponents build upon the assumption that co-housing might enable a lower ecological footprint compared to other housing forms (Chatterton 2013; Tummers 2017). Particularly, co-housing is conceived as a way of both ensuring a more resource-efficient residential design and as part of promoting a pro-environmental lifestyle within the building itself. Collective forms of living and sharing of both stuff and spaces can minimize the need for private consumption – which Lietaert (2010) sees as enabling 'efficient sharing habits', and what Vestbro (2012) calls 'saving by sharing'. Marckmann et al. (2012) point to four sustainability claims in co-housing that they critically explore: 1) the potential of adopting more sustainable technologies; 2) small compact dwellings; 3) whether co-housing mutually supports pro-environmental behaviour; and 4) co-housing as providing environmental advantages for small households. Chatterton (2013) moreover underlines the potential (and challenges) for co-housing communities to foster a 'post-carbon value change', while Lietaert (2010) and Hagbert (2018) explore the possible links between co-housing and degrowth – as the equitable downscaling of the economic throughput of society to keep within environmental limits. As such, co-housing is also posited as part of more radical transitions, challenging socio-technical and economic systems.

Following on critiques of co-housing as serving a rather privileged group (Lang et al. 2018; Jakobsen and Larsen 2018), an intersectional perspective nevertheless also needs to consider the implications of how different ways of living are framed in relation to prevalent sustainability discourses. As noted by Bradley (2009), current mainstream strategies for sustainability are underpinned by middle-class norms. This entails processes of (self)disciplining and normalisation of 'the other' – such as when immigrants are targeted in education programs in order to act more sustainably (despite the fact that their average ecological footprint is often lower than the environmentally conscious middle class) – rather than appreciating the 'multiple ways we can save natural resources [...] more attuned to social and cultural diversity' (ibid.: non paginated abstract).

In light of this, how can co-housing be understood in the strive for a just distribution and use of resources within planetary boundaries? Or, as expressed by Lietaert (2010: 1), 'as a model to make life more social and greener in an urban context'. This chapter explores whether co-housing, as it is conceived by the residents themselves and in the ways in which it is represented in new urban development, can be seen as part of a more fundamental transition to a sustainable society within planetary boundaries, or whether it rather might serve as an example of incremental, yet insufficient change within current systems.

The chapter starts with outlining key analytical frameworks of 'weak' and 'strong' sustainability, and the often-stated dichotomy between collective action and individual responsibilisation, drawing upon previous research and linking this particularly to housing. Utilising these frameworks in an integrative manner, the potential of co-housing to contribute to socio-ecological sustainability is then explored, focusing particularly on climate targets, a just distribution of housing resources and the role of community, rather than seeing affordability as the primary social sustainability issue in co-housing (instead discussed further in the Conclusion of this volume). The chapter looks specifically at key sustainability claims often made in co-housing – exploring aspects of sharing; community innovation; social pressures; and whether co-housing should be understood as merely a more resource efficient form of housing, or a as a different way of 'doing' urban sustainability. The chapter then concludes with a discussion of in what way co-housing can be understood as a sustainable way of living: does it propose a radical socio-ecological alternative or is it merely a 'greener' middle-class lifestyle choice?

'Weak' or 'strong' sustainability in housing

Previous research has underlined the need to distinguish between a framing of 'weak' or 'strong' sustainability (Hobson, 2013a). The main issue of interest is whether sustainable development pathways are to rely on voluntary, incremental change, or whether more profound societal changes are needed, with 'deep green' calls for radical transitions on multiple levels. As pointed out by Lovell (2004), Gram-Hanssen and Jensen (2005) and Jensen and Gram-Hanssen (2008), drawing on examples from the UK and Denmark respectively, the discourse on sustainable housing development has shifted during recent decades. In the late 1970s and 1980s, a prevalent deep ecological understanding, anchored in residents' values of environmental stewardship (and/or solidarity), were translated into grassroots projects, manifested in for example eco-villages and urban eco-building projects. The mainstream discourse, particularly in Scandinavia, has since shifted towards a wider eco-modernist framing (Lidskog and Elander 2012), emphasising sustainable (housing) consumption and the resident as an empowered consumer, which in conjunction with top-down policy approaches to address a multitude of societal challenges also has led to the institutionalization of sustainability discourses within the housing sector (Lundqvist 2004).

Through the promotion of eco-efficiency and urban densification, financial incentives for investors and builders are key drivers for urban sustainable development, in line with ecological modernisation (Spaargaren 2000). Environmental consideration in the housing sector has now in many aspects become a 'hygiene factor' in new construction, meaning that it is seen as a (technical) standard to simply be fulfilled. Particularly in countries such as Sweden, lauded to be at the forefront of environmental management, few actors see ecological sustainability goals as controversial (Hagbert et al. 2013). Apart from being driven by the building industry itself, this is further spurred by for example new EU directives, national regulations and subsidies regarding energy efficiency measures in the existing stock and building performance requirements in new construction. The idea that technological advances, enabling incremental adjustments, can achieve a reduced environmental impact without altering living standards, or the need for more radical societal changes, is prevalent. This relates both to a logic within the building industry that incremental implementation of efficient technologies minimizes the need to more radically modify current production practices and processes (Lees and Sexton 2013), and upholds middle-class household norms (Bradley, 2009) without having to challenge current residential comforts and conveniences (Gram-Hanssen and Jensen 2005). This constitutes a powerful story, upheld by the different actors involved, where a certain framing of eco-efficient urban development contributes to a hegemony of what is understood as sustainable, and in turn, what is not (Hagbert and Bradley 2017).

The reliance on efficiency measures and constant technological innovation is, nonetheless, argued to be inadequate in meeting the sustainability challenges facing society, including keeping within planetary boundaries. Rebound effects, tokenism and belief in techno-salvation are some of the obstacles for a sustainable development (Huesemann and Huesemann 2008; Gifford, 2011). Among critics of a growth-based understanding of development, decoupling of continued economic growth (as measured by the value of the goods and services produced) from further environmental pressure is increasingly seen as unattainable (Jackson 2009; Xue 2012).

As found in the studies of sustainable urban development projects relating to co-housing presented in previous chapters in this book, there is also a distinct contradiction between an understanding of economic sustainability as growth, and social sustainability aspects such as housing affordability and notions of social mixing (see Chapter 5 and Scheller and Thörn 2018). Xue (2015) suggests that continued growth in the housing stock provides only weak decoupling from absolute environmental impact, and instead calls for reduced expansion of the total volume of housing. Taken together, such perspectives indicate that a more radical approach is needed, including fundamentally rethinking ways of residing and the distribution of housing resources, while minimising total environmental claims, calling for a reinterpretation of sustainable housing beyond a growth logic (Hagbert 2018).

The paradox regarding resource efficiency in housing, in relation to a maintained or even increased and more individualised demand of housing functions, is in this respect especially relevant to address. Social norms regarding 'the good life' and the image of the comfortable and yet resource and energy intense modern home is hard to challenge, particularly in a dominant framing of sustainable housing as mainly a technological or building performance issue (Hagbert 2016). The ecological impact of modern ways of living goes beyond the buildings themselves. A narrative turn in energy research (Janda and Topouzi 2015) for example underlines the need to explore everyday practices and what people do in and through their homes (Hagbert 2018), rather than solely focusing on technical provision and buildings' energy performance. This includes critically exploring norms surrounding home and notions of comfort, as well as the market-driven framing of living standards in relation to households' 'willingness-to-pay', which uphold unsustainable and inequitable patterns of residential resource use. The continued increase in spatial and material demands (Vale and Vale 2010), and the rise in use of home appliances (Marsh et al. 2010), for example, pose large challenges. Shifting demographics, such as an increase in single households in many countries, also puts strain on existing and future housing resources (Kabisch and Haase 2011), implying a larger spatial demand and resource intensity in satisfying individual needs compared to households where functions and resources are shared.

Collective action and individual responsibility

While it is acknowledged that the transitions needed to meet challenges of living within planetary and social boundaries will require changes in all areas and sectors of society, the debate on responsibility in sustainable development is divided. On the one hand, calls for large-scale socio-technical transitions point to the inadequacy of individual actions and governance models that support an economistic framing of change (Shove 2010), and instead underline the importance of limiting total consumption (Alfredsson 2004; Lorek and Spangenberg 2014), and the role policy and planning, including a range of different actors, might play (Avelino and Wittmayer 2016; Isaksson and Heikkinen 2018). On the other hand, there is an increasing interest in 'behavioural change', also within housing, as more actors realize the limitations of building performance improvements on their own in reducing the ecological footprint from the residential sector. Often, these behavioural framings assume an evolutionary economical, rational choice model, such as 'nudging', to encourage certain behaviours among residents (Hobson 2013a; Reid and Ellsworth-Krebs 2018).

A main driver in the current market-oriented housing development is the notion of an informed customer creating demand for more 'eco-friendly' ways of living (Hagbert et al. 2013), which relies on a framing of residents as consumers rather than co-actors (Hagbert 2016). This can further be related to developments towards on the one hand a more individualized global consumerism, but on the other hand calls for common efforts for sustainability (Middlemiss 2014). The framing of 'responsible consumers', but also of 'green citizens', can be seen in relation to general processes of individualization in much of the (Western) world (see also Introductory chapter). It can moreover be understood within a green governmentality framework, emphasising the voluntary adoption of pro-environmental behaviour and 'green lifestyles', and the enrolment of individuals to think and act in ways that align with governmental aims (Soneryd and Uggla 2015; Hobson 2013b). Within a context of advanced liberal governance, Scheller and Thörn (2018) further point towards a mode of governance in sustainable urban development of shifting responsibility from state agencies to the encouragement of self-government among individuals and civil society groups to engage with and carry out political responsibilities regarding urban sustainability, such as the provision of low-impact, affordable housing.

The role of collective action, as framed in the formation of 'community', can moreover be examined in light of this concept of responsibilisation. It has been underlined that the development, and particularly the wider adoption, of less impactful ways of living must be understood as relying on social support (Seyfang 2009), emphasizing the need to contextualize potential transitions within various communities. Individual motivations and potentials for action are in this sense connected to what are seen as pathways to more systemic transformations, in the creation of collective capacity to act and challenge current socio-technical, economic and political paradigms. This, in a sense, can be seen as a middle ground between structuralist and behaviourist dichotomies, where the framing of collective action within a community provides a basis for change, situated in people's everyday lives. As Seyfang and Smith (2007) express it: '[c]ommunity action is a neglected, but potentially important, site of innovative activity', and should be studied further to also influence policy in sustainable housing.

In the Scandinavian context, historically prevalent norms and social practices surrounding frugality, collectivism and a culture of consensus could be seen in relation to the potential acceptance for various forms of collaborative practices in everyday life (Mont 2004). While collaborative forms of production and consumption is today often linked to digital platforms and open networks of peer-to-peer exchange, it has nonetheless been stressed that urban sharing of spaces, stuff and skills – based on principles of reciprocity – also calls for solutions at the neighbourhood level, supported by municipal policy and planning to ensure an inclusive development (Hult and Bradley 2017).

The limits of individual action as 'responsible consumers', but also of building community capacity and framings of green citizenship, should be reflected upon in relation to processes responsibilisation. There is a need to recognize that different groups of people might face different challenges in 'living more sustainably' (Barr and Gilg 2006). It is especially important to consider 'lifestyles' as more than merely an aggregate of individual consumer choices. Everyday practices are reproduced and locked in by societal structures simultaneously (Sanne 2002). This includes assumptions regarding what lifestyle is perceived as 'correct' in relation to the norm. As explored by Bradley (2009), the discourse on urban sustainability, and its practical implementation in planning, building and various resource saving programs, needs to be understood as normatively framed. The reproduction of middle-class norms, particularly in regards to environmental consciousness, means that other groups – along with certain types of dwellings and urban districts, not branded as 'green' – are either directly or indirectly seen as not aligning to the norm of what a 'sustainable' resident does or where they live.

What is lacking is a more fundamental approach to housing as a part of organising a sustainable society within planetary boundaries, incorporating dimensions of what economic activities that are assumed to take place, as well as social justice perspectives in the strive for a safe and just distribution and use of resources (Hagbert 2016; Hagbert 2018). The question is whether co-housing provides this? Using the frameworks of weak/strong sustainability and collective/individual action in an integrative manner, the potential of co-housing to contribute to socio-ecological sustainability (focusing on climate targets and just access to housing in particular), is explored in the following sections, looking specifically at claims regarding: resource sharing; community innovation; social pressures; and problematising whether co-housing should be understood as merely a more resource efficient form of housing, or a as a different way of 'doing' urban sustainability.

Sharing: a key strategy or a marginal benefit?

A key notion in co-housing is the social and environmental benefits of sharing that the community might provide. Co-housing has been suggested to offer an alternative way of organising everyday life (Jarvis 2011) and communities in a way as to reduce resource use (Chatterton 2013). As such, it does tie into responsibilisation processes in contemporary green governmentality with respect to the focus on the everyday and self-management, but also proposes a strong idea of collaboration and collective action at the community level. Based in this belief in collaboration, co-housing projects are often thought to gather smaller households to reduce private ownership in favour of more shared use – households that could otherwise be assumed to live in more isolated ways were such sharing was more difficult, at least in their everyday domestic environment. Findings from Marckmann et al.'s (2012) study of Danish co-housing in the form of eco-villages, however, point to that this potential is somewhat lost – at least in this context – as there is an over-representation of families with children, rather than single households or couples without kids. They give some possible explanations, including the suburban or rural location and child-dominated community activities, which might be less attractive to single persons and child-free couples, but also propose that 'those living in one-person households may lack the economic or social resources needed to fit in and be accepted into a co-housing community' (ibid.: 424).

In her review of co-housing research in relation to resource use, Tummers (2017) finds that while energy-related savings in co-housing have not been studied to any greater extent, the few studies that have been made are 'promising'. The benefits of sharing activities and spaces has a potential of reducing the ecological footprint compared to other housing, to some extent due to the everyday practices that residents engage in, but also for example through the reduced spatial heating needs (Sundberg 2014). The inherent potential of reducing space and private consumption in co-housing due to sharing is often stressed. Vestbro (2012) refers to a study of Swedish co-houses from the middle of the 1980s, which found that individual apartments in co-housing were smaller than average Swedish apartments, and that residents instead have access to common spaces. Vestbro further discusses that it is not only a question of reducing spatial standards, but of accepting fewer rooms within the private dwelling, something he considers Swedish co-housing encourages.

Considering that we will need to live smaller, share more and live 'simpler' to meet climate targets (Hagbert 2016), the promise of co-housing practices can be seen as a step in the right direction. Yet, the current benefits of sharing seen in co-housing are at best to be understood as incremental improvements. Compared to the absolute reductions in emissions from housing consumption needed to meet the climate target, the spatial savings in co-housing discussed by Vestbro (2012) are insufficient. Saving around 10% of private space to maximize shared space and common facilities in co-housing does not necessarily reduce the total amount of heated space to the extent that is needed. A collaborative economy scenario (in which co-housing is considered key, and broadly adopted) to meet climate targets for the built environment in Sweden 2050, as explored by Francart et al. (2018), suggests that an approximately 40% reduction in average floor area per person is needed (going from the current Swedish average of $42m^2$ to $26m^2$), even if energy efficiency measures are widely adopted.

In addition, other important strategies to meet the climate target in such a scenario include extensive sharing of appliances and a decrease in the use of domestic appliances overall (countering the current trend). This implies that people not only share space, but actually cut down on the number of appliances they own or use privately. A study of extended family households (not co-housing as such, but an indication of shared living), however point to the limited savings achieved, as 'cultural values of privacy, space, and independence – and the sanctity of the nuclear family – have led to the duplication (and even multiplication) of household spaces, appliances, and resources' (Klocker et al. 2012). This suggests that caution needs to be taken not to over-emphasise the resource savings made in shared living configurations, although it could be argued that compared to households living in 'normal' isolated dwellings, co-housing offers an alternative where sharing both space and other things is enabled in a different way. The collaborative practices encouraged in co-housing could thus be part in leading the way, as a blueprint for a sustainable future scenario where this is the new norm. Yet, today, it remains marginal, at best – and would need to be further developed for co-housing to offer the savings required to meet climate targets.

Community innovation for systems change

While research has specifically pointed to the potential normative aspects of co-housing, as challenging norms on multiple levels that might have resource impacts, the role co-housing projects and residents might play in ushering transitions in for example energy provision has also been underlined (Tummers 2017). A major challenge in meeting climate targets for the built environment is to move towards a fossil free energy mix (Francart et al. 2018). This includes a major overhaul of energy infrastructure and systems of provision, yet will also depend on a reimagined role of actors and agency in the energy system (Janda and Topouzi 2015), as well as for example applying a participatory and intersectional perspective on energy transitions, not the least with respect to gender (Fraune 2015; Tjørring 2016).

As suggested in the empirical analysis by Marckmann et al. (2012), the most important, and what they see as the most direct advantage of co-housing in relation to sustainability claims, is that co-housing communities are more motivated to choose more sustainable and experimental technologies, including solar energy solutions. Tummers (2017) argues that the potential lies in co-housing communities and other collaborative, self-organised forms of housing pursuing alternative energy solutions, including renewables, where the community members are to be seen as co-actors rather than end consumers or merely residents of a building. This can be illustrated in the Swedish co-housing Stacken in Gothenburg, an older high-rise building that has undergone a major energy-efficiency renovation to passive house standards, and an installation of solar PV panels on the façade and roof, reducing the need for bought energy for heating (from district heating) by 70%, and providing a surplus production of electricity sold back to the grid. This type of project was made possible due to engaged residents going together. The fact that Stacken is self-managed and self-owned in the form of a non-profit cooperative rental association is an important aspect, where residents together made the decision to renovate their property based in an expected long-term return on investment (something private as well as public property owners can struggle significantly with, as such investments often need to be weighed against potential profits in a much shorter term). Important to note, the renovation was funded in part through a loan via an ecologically oriented bank, but also through the financial support of a range of organisations and authorities seeing this as a pilot project to renovate a high-rise building in the existing stock to low-energy standards (see Chapter 1 and Chapter 5 for further details on Stacken).

Following on Tummers' (2017) point that resident-led housing projects can lead the way as pioneers in energy transitions, co-housing can be seen as offering a platform for pursuing these types of frontline projects. It is yet important to consider that the potential to 'choose' more sustainable technologies is dependent on what legal and practical influence co-housing communities have over this matter. While housing cooperatives (as common in the Danish context studied by Marckmann et al. 2012) or cooperative rental associations (as the example of Stacken) own their buildings collectively, co-housing communities in rental apartments have little control over the facilities management and are rarely able to influence such technical choices, unless these solutions are pushed for actively in the refurbishment or new development of a co-housing project, and actively negotiated between the community and the developer. As underlined in other chapters in this book (see for example Chapters, 1, 2 and 5), tenure form once again appears to be a contingent for assumptions regarding sustainability, in that certain pro-active co-housing residents can take on the role as 'pioneers' (addressed further below).

Nonetheless, these types of projects also show relevant and important examples of energy transitions in practice, with a potential to contribute to a repertoire of community-led, grassroots innovations, which Seyfang and Smith (2007) see as key in driving the development and policy on sustainable housing forward. As such, they offer something more than just energy savings or renewable alternatives for the residents of a particular co-housing community. The example of Stacken also pushes the boundaries of what is perceived as possible to do in an older building, where energy transformations of the existing stock is a pertinent issue, particularly with respect to democratising the process, and challenging the energy efficiency measures that are driving renovictions in the rental stock (Mangold et al. 2016).

Individual responsibilisation and social pressure within co-housing communities

Another key idea of co-housing, according to our definition in this book, is the stress on community and collectivity (Droste 2015). Empirical insights from the negotiation of family and emotional labour in co-housing communities (see Chapter 7), illustrate what Gauvain and Altman (1982) describe as important social-physiological features of home more generally, and the opposing interests of on the one hand guarding one's individuality against external pressure, while on the other hand simultaneously seeking belonging. This dialectic between individuality and communality is interesting to examine in co-housing, not the least in what implications it has for the potential to create alternative configurations of everyday life and seek low-impact ways of living. Linking it also to a more dialectic understanding of individual responsibilisation and collective action in co-housing, an emphasis can further be placed on how on the one hand residents are assumed to shift behaviours, in line with the community – and governance ideals at large – and on the other hand how individuals, together constituting the community, can in turn influence practices and challenge paradigms that go beyond the co-housing project itself. As expressed by Vestbro:

> This type of living can be assumed to facilitate behaviour change on the grounds that community cooperation is already established and that consumerist lifestyles are often not highly valued.
>
> (Vestbro, 2012: 2)

The importance of home to both individual and collective identity is multi-faceted, with social as well as resource-related consequences. Commonly constructed meanings of home, as outlined by among others Després (1991), for example show how home is made sense of as a reflection of one's ideas and values, and can be perceived as an indicator of personal status – with problematic implications as it is entangled with domestic consumerism and financialisation of housing (Hagbert 2018). Formed in relation to the external, the identity of home is created within and in tension with place, the built environment and the manifestation of embedded social constructs (Hagbert 2016). In co-housing, the upholding of community is moreover often (but not necessarily) intrinsically tied to the everyday, and the reproduction of self in everyday domestic life.

Following upon the claim of resource-sharing, shared activities such as cooking dinner in the co-housing community several times a week is thought to contribute to reducing the need for kitchen equipment in the private apartment kitchens. However, unresolved debates regarding whether or not to restrict communal meals to a vegetarian diet, such as in one Swedish co-housing community that we studied that eventually disbanded communal meals altogether, also show the difficulty of addressing and negotiating certain aspects of individual identity and practices. While the practice of shared meals in itself might be considered pushing the boundaries of social norms compared to conventional dwellings, the idea to forgo meat one or a few meals a week apparently encroaches on some co-housing members individual identity and autonomy to the extent that collective decision-making regarding the meals came to an impasse.

Yet, insights from other co-housing communities illustrate that the collective negotiation and action actually pushes certain pro-environmental practices forward, which draws upon the social pressure created to do 'right' and behave in line with the common identity. This is not unique to co-housing, as such effects can be seen also on a neighbourhood level, where social capital and community-level dynamics are found to be an important aspect for pro-environmental practices (Macias and Williams 2014). Yet, as explored by Sanguinetti (2013), in a study of co-housing in the United States, connection to community and connection to nature is found to correlate, and are moreover seen as 'characteristic of sustainable lifestyles in co-housing'. How successful a community is, can in this sense be framed as how successful all members are individually, where key behaviours will relate to both personal outcomes, such as well-being and quality of life, and collective outcomes, such as ecological sustainability. This is seen to 'promote a sense of awareness and understanding of the interdependence between individuals and their sociophysical community' (ibid.: 2).

Sanguinetti (2013) further finds what she calls transformational practices in co-housing, seen as contributing to an enhanced connection to community and/or nature. This includes among other things sharing, as discussed above, but also refers to aspects of culture, fellowship and stewardship, with respect to both nature and the built environment. Sanguinetti finds that the size of the co-housing community, and the cooperative culture that exists, is conducive to sustainable practices related to for example choosing renewable energy solutions (as also discussed above), growing food, and recycling. This underlines a main assumption that sustainability is promoted through an 'enhanced interdependence between the individual, society, and the environment' (ibid.: 15).

Within this understanding of co-housing residents as contributing to a community that also supports them in shifting practices, an implicit responsibility is put on the individual level. It suggests that the change needed is precisely this type of new, more ecologically and socially considerate practices, carried out in the everyday. What is more seldom discussed in this type of behaviourally oriented or sociopsychological research is the need for structural changes and responsibility placed at a governance level. Instead, an important role is given to individuals, through forming communities as a type of meso-level of collective action, to drive the development. Here, it is relevant to also explore this community-driven action a bit deeper. Even if people act collectively, the responsibility tends to be placed on a few individuals to uphold it. As in the case of the co-housing Stacken (described briefly above), it was evident that the passive house renovation project was driven by a few initiated individuals, that managed to convince the rest of the co-housing community. These individuals happen to be knowledgeable, and with some professional experience, in matters relating to energy. While the decision was made collectively, the project was spurred and aided by these individuals. The current identity of Stacken as a passive house building is furthermore negotiated in relation to individual co-housing residents' own identities and lives, where the same narrative is not shared by everyone, as some feel less involved or have had to adapt to for example changes in the building envelope, such as changed window fittings, that run counter to their own intentions to self-manage their own apartment.

The argument that co-housing offers a social pressure that influences practices can also be seen in a spatial aspect. As explored in Chapter 8, the spatial organisation of co-housing may influence the type of social logic created. Vestbro further links this spatial organisation to social control, 'which in turn may constitute a determining factor for pro-environment behaviour' (Vestbro 2012: 1). Referring to the concept of 'social contact design', coined by McCamant and Durrett in 1994, Sanguinetti (2013) also describes how the built environment can promote certain types of social interactions in co-housing. This can be more general in the form of common spaces that can accommodate shared activities that support community. But it can also refer to design features such as whether houses face each other or the placing of a shared path (keeping in mind the US context for Sanguinetti's study, characterised by clustered houses around a common yard, rather than the Swedish model of high-rise co-housing, see Chapter 8). Vestbro (2012) also refers to a study by Palm Lindén in 1999 that explores how the spatial structure of Swedish eco-villages influences social contacts and the social pressure seen as relevant for promoting pro-environmental behaviour. This research points to for example the importance of placing of entrances so that residents meet face-to-face – and the placement of recycling, shared bike rooms etc, to promote certain practices. Again, this underlines the role played by the community in enacting social pressure on individuals, but also the shaping of the organisation of the community itself to also facilitate the types of practices collectively agreed upon.

Beyond co-housing as a sustainable housing form

Vestbro (2012) stresses the urban context of most Swedish co-housing projects, where aspects such as land-use, density, infrastructure and location, as well as a compact building design are suggested to facilitate a more efficient use of resources. This can be linked to a discourse in sustainable building and planning emphasising the compact city idea. However, this urban sustainability discourse has also been challenged, questioning the focus on urban form and instead emphasising the role of social practices, that is, what people actually do in the built environment (Jensen et al. 2011). It is especially relevant to elaborate on the limitations of current urban design and technological solutions in co-housing, compared to the more fundamental changes in residential patterns and consumer practices needed. This includes lock-ins in large-scale technical systems and growth-based narratives that perpetuate increased, albeit more efficient, consumption rather than proposing radically different ways of structuring society and everyday life that might also challenge the urban norm (Hagbert and Bradley 2017).

Exploring critical questions of lifestyle and income in relation to narratives of sustainability, as raised by Bradley (2009), for example suggests that attention should be placed on what middle-class norms and notions of the 'green citizen' that are upheld. This is relevant to address also in contemporary co-housing projects that frame themselves as sustainable, or that are governed as part of urban sustainable development schemes. Bradley particularly highlights the need to critically explore the political in sustainability strategies, and to paint a broader picture of possible alternative futures, that could include other ways of doing that offer more progressive socio-ecological pathways.

Co-housing, as argued by Lietaert (2010) and others, could offer a critique of current economic and social systems, with a potential for more radical socio-ecological transitions. This is also echoed in Vestbro's (2012) claim that counter to what is hinted at above (and throughout this book), co-housing inhabitants – while well-educated and often with high social capital – should not be understood as having moved to co-housing to represent middle-class norms and values, but rather as belonging to what he sees as a group of 'post-materialists', who shun a consumer-oriented society and instead 'favour values, such as time with children, good social contacts, cultural and recreational activities' (Vestbro 2012: 12). This potential of co-housing that Vestbro puts forward is as a post-materialist experiment, of interest also to other groups that might be marginalized or isolated in society. Yet, as illustrated for example in the case of mainstreaming Danish co-housing (see Chapter 1), this might not always be the bearing idea. Or as also concluded by Marckmann et al. (2012) in their study of Danish co-housing in eco-villages:

> co-housing does not succeed in addressing the general growth in consumption, which has historically been the main reason why it has not yet been possible to realize significant reductions in residential resource use. Thus, co-housing does not seem to hold the 'critical potential' for more profound changes in consumption practices and lifestyle that could potentially challenge modern consumer culture.
>
> (Marckmann et al. 2012: 428)

A key aspect to bear in mind here is the relative homogeneity of co-housing communities, where the 'alternative' lifestyle of living together is not necessarily indicative of a diversity of other ways of approaching sustainability, as outlined by Bradley (2009). As such, the question remains whether co-housing should be understood as merely a marginally more resource efficient form of housing, or if it could constitute a radically different way of 'doing' (urban) sustainability – beyond a middle-class norm.

Conclusion: co-housing as a radical alternative or a green lifestyle choice?

The sustainability claims made in relation to co-housing are manifold. Previous research points particularly at the resource efficiency of co-housing as a denser form of dwelling, with a higher degree of sharing space and things than in conventional housing, and the potential of co-housing in fostering also other pro-environmental practices. Such claims relate to rather incremental environmental and social benefits, with an understanding of sustainability as situated in everyday life. While this could be said to follow an individual responsibilisation narrative, and a 'weak' rather than 'strong' framing of sustainability, co-housing is nonetheless also sometimes positioned as a more radical alternative, challenging current socio-technical, economic and social paradigms. While the empirical insights to support this more transformative potential remain few, particularly given that many co-housing communities on the contrary are quite homogenous and could be seen as perpetuating middle-class norms also with regards to framings of sustainability, there are nevertheless several aspects where co-housing projects might offer relevant aspects for sustainability transitions.

Even though it might be still marginal, the 'saving by sharing' claim in co-housing is not insignificant. If pursued further, co-housing can offer an alternative social and spatial configuration that facilitates sharing, and could provide a practical example of the type of collaborative practices that will be essential in a sustainable future that ensures just distribution and use of resources within planetary boundaries. Another aspect is the role co-housing might play in community innovation for systems change for example in energy infrastructure and provision – where the collective action of residents going together can be seen as part of a renegotiated responsibility and reimagined sense of agency, but also a more participatory and democratic energy transition. This includes framing co-housing residents as co-actors rather than merely responsible consumers, which in turn point to the importance of tenure forms in shaping residents' ability to participate in decision-making processes. Projects that can act as pioneering examples hold a symbolic value, and could contribute to broadening the repertoire of community-led initiatives that also offer a leverage point for pushing policy forward when it comes to for example low-energy developments or renovation of the existing housing stock. However, the reliance on engaged and often highly educated, knowledgeable, individuals to drive such projects – often centred on technical issues of energy efficiency or local renewable energy production – might further frame a certain narrative of who and what type of knowledge is considered 'sustainable'.

There is furthermore an understanding of co-housing as contributing to creating a community, which can also support individual residents to shift practices. Co-housing can to some extent be seen as enforcing an identity or lifestyle, where the individual's sense of self is mediated in relation to the community. An underlying question is whether co-housing residents act on environmental and social sustainability imperatives to a larger extent than other, average residents? While it might be a stretch to claim that simply living in co-housing is ecologically sustainable per se, there is a potential for enabling more significant sustainability transitions, based in principles of anti-consumerist, collaborative, and low-impact everyday practices. While this could be seen as putting responsibility on the individual level, implying that the type of change needed is connected to lifestyles and active 'choices' in everyday life, the collective action created at the meso-level of the co-housing community is an important arena. Connecting this further to the type of wider political activism and alliance with urban social movements described in Chapters 3, 4 and 6, co-housing must also be understood contextually, as an alternative to the contemporary market-driven consumer-oriented housing provision that otherwise characterises urban development.

Transitions to a sustainable future are needed on multiple levels, and moreover need to be inclusive and just. This cannot rely of weak, incremental developments, or individual actors, but will demand structural changes and imply shifting power relations in society. What this sustainable society might look like, however, needs to be critically discussed and will rely on the ability to reimagine established pathways, norms and institutions. As seen in the chapters throughout this book, co-housing can on one hand suggest alternative imaginaries that are put into practice and negotiated at the junction of everyday life, social justice struggles and access and use of housing resources, and on the other hand constitute a less radical type of mainstreaming of collaborative housing in line with eco-modernist urban governance. Perhaps the most important claim of co-housing is thus if it might answer the call made by Bradley and Hedrén (2014), providing examples of 'contemporary green utopian practices and subversive strategies [...] which together may spark discussions about possible futures' – proposing something more than merely a 'greener' middle-class lifestyle, and instead offering a radical socio-ecological alternative.

References

Alfredsson, E. C. (2004) '"Green" consumption—no solution for climate change', *Energy*, vol. 29, no. 4, pp. 513–524.

Avelino, F. and Wittmayer, J. M. (2016) 'Shifting Power Relations in Sustainability Transitions: A Multi-actor Perspective', *Journal of Environmental Policy & Planning*, vol. 18, no. 5, pp. 628–649.

Barr, S. and Gilg, A. (2006) 'Sustainable lifestyles: Framing environmental action in and around the home', *Geoforum*, vol. 37, no. 6, pp. 906–920.

Bradley, K. (2009) *Just environments: politicising sustainable urban development* (PhD thesis), KTH, Stockholm.

Bradley, K. and Hedrén, J. (2014) 'Utopian thought in the making of green futures', in K. Bradley and J. Hedrén (eds) *Green Utopianism: Perspectives, Politics and Micro-Practices*. New York: Routledge.

Chatterton, P. (2013) 'Towards an Agenda for Post-carbon Cities: Lessons from Lilac, the UK's First Ecological, Affordable Cohousing Community', *International Journal of Urban and Regional Research*, vol. 37, no. 5, pp. 1654–1674.

Després, C. (1991) 'The meaning of home: Literature review and directions for future research and theoretical development', *Journal of Architectural and Planning Research*, vol. 8, no. 2, pp. 96–115.

Droste, C. (2015) 'German co-housing: an opportunity for municipalities to foster socially inclusive urban development?', *Urban Research & Practice*, vol. 8, no. 1, pp. 79–92.

Fraune, C. (2015) 'Gender matters: Women, renewable energy, and citizen participation in Germany', *Energy Research & Social Science*, vol. 7, pp. 55–65.

Francart, N., Malmqvist, T. and Hagbert, P. (2018) 'Climate target fulfilment in scenarios for a sustainable Swedish built environment beyond growth', *Futures*, vol. 98, pp. 1–18.

Gauvain, M. and Altman, I. (1982) 'A cross-cultural analysis of homes', *Architecture & Comportement/Architecture & Behaviour*, vol. 2, no. 1, pp. 27–46.

Gifford, R. (2011) 'The dragons of inaction: Psychological barriers that limit climate change mitigation and adaptation', *American Psychologist*, vol. 66, no. 4, pp. 290–302.

Gram-Hanssen, K. and Jensen, J. O. (2005) 'Green Buildings in Denmark - From radical ecology to consumer oriented market approaches?', in S. Guy and S. A. Moore (eds) *Sustainable Architectures: Cultures and Natures in Europe and North America*, pp. 165–182. New York: Spon Press.

Hagbert, P. (2016) *A sustainable home? Reconceptualizing home in a low-impact society* (PhD thesis), Chalmers University of Technology, Göteborg.

Hagbert, P. (2018) 'Rethinking home as a node for transition', in A. Nelson and F. Schneider (eds), *Housing for degrowth: Principles, Models, Challenges and Opportunities*. New York: Routledge.

Hagbert, P. and Bradley, K. (2017) 'Transitions on the home front: A story of sustainable living beyond eco-efficiency', *Energy Research & Social Science*, vol. 31, Supplement C, pp. 240–248.

Hagbert, P. and Femenías, P. (2016) 'Sustainable homes, or simply energy-efficient buildings?', *Journal of Housing and the Built Environment*, vol. 31, no. 1, pp. 1–17.

Hagbert, P., Mangold, M. and Femenías, P. (2013) 'Paradoxes and Possibilities for a "Green" Housing Sector: A Swedish Case', *Sustainability*, vol. 5, no. 5, pp. 2018–2035.

Hobson, K. (2013a) '"Weak" or "Strong" Sustainable Consumption? Efficiency, Degrowth, and the 10 Year Framework of Programmes', *Environment and Planning C: Government and Policy*, vol. 31, no. 6, pp. 1082–1098.

Hobson, K. (2013b) 'On the making of the environmental citizen', *Environmental Politics*, vol. 22, no. 1, pp. 56–72.

Huesemann, M. H. and Huesemann, J. A. (2008) 'Will progress in science and technology avert or accelerate global collapse? A critical analysis and policy recommendations', *Environment, Development and Sustainability*, vol. 10, no. 6, pp. 787–825.

Hult, A. and Bradley, K. (2017) 'Planning for sharing – Providing infrastructure for citizens to be makers and sharers', *Planning Theory & Practice*, vol. 18, no. 4, pp. 1–19.

Isaksson, K. and Heikkinen, S. (2018) 'Sustainability Transitions at the Frontline. Lock-in and Potential for Change in the Local Planning Arena', *Sustainability*, vol. 10, no. 3, p. 840.

Jackson, T. (2009) *Prosperity without Growth: Economics for a Finite Planet*. London: Earthscan.

Janda, K. B. and Topouzi, M. (2015) 'Telling tales: using stories to remake energy policy', *Building Research & Information*, vol. 43, no. 4, pp. 516–533.

Jakobsen, P. and Larsen, H. G. (2018) 'An alternative for whom? The evolution and socio-economy of Danish cohousing', *Urban Research & Practice*, doi: 10.1080/17535069.2018.1465582

Jarvis, H. (2011) 'Saving space, sharing time: integrated infrastructures of daily life in cohousing', *Environment and Planning A*, vol. 43, no. 3, pp. 560–577.

Jensen, J. O. and Gram-Hanssen, K. (2008) 'Ecological modernization of sustainable buildings: a Danish perspective', *Building Research & Information*, vol. 36, no. 2, pp. 146–158.

Jensen, J. O., Christensen, T. H. and Gram-Hanssen, K. (2011) 'Sustainable urban development–compact cities or consumer practices?', *Danish Journal of Geoinformatics and Land Management*, vol. 46, no. 1, pp. 50–64.

Kabisch, N. and Haase, D. (2011) 'Diversifying European agglomerations: evidence of urban population trends for the 21st century', *Population, Space and Place*, vol. 17, no. 3, pp. 236–253.

Klocker, N., Gibson, C. and Borger, E. (2012) 'Living together but apart: Material geographies of everyday sustainability in extended family households', *Environment and Planning A*, vol. 44, no. 9, pp. 2240–2259.

Lang, R., Carriou, C. and Czischke, D. (2018) 'Collaborative Housing Research (1990–1992017): A Systematic Review and Thematic Analysis of the Field', *Housing, Theory and Society*, doi: 10.1080/14036096.2018.1536077

Lees, T. and Sexton, M. (2013) 'An evolutionary innovation perspective on the selection of low and zero-carbon technologies in new housing', *Building Research & Information*, vol. 42, no. 3, pp. 276–287.

Lidskog, R. and Elander, I. (2012) 'Ecological Modernization in Practice? The Case of Sustainable Development in Sweden', *Journal of Environmental Policy & Planning*, vol. 14, no. 4, pp. 411–427.

Lietaert, M. (2010) 'Cohousing's relevance to degrowth theories', *Journal of Cleaner Production*, vol. 18, no. 6, pp. 576–580.

Lorek, S. and Spangenberg, J. H. (2014) 'Sustainable consumption within a sustainable economy – beyond green growth and green economies', *Journal of Cleaner Production*, vol. 63, no. 0, pp. 33–44.

Lovell, H. (2004) 'Framing sustainable housing as a solution to climate change', *Journal of Environmental Policy & Planning*, vol. 6, no. 1, pp. 35–55.

Lundqvist, L. J. (2004) '"Greening the People's Home": The Formative Power of Sustainable Development Discourse in Swedish Housing', *Urban Studies*, vol. 41, no. 7, pp. 1283–1301.

Macias, T. and Williams, K. (2014) 'Know Your Neighbors, Save the Planet: Social Capital and the Widening Wedge of Pro-Environmental Outcomes', *Environment and Behavior*, vol. 48, no. 3, pp. 391–420.

Mangold, M., Österbring, M., Wallbaum, H., Thuvander, L. and Femenias, P. (2016) 'Socio-economic impact of renovation and energy retrofitting of the Gothenburg building stock', *Energy and Buildings*, vol. 123, pp. 41–49.

Marckmann, B., Gram-Hanssen, K. and Christensen, T. H. (2012) 'Sustainable living and co-housing: Evidence from a case study of eco-villages', *Built Environment*, vol. 38, no. 3, pp. 413–429.

Markard, J., Raven, R. and Truffer, B. (2012) 'Sustainability transitions: An emerging field of research and its prospects', *Research Policy*, vol. 41, no. 6, pp. 955–967.

Marsh, R., Larsen, V. G. and Kragh, M. (2009) 'Housing and energy in Denmark: past, present, and future challenges', *Building Research & Information*, vol. 38, no. 1, pp. 92–106.

Middlemiss, L. (2014) 'Individualised or participatory? Exploring late-modern identity and sustainable development', *Environmental Politics*, vol. 23, no. 6, pp. 929–946.

Mont, O. (2004) 'Institutionalisation of sustainable consumption patterns based on shared use', *Ecological Economics*, vol. 50, no. 1–2, pp. 135–153.

Raworth, K. (2012) 'A safe and just space for humanity. Can we live within the doughnut?' Oxfam Discussion Papers. Oxford.

Reid, L. and Ellsworth-Krebs, K. (2018) 'Nudge(ography) and practice theories: Contemporary sites of behavioural science and post-structuralist approaches in geography?', *Progress in Human Geography*, vol. 43, no. 2, pp. 295–313.

Sanguinetti, A. (2013) *Cohousing: A Behavioral Approach, Transformational Practices, and the Retrofit Model* (PhD thesis), University of California, Irvine.

Scheller, D. and Thörn, H. (2018) 'Governing "Sustainable Urban Development" Through Self-Build Groups and Co-Housing: The Cases of Hamburg and Gothenburg', *International Journal of Urban and Regional Research*, vol. 42, no. 5, pp. 914–933.

Seyfang, G. (2009) *The New Economics of Sustainable Consumption: Seeds of Change*. Basingstoke: Palgrave Macmillan.

Seyfang, G. and Smith, A. (2007) 'Grassroots innovations for sustainable development: Towards a new research and policy agenda', *Environmental Politics*, vol. 16, no. 4, pp. 584–603.

Shove, E. (2010) 'Beyond the ABC: climate change policy and theories of social change', *Environment and Planning A*, vol. 42, no. 6, pp. 1273–1285.

Soneryd, L. and Uggla, Y. (2015) 'Green governmentality and responsibilization: new forms of governance and responses to "consumer responsibility"', *Environmental Politics*, vol. 24, no. 6, pp. 913–931.

Spaargaren, G. (2000) 'Ecological modernization theory and domestic consumption', *Journal of Environmental Policy and Planning*, vol. 2, no. 4, pp. 323–335.

Storbjörk, S., Hjerpe, M. and Isaksson, K. (2018) '"We cannot be at the forefront, changing society": exploring how Swedish property developers respond to climate change in urban planning', *Journal of Environmental Policy & Planning*, vol. 20, no. 1, pp. 81–95.

Sundberg, F. (2014) *Cohousing and Resource Use: A Case Study of the Färdknäppen Cohouse* (Master Thesis), KTH Royal Institute of Technology, Stockholm.

Tjørring, L. (2016) 'We forgot half of the population! The significance of gender in Danish energy renovation projects', *Energy Research & Social Science*, vol. 22, pp. 115–124.

Tummers, L. C. (2017) *Learning from co-housing initiatives – Between Passivhaus engineers and active inhabitants* (PhD Thesis), Delft University of Technology, Delft.

Vale, B. and Vale, R. (2010) 'Domestic energy use, lifestyles and POE: past lessons for current problems', *Building Research & Information*, vol. 38, no. 5, pp. 578–588.

van den Bergh, J. C. J. M., Truffer, B. and Kallis, G. (2011) 'Environmental innovation and societal transitions: Introduction and overview', *Environmental Innovation and Societal Transitions*, vol. 1, no. 1, pp. 1–23.

Vestbro, D. U. (2012). *Saving by Sharing – Collective Housing for Sustainable Lifestyles in the Swedish Context*, paper presented at the 3rd International Conference on Degrowth for Ecological Sustainability and Social Equity, Venice, 19–23 September 2012.

Xue, J. (2012) 'Potentials for decoupling housing-related environmental impacts from economic growth', *Environmental Development*, vol. 4, pp. 18–35.

Xue, J. (2015) 'Sustainable housing development: decoupling or degrowth? A comparative study of Copenhagen and Hangzhou', *Environment and Planning C: Government and Policy*, vol. 33, no. 3, pp. 620–639.

Constraints and possibilities for co-housing to address contemporary urban and ecological crises

A conclusion

Håkan Thörn, Henrik Gutzon Larsen, Pernilla Hagbert and Cathrin Wasshede

In this book, we set out to provide a critical analysis of different forms and practices of European co-housing in relation to the discourse of sustainable urban development, as adopted in the context of local urban governance world-wide. We have argued that an important feature of new co-housing initiatives in Europe is that in several contexts they have attracted significant interest and support from municipalities and city planners, who have identified co-housing as an avenue to both socially and ecologically sustainable cities. In our research, we have found that the renewed interest in co-housing, expressed by architects, urban planners and co-housing activists, as well as the interest in the new emerging research field of co-housing, is repeatedly motivated with reference to sustainability agendas. But what does co-housing mean *in practice* in Europe today, and how does it relate to the discourse of sustainable urban development?

Our contribution has emphasized contextual dimensions that have been identified as an under-researched aspect of co-housing. More specifically we argue that the housing needs, values and political ideas expressed in practices of co-housing, and how both ideas and practices may vary, need to be understood in relation to the specific contextual conditions of civil society and urban governance. While we have demonstrated in this book that definitions of co-housing as well as co-housing practices in different European countries vary according to different political, economic and cultural contexts, we propose that there are some general lessons to be learnt for anyone interested in understanding or practising co-housing in the context of advanced capitalist societies.

This conclusion has three parts: First, we address the questions asked in the introduction regarding the relation between contemporary co-housing ideas and practices and the discourse on sustainable urban development. Second, we address the questions asked in the introduction regarding the two key dimensions of co-housing, community and autonomy, as understood in relation to the broader contexts of civil society and urban governance. Third, we will conclude by paying particular attention to the constraints on co-housing produced by contemporary urban development regimes as well as the potential of co-housing to contribute towards more just and ecologically sustainable cities.

Co-housing and sustainable urban development discourse, policy and practice

As part of our empirical investigation, focusing on Gothenburg and Hamburg in particular, we examined the meanings ascribed to 'sustainable urban development' in the context of co-housing projects, including local government support for, or partnerships surrounding, co-housing. The result of this is a definition that included both analytical and descriptive components. On the one hand, we distinguish between the meanings attached to 1) the social and ideological functions of sustainability discourses; and, on the other hand, 2) sustainability practices. In addition, we discerned 3) a number of inherent contradictions between different dimensions of sustainability (the ecological, social and economic dimensions); and 4) conflicts between different definitions articulated by various actors (Chapter 5; for a detailed analysis, see Scheller and Thörn, 2018).

First, analyses of policy documents and interviews with politicians and civil servants demonstrated that the concept of sustainable urban development clearly functions as an empty signifier, understood as a discursive nodal point uniting the fields of urban planning and urban restructuring. Its social function consists in mobilizing and integrating various actors with different interests, ideas and strategies. This means that the notion could also have an ideological function, in the sense that it can create the appearance of a broad consensus in a policy field defined by conflict and unequal power relations.

Second, such a general conclusion does not imply that studies of the actual meanings ascribed to sustainability are irrelevant. The notion of an 'empty' signifier in this context means that the meaning of sustainability is not fixed. Instead, we find that it is necessary to establish empirically how the discourse actually works – and varies – when it is translated into governing strategies and practices in the local contexts of urban governance.

In our research, we find that the meaning of ecological sustainability in this context is quite coherent and is shared by politicians, planners, architects and co-housing communities: buildings should have a low climate impact; and co-housing as a collective form of living is associated with resource-saving, emphasizing urban sharing. Further, we find four recurring dimensions of social sustainability in connection with co-housing practices – creating community, self-governance (or autonomy), affordability and social mixing within the co-housing project. However, co-housing activists do not necessarily share the interest of policy makers in using middle-class projects to improve the social mix of poor areas; instead, they fear that this could have gentrifying effects. There is also a shared view that co-housing could be a way of creating affordable housing, but with one key difference regarding the importance given to this goal. Residents tend to define this under the category of economic sustainability. From their perspective, the most important goal of co-housing is first and foremost to create a stable economic situation that enables affordable (and, thus, non-speculative) housing. Politicians and civil servants, on the other hand, define economic sustainability in terms of economic growth. Economic sustainability goals that are supposed to be addressed by self-build co-housing, are often formulated by local governments according to a smart growth formula, as 'a way of organizing disparate elements of land-use planning goals' (Krueger and Gibbs 2008: 1266; Scheller and Thörn 2018), and approaches such as open space preservation, regeneration, business improvement districts and the use of existing infrastructure.

We found that there was a distinct contradiction between economic sustainability, as growth, and social sustainability, which is primarily concerned with housing costs, but also autonomy and social mixing of groups with different income levels. On the other hand, and contrary to what is usually assumed, we found that there is not necessarily a contradiction between ecological sustainability and social sustainability in the form of affordable housing.

Forms of community: activism, solidarity and notions of 'the good home'

Our empirical research, presented in the various chapters of this book, provides insights into several relevant aspects of the forms of community, and the associated dilemmas, that shape co-housing practice. As explored in Chapter 8, the tension between creating and upholding internal and external solidarity in co-housing communities has both a spatial and social dimension. This can first of all be discussed in regard to the internal organization of space, where the distribution of private space (such as individual apartments) in relation to shared space (such as a common kitchen, laundry, library, play room, workshop etc.) varies in the co-housing examples studied. The relation between being able to have privacy, and the level of social control within the community is something residents have to handle in a very concrete way and on a day-to-day basis. As described in Chapter 7, different narratives from co-housing residents point to the mediation of social relations in everyday family life. Residents' emotional boundary work around the node of 'family' reveals conflicts and tensions surrounding individuality and different kinds of collectivity, and in the sense that co-housing communities are both semi-public and semi-private spaces that have to be negotiated. Residents in co-housing communities in our empirical material often have, or strive for, a sense of extended family, but at the same time they generally want to protect their own nuclear family from becoming too dissolved.

While many co-housing projects seek to be open to the neighbourhood, at the same time they struggle to uphold the boundaries of what is defined as the collective identity of the co-housing community. As seen in a new Swedish co-housing project in Malmö, for example (Chapter 8), from a planning perspective the potential of co-housing as a 'catalyst' in urban regeneration is built around the idea that co-housing, conceived as the highest degree of sharing space in a housing block, offers a different engagement with the streetscape and contributes more to social life in the district than regular housing developments do. This posits co-housing as a particularly social form of living, something that is often also reflected in the ideas of the communities and residents themselves. How this corresponds to external solidarity with the neighbourhood, or beyond, is however not as straightforward. In our empirical material we also found examples of tensions between the idea of openness to the surrounding context and the idea of safety for the residents in the house. Sometimes, the residents of the co-housing communities feel an urge to protect themselves and their community from the surrounding neighbourhood, for example by locking doors and gates. Internal discussions about where to draw the line, for example around the use of a youth room or a trampoline, or whether or not to install a gate to the backyard, are also taking place.

We have, moreover, found that an emphasis on opening up the community's shared spaces not only to the neighbourhood, but making them public in the sense of being available to residents from the wider city, is particularly prevalent where co-housing is connected to urban activism and housing struggles. For example, a shared space in one co-housing project in Berlin that we visited could be booked for the purpose of meetings by activist groups from all over the city; and a Baugemeinschaft in Hamburg planned to organize concerts in their house. Similar examples were found in Swedish co-housing, with organized activities that were also open to marginalized communities, such as newly arrived migrants. In some of the co-housing communities we have visited, the collaborative act of cooking and eating together – seen as a cornerstone of creating a sense of collectivity within co-housing – is also opened up to others outside the immediate co-housing community.

As underlined in Chapters 3, 5 and 6, we would argue that overall there is a significant difference between those co-housing projects that articulate their collective identity in 'activist' terms, i.e. whose identity is primarily defined in terms of a political project, and those that emphasize co-housing in 'associational' terms, as a 'community-building' project, often driven by personal longings to create a good home together with other people. In the former case, co-housing and the construction of a sense of community is part, or a result, of an urban activism that may resist urban restructuring and gentrification, and articulate demands for affordable housing and the democratization of urban space. In the latter case, collective identity is tied to co-housing as a goal in itself, embodying values such as a sense of community in everyday life and alternative ways of urban living. The extent to which the former or the latter form of collective identity tends to dominate co-housing projects in a particular city is, not surprisingly, related to the wider characteristics of community and associational life in the neighbourhood and the city. In Chapter 5, for example, we demonstrate how strong links to the wider community of co-housing projects with an activist collective identity in Hamburg needs to be seen in relation to an urban civil society defined by decades of housing and squatting activism (see also Chapter 6). On the other hand, relatively weak links to the wider community of co-housing projects in Gothenburg can be seen in light of the relative absence of urban movements in the city. As shown in Chapters 4 and 6, the connection between co-housing and housing and neighbourhood activism is also strong in Barcelona.

Forms of autonomy: three ownership models

As found in our studies across the different cases, ownership form is a decisive factor in determining to what extent co-housing projects can realize the values that define their projects. Reflecting this insight, we have chosen to discuss the relation between co-housing and urban governance, and the different forms and degrees of autonomy in co-housing projects, by outlining *three models of ownership*. Ownership is shaped by dominant forms of urban governance in the sense that it is conditioned by housing legislation, housing policies and predominant forms of housing provision in the respective national contexts. Ownership is about control in the most profound sense, which is why it is a key for understanding both the constraints and the opportunities for autonomous self-governance in contemporary society. In the following we will present the three models identified in our research, followed by a brief comparison of how the different ownership forms affect constraints and possibilities for co-housing to address contemporary urban and ecological crises.

1) The private ownership model

Here we refer to co-housing projects that involve private ownership, the defining element being that individual units are exchanged at market price. Legal and tenure forms can vary, from owner-occupation (e.g. in Germany and Denmark), to the 'privatized' cooperatives in Sweden, in which members are allowed to sell their apartments on the housing market (which make them similar to condominiums). We found that there is a conflict in the European co-housing movement regarding to what extent housing with a speculative element should be included in the definition of co-housing. In both the German and Swedish co-housing movements, there is a widespread idea that speculation is in conflict with the values on which co-housing is based. This is also a characteristic, almost defining feature of the emerging co-housing movement in Barcelona. Below, we will argue further that this scepticism is justified, at least if co-housing is regarded as contributing to making urban development sustainable. On the other hand, the fact that parts of the co-housing movement (as well as co-housing research) do include owner occupation (and similar ownership forms allowing speculation) means that it is hard to exclude it from the definition of co-housing. For a few of those who have sought to define co-housing, 'non-speculative' is a key characteristic (e.g. Tummers 2015); for most others, this is not a characterizing feature (e.g.

McCamant and Durrett 2011). Jarvis (2015: 95) argues, for example, that 'it is important to recognize that the underlying concept [of co-housing] is essentially socio-spatial rather than specifying a particular legal and financial model of land purchase or construction'. Co-housing cannot be reduced to questions of ownership forms, of course. But our research has shown that ownership structure is of key importance if co-housing is to develop into an affordable and inclusive housing form (see also Larsen 2019). Private ownership is in this respect the least socially sustainable form of co-housing.

2) The cooperative model

Here we refer to cooperatives that involve collective, non-speculative ownership, which in many (but not all) cases means that individuals need to purchase a 'share' to become a member, but that shares cannot be sold at market price. We found versions of this ownership form in co-housing in all our case countries. In Hamburg it is the dominant ownership form for co-housing projects. Here, large and small cooperatives have a long history, going back to the early years of the workers' movement, while The Mietshäuser Syndikat's solidarity network is a product of the autonomous squatting movement (see Chapters 3 and 5). In the case of both large and small cooperatives, there is a rental contract between the cooperative and the individual co-housing project, which sublets apartments to members. In the German context, the Syndikat is not a cooperative in the formal sense, as it has a different legal status. But in many respects, it functions in a similar manner to a cooperative. It is organized as a non-profit Limited Liability Company with two collective shareholders. No private equity is necessary to join a co-housing project, which sublets apartments to its members. Like Germany, Denmark, Sweden and Spain all have a history of housing cooperatives emerging as part of the workers' movements in the late nineteenth or early twentieth century, but have followed different trajectories since then. In Denmark, a housing cooperative (*andelsbolig*) implies that the property is owned collectively and that members have a right of use to a housing unit (see Chapter 1). In addition to a monthly fee, members must buy a share (*andel*) to gain access. This system was central to the expansion of Danish co-housing in the 1980s. Since the early 2000s, however, share prices have generally increased significantly, but it is still prohibited to exchange housing cooperative shares at 'market rate'. In Sweden, the cooperative housing model introduced by the workers' movement was exposed to change back in 1971, when a new law opened the way for market pricing. This development has meant that relatively few co-housing projects are interested in applying this model. The fact that the early development of co-housing in Sweden in most cases involved cooperation with municipal housing companies has most likely influenced the fact that cooperatives, either in speculative or non-speculative ownership form, are a rare species. The most well-known case of a cooperative with a non-speculative ownership form, Stacken (see Chapters 2, 5 and 8), applies a symbolic fee for shares

(EUR 10), and sublets apartments to its members. While the cooperative movement in Spain was suppressed by the Franco regime, co-housing movements in and around Barcelona are currently pioneering 'right-of-use' housing cooperatives as a non-speculative housing form, which in a small but symbolically significant way challenges the near hegemony of private ownership in the Spanish housing system (Chapter 4).

3) The public-private partnership model

Here we refer to co-housing projects that cooperate with public or private housing companies, which own the property. In the Swedish variant of this model the co-housing association has a rental contract with the housing company and sublets to its members (see Chapter 2). Of the countries we have studied, this model is mostly associated with Sweden, though it also exists in Germany (Schröder and Scheller 2017). In Sweden, where the civil society sector's involvement in housing remains rather small, alliances between co-housing initiatives and municipal housing companies or especially inclined developers have historically been an important factor in realizing new co-housing projects. These developments continue and have strengthened in connection with the second wave of co-housing. In several Swedish cities, municipal housing companies have cooperated with co-housing associations in constructing new co-housing, which is to be owned by the companies, who then let to the co-housing residents as individual tenants. As described in Chapter 5, we also found an example of how a private housing company, specializing in sustainable housing, cooperated with a co-housing association following a slightly different model: tenants rent their apartments from the private housing company, while the co-housing association has an agreement with the company concerning responsibilities for the self-maintenance of the house. In Denmark, several senior co-housing projects and some intergenerational co-housing projects have been established as branches of non-profit housing associations. While these associations are civil society organizations, they are both directly and indirectly dependent on the (local) state. Similarly, several of the 'right-of-use' co-housing projects that are being established in Barcelona rely on long-term leases of land from the municipality.

Consequences of ownership forms for co-housing's possibilities to address sustainability

How, then, do the different ownership forms compare when it comes to the opportunities and constraints for co-housing to address contemporary urban and ecological crises? Across our cases, we found that the non-speculative cooperative ownership form has the greatest possibilities for realizing values that are associated with sustainability. Obviously, this ownership form means a high degree of autonomy, as the group can affect all aspects of housing. In particular, this ownership form tends to support the realization of those values that we have identified as being most commonly referred to in the context of social sustainability and economic sustainability (as defined by co-housing projects): self-governance, affordability, social cohesion, and (internal) social mixing (with a link between affordability and internal mixing). For example, studies have suggested that cooperative-tenure co-housing communities in Denmark were more diverse than owner-occupied communities with respect to age, income, occupation and family structure (see Chapter 1). In Germany, the large cooperatives can offer lower shares to their members as well as more affordable rents, because capital is available to compensate for the costs of new builds. Moreover, we found examples of how small cooperatives could be more 'creative' in their efforts to remain or become affordable, for example, by recruiting solidarity members who buy shares (probably at a low interest rate) without living there, or through crowdsourcing projects (see Chapter 5). Similar models have also been used in Barcelona (Chapter 4).

Regarding the realization of ecological values, we found that in a few cases in Hamburg, affordability conflicted with measures to realize sustainability goals. On the other hand, the Stacken co-housing project in Gothenburg demonstrated that a non-speculative cooperative can combine the introduction of improved energy performance measures (including the installation of solar panels), while keeping rents affordable.

While the private ownership model undoubtedly also involves a high degree of autonomy (which importantly is restricted by the fluctuations of the housing market), current prices in the housing market impact negatively on affordability and social mixing (of different income groups), and most likely also on social cohesion (since the co-housing group can exercise less control over who moves in when an apartment is sold).

Regarding the public-private partnership model, we found that a substantial number of Swedish co-housing projects that rented municipal housing could offer their members affordable rents. It should be emphasized, however, that these houses were built during the post-war era, during which Swedish housing policy was steered towards industrialized production and favourable state loans to produce affordable housing (the rents in these houses are still largely determined by regulations that this policy created). For those co-housing projects that rent houses built after the roll-back of this policy, housing is significantly less affordable. The same goes for housing recently built by a private housing company that we studied in Gothenburg (see Chapter 5). While affordable co-housing in our limited study was thus primarily associated with non-speculative cooperatives and municipal housing companies, we also found that the latter tend to restrict the autonomy of co-housing communities in various ways. This was also true to some degree for what are known in Germany as 'large cooperatives', in which co-housing projects were often subjected to policies decided by the central organization (see Chapter 5).

To sum up: in the introduction to this book we emphasized how a lack of affordable housing is a main feature of the contemporary urban crisis in big

European cities. Consequently, in order for co-housing to address this crisis, it has to be able to make co-housing affordable. The same goes for the ecological crisis. If co-housing is to be part of a substantial solution to make housing more ecologically sustainable, it has to address the just distribution of housing resources on a large scale, enabling transitions on multiple levels. Following this, we found that those co-housing projects that manifest a political will to provide affordable housing, either from 'above' (public housing companies) or from 'below' (non-speculative cooperatives), are also the most promising. This being said, non-speculative cooperative ownership is not a panacea. Housing cooperatives can become capitalized (Larsen and Lund Hansen 2015). Whether they do or not depends on ideological commitment, organizational structures and legal frameworks that are subject to political change. This is recognized by some co-housing activists, for example in Hamburg and Barcelona (Chapters 3 and 4). And with regard to public housing policies that promote affordable housing, they can change with political shifts in interest. Still, our research suggests that the political avenue towards affordable co-housing could involve a combination of policies that support both the growth of non-speculative cooperatives and cooperation between co-housing projects and public housing companies or non-profit housing associations.

Realizing (sustainable) co-housing in prevailing urban development patterns

An important result is that the fundamental conditions for realizing co-housing in current urban environments have changed profoundly compared to the first post-war wave. One major aspect – to which co-housing can partly be seen as a reaction (but not necessarily a solution) – is the lack of affordable housing in many European cities. We have seen that new co-housing communities try to find different ways of developing more affordable alternatives, for example in the constitution of co-housing communities as self-build projects (seen in all countries to varying degrees), which is to say that the development process is driven to a large extent by the residents themselves, often in cooperation with housing companies, architects and municipal civil servants. Yet the prevailing urban development patterns – characterized by rising land prices, property speculation and gentrification – make it difficult if not impossible to build and live collectively in affordable newly built housing.

As a conclusion, we argue that, in the contemporary urban context of the Global North, pockets of co-housing can provide marginal alternatives to dominant forms of housing. But the examples we have studied across the four countries also show how even such a modest target is not without difficulties or struggles, particularly concerning the possibilities for making such housing affordable and inclusive in the context of current economic and political logics of urban governance. On the basis of our analysis, we argue that 'successful' co-housing can even contribute to processes of gentrification, as groups that are relatively strong in economic and cultural capital displace weaker groups. We also found that where there was a strong political will to support self-build projects and co-housing as part of an overarching sustainability strategy (such as in Hamburg), this was not sufficient to counteract the above-mentioned tendencies. Further, in some cases, local or national governments use their support for co-housing as a way to legitimize economically, socially and ecologically unsustainable large-scale urban restructuring. This is mainly due to the fact that the third pillar of the sustainability agenda, economic sustainability, is defined and practised in terms of 'growth first' (Mayer, 2017). On the other hand, examples such as the right-of-use model being explored and developed by housing cooperatives in Barcelona, based on long-term leases of municipally owned land paired with certain socio-economic criteria, propose local government-supported measures that could help to prevent co-housing from becoming enclaves for the economically privileged.

Is co-housing an answer to the need to create just and sustainable cities?

A critical analysis of the notion of sustainability that is conceived in relation to co-housing, as presented in Chapter 9, underlines the need to problematize the extent to which co-housing can be understood as part of more fundamental socio-ecological transitions, particularly regarding the norms and practices that are reproduced. The potential of co-housing to be an ecologically sustainable alternative relies on more than project-specific building solutions and sharing; it links to the engagement of co-housing communities in for example pushing social norms, questioning spatial and material standards and enacting low-impact everyday practices, with synergies between social and ecological sustainability in the framing of co-housing as a social and political project, as well as a less resource-intense way of organizing everyday life.

This underlines another important aspect regarding the framing of co-housing, and what question it can be seen to answer. As described by Sargisson (2011), referring primarily to the works of McCamant and Durrett, the American roots of co-housing – as opposed to the European origins, in their view – are purposefully 'anti-radical', meaning that co-housing is not primarily a political project or an ideological statement, but rather a pragmatic approach to housing that offers some practical everyday living and social benefits. In contemporary Europe, however, co-housing runs the risk of becoming a largely middle-class phenomenon with precisely such a pragmatic framing. This is particularly evident in Denmark and Sweden, but also in some examples of new self-build co-housing projects from Hamburg. As such, the radicalness and political potential of co-housing today is perhaps not as obvious in many countries as in previous waves of European co-housing. Co-housing is on one hand proposed as an alternative within current systems, in line with an incremental, eco-modernist approach and framework of urban governance. Yet on the other hand, in a few countries, co-housing projects embedded in urban activism and social movements, such as in

Barcelona and Hamburg, still offer radical challenges to prevailing structures, including political struggles for access to housing and the right to the city, as well as alliances to fight racism, sexism, etcetera.

What then are the prospects for co-housing to expand beyond a mere middle-class phenomenon, in order to become an avenue to just and sustainable cities in the sense of contributing to fulfilling a need for affordable, low-impact housing? In Gothenburg, the local council recently assigned its municipal housing companies, which own 50% of the rental apartments in the city, to investigate the possibilities for tenants to self-organize in co-housing units (based on the public ownership model discussed above). In our interviews with representatives of the municipal housing companies we encountered scepticism, as it was argued that there is not sufficient demand for this form of housing at the scale at which they are operating (see also Scheller and Thörn 2018). One example of this is a failed project in a poor Gothenburg suburb in which a municipal housing company cooperated with a co-housing association. The project failed because the co-housing association could not find a sufficient number of tenants. The reason was that those who expressed interest in living there, mostly people already living in the suburb, could not afford it, and those who could afford it, did not want to live in that particular area (a stigmatized suburb).

Based on our research, we argue that co-housing is not *the* solution to the housing crisis, at least not in the present situation. It may nevertheless be *one* of many solutions. And even as a housing phenomenon on a relatively small scale, it may offer important insights for those who are making efforts on a larger scale to create sustainable cities for people, not for profit.

References

Jarvis, H. (2015) 'Towards a deeper understanding of the social architecture of co-housing: evidence from the UK, USA and Australia', *Urban Research & Practice*, vol. 8, no. 1, pp. 93–105.

Krueger, R. and Gibbs, D. (2008) '"Third wave" sustainability? Smart growth and regional development in the USA', *Regional Studies*, vol. 42, no. 9, pp. 1263–1274.

Larsen, H. G. (2019) 'Three phases of Danish cohousing: tenure and the development of an alternative housing form', *Housing Studies*, vol. 34, no. 8, pp. 1349–1371.

Larsen, H. G. and Lund Hansen, A. (2015) 'Commodifying Danish housing commons', *Geografiska Annaler B*, vol. 97, no. 3, pp. 263–274.

Mayer, M. (2017) 'Neoliberal urbanism and uprisings across Europe', in M. Mayer, C. Thörn and H. Thörn (eds) *Urban Uprisings: Challenging Neoliberalism in Europe*, pp. 57–92. Basingstoke: Palgrave Macmillan.

McCamant, K. and Durrett, C. (2011) *Creating Cohousing: Building Sustainable Communities*. Gabriola Island: New Society Publishers.

Sargisson, L. (2011) 'Cohousing evolution in Scandinavia and the USA', in S. Bunker, C. Coates, M. Field and J. How (eds) *Cohousing in Britain: A Diggers & Dreamers Review*, pp. 23–42. London: Diggers and Dreamers Publications.

Scheller, D. and Thörn, H. (2018) 'Governing "Sustainable Urban Development" through self-build groups and co-housing: the cases of Hamburg and Gothenburg', *International Journal for Urban and Regional Research*, vol. 42, no. 5, 914–933.

Schröder, S. and Scheller, D. (2017) 'Abgesicherte Fürsorge und fürsorgliche Absicherung in Gemeinschaft. Mehrgenerationenwohnprojekte als neue Formen der städtischen Reproduktion?', *sub\urban*, vol. 5, no. 3, pp. 23–42.

Tummers, L. (2015) 'Understanding co-housing from a planning perspective: why and how?', *Urban Research & Practice*, vol. 8, no. 1, pp. 64–78.

Index

For Product Safety Concerns and Information please contact our EU
representative GPSR@taylorandfrancis.com
Taylor & Francis Verlag GmbH, Kaufingerstraße 24, 80331 München, Germany

www.ingramcontent.com/pod-product-compliance
Ingram Content Group UK Ltd.
Pitfield, Milton Keynes, MK11 3LW, UK
UKHW021302190926
475701UK00009B/606

* 9 7 8 1 0 3 2 0 8 5 2 3 4 *